Technical
and
Business Writing

Technical
and
Business Writing

Clarence A. Andrews

Director, Technical Writing and Communications
Michigan Technological University

HOUGHTON MIFFLIN COMPANY BOSTON
Atlanta   Dallas   Geneva, Illinois   Hopewell, New Jersey   Palo Alto   London

Library of Congress Catalog Card Number: 74-15589
ISBN: 0-395-18603-X

Contents

Contents

Preface

Technical and Business Writing is an example of the "how-to-do-it" kind of technical and business writing discussed in Chapter 9. Its specific purpose is to show you how to write and illustrate the patterns of technical and business information that you will be called upon to provide on the job. The book proceeds from the simplest pattern—the face-to-face or telephone report—to the most complex—the feasibility report or the magazine article. Within this range are letters, memorandums, specifications, technical description, technical illustrations, the process paper, instructions, and various kinds of informal and formal reports.

The selection of materials is based on my own experience as technical and business writer, and on my teaching experience in the technological and business programs of three universities and also in a community college. This experience has been augmented by continued discussions with industrial and government people about the writing they do.

Examples are taken primarily from the work of freshman technological students, from the magazines or books available in two-year colleges, and from industry itself. The skills outlined are based on my own experience in writing not only the kinds of materials discussed here but also textbooks, newspaper and magazine articles, journal articles, and the like. The guidelines given here are those I follow in my role as a professional writer.

Chapters 2 and 3 on the "technical sentence" and the "technical paragraph," as well as the discussion of the "block pattern," offer positive advice on constructing these patterns. Very little is said in the text about writing "errors"; it is my belief, supported by years of classroom work, that the variety of possible errors is so large as to prohibit discussion in a small book. You are best advised to discuss writing problems with your teacher, as a lesser alternative, to consult a reliable handbook.

To conclude, keep in mind that writing doesn't come easily—not even to the professional. But good writing, done on the job or in the classroom, has its compensations. It is my sincerest wish that you will discover these compensations in the course of your own writing.

To three people—Jix Lloyd-Jones, Irving Herman, and my wife, Ollie—I am deeply obligated.

1 | What This Book Is About

The Boeing 747 is an engineering marvel. Designed to carry as many as 490 passengers and as much as 6,000 cubic feet of cargo, it is 231.4 feet long (longer than a professional football player can punt), it has a wingspan of 195.8 feet (the length of two basketball courts), and it has a height at the tail of 63 feet (higher than a five-story building). Its maximum weight in flight is 710,000 pounds.

With the four mammoth engines, the electric motors and hydraulic gear, the electrical cable, and the interior furnishings, the 747 is a lot of *hardware*.

The first models took between four and five years to build. At times, crews were working at four different levels on the plane. Hundreds of thousands of manhours—perhaps millions—went into the plane. That's a lot of manhours. The income derived from those manhours made a significant contribution to the wealth of a very large city.

Thirty-one million sheets of paper were used by Boeing in building the 747—31,000,000 sheets of instructions, plans, diagrams, specifications, change orders, parts lists, and so on. Those 31,000,000 sheets contained many millions of words, symbols, figures, and ideas. Taken as a whole, this information is technical *software*.

These are the ingredients of America's massive technology—hardware, manpower, ideas, and symbols. It took all these elements to build our expressway systems. It took all of them to build the Verrazano Narrows Bridge, one of the world's largest bridges. It takes all three ingredients to build and maintain automobiles, solid-state television sets, quadrasonic stereos, and motorbikes. And it will take these same elements to solve our needs for energy and our pollution problems.

What Is "Technical Software"?

The word "software" refers to the written or printed data, such as programs, routines, and symbolic languages, essential to the operation of computers.[1] The word also refers to the manuals, circuit diagrams, and flow charts used in the maintenance and operation of computers. By extension, then, "technical software" refers to the language, symbols, ideas, drawings, manuals, and so on used in technology.

Technology begins with technical software in one form or another. "Joe, here is what we have cut out for us today," your boss might say as you report in the morning for work. Or, if you

---

[1] *The American Heritage Dictionary of the English Language* (Boston: Houghton Mifflin, 1971), p. 1227.

O'LEARY MANUFACTURING CORPORATION

1208 East Industrial Way

Steel City, Indiana 47036

(1) 319-827-7675

.   Forgings   .   Stampings   .   Castings   .   Machining   .

Mr. Walter Mytty

87302 Speedway

Copper City, Michigan

48302

Dear Mr. Mytty:

Your letter to Mr. Robert Byrne, inquiring about employment with our firm, has been turned over to the Personnel Department.

At present it appears that we will be hiring three
technical associates early in the summer of 1975. In order to consider
your application we will need the following:

A vita sheet;

Three letters of reference;

A statement about your career interests, your interest in

our firm, and the salary you expect.

If, after a review of your materials, it appears that you
are eligible for one of these positions, we will get in touch with you
to set up a personal interview at our plant. The expenses of such a
trip would be paid by us.

If you have any further questions, please get in touch
with me either by letter or by telephone.

Very truly yours,

Roger Porterfield

Roger Porterfield
Engineering Employment Division

FIGURE 1.1 Technical letter demonstrating the letter pattern and standard English.

have your own shop, you might come to work thinking, "Today, I've got to iron the wrinkles out of that system, or else."

Technology moves on technical software. Letters to read and answer, telephone calls to make, meetings to attend, and proposals, reports, and specifications to read and write.

Technology ends with software. "Well, we got it licked," you tell your boss at the end of the day. "Ship it out tomorrow." Or you say to yourself, "I knew I could whip that problem if I thought about it long enough."

The point is this: Technical hardware does not exist in a vacuum. Technologists cannot work with hardware alone. Technical hardware and technologists require technical software, without which hardware and work probably could not exist or take place.

Kinds of Language

Look at these sentences again:

"Joe, here is what we have cut out for us today."
"Well, we got it licked."
"I knew I could whip that problem if I thought about it long enough."

These sentences are examples of the *informal* language most of us use to conduct our day-to-day business. Informal language is widely used not only at work, but also at play, in contests, while watching TV, even in many of your college classrooms.

Informal language is comfortable. It's like a pair of old shoes that we put on when we come home at the end of a day of hard work. It's the language we use with our families and friends.

Now look at the letter in Fig. 1.1. This letter is written in standard English. The language of the letter is more formal and more precise than the language used in ordinary speech, and it gives the effect of an efficient, businesslike way of doing things. It is standard for letters in industry, government, and business. It is also used in many other technical patterns.

The engineering drawing in Fig. 1.2 uses some of this standard English. But it also uses other kinds of "language"—numbers and symbols. These numbers and symbols communicate meaning to the person trained to read them, just as the words in the letter communicate meaning to the person trained to read *them*.

Look at the illustrations in Fig. 1.3. There are no words here, only symbols and lines. When they are appropriately placed—along an expressway, for example—the signs also communicate. "No Trucks," "No Left Turn," "No U Turn," "No Bicycles," they say plainly.

And, as you know, computers have their own languages.

All languages, such as computer language, the language of engineering drawings, the symbolic languages of highway road signs, and standard English, must be learned. To learn them requires extra effort and even hard work in some cases.

If we fail to learn them, we may find ourselves in the dilemma of the jeep driver in Fig. 1.4. As the cartoon shows, we must get the message that "language" has for us, or someone else is likely to end up "in the driver's seat." But once we have learned the languages, they stay with us and become as easy to use as our informal language.

There are two sides to this coin. Just as the language on the road signs must have a specific meaning, and just as the symbols on the engineering drawings must have a specific meaning, so, too, the language you use must be specific. When you work with engineers, technologists, or anyone, the language you use must be specific— it must say exactly what you mean.

Patterns

In industry, business, and government, technical software assumes a variety of *patterns*.

A *technical software pattern* is the result of organizing words, pictures, symbols, figures, and ideas in a given order to convey certain information to a predetermined audience (one or

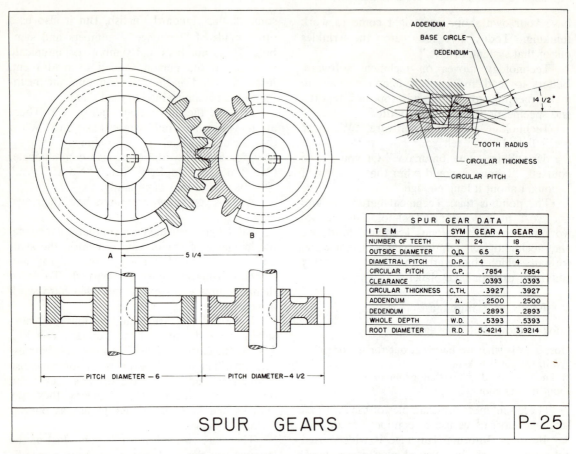

SPUR GEAR DATA			
I T E M	SYM	GEAR A	GEAR B
NUMBER OF TEETH	N	24	18
OUTSIDE DIAMETER	O.D.	6.5	5
DIAMETRAL PITCH	D.P.	4	4
CIRCULAR PITCH	C.P.	.7854	.7854
CLEARANCE	C.	.0393	.0393
CIRCULAR THICKNESS	C.TH.	.3927	.3927
ADDENDUM	A.	.2500	.2500
DEDENDUM	D.	.2893	.2893
WHOLE DEPTH	W.D.	.5393	.5393
ROOT DIAMETER	R.D.	5.4214	3.9214

SPUR GEARS   P-25

FIGURE 1.2 Engineering drawing. (Reproduced by permission of Robert Stebler.)

more people). Bad technical patterns produce confusion. Good technical patterns produce order and sense.

A sentence is a pattern. Technical sentences are built from units (nouns, verbs, modifiers, clauses, phrases) to produce meaning and emphasis.

A paragraph is a pattern. Technical paragraphs are produced from technical sentences to enlarge or expand meaning.

Sentences and paragraphs become parts of larger technical patterns. One of these patterns is the letter (Fig. 1.1). The pattern of the letter begins with the address of the writer and the date of the letter; it then continues with the name and address of the person to whom the letter is being sent, the message, the signature, and other relevant information (see Chapter 4).

Another technical pattern is the engineering drawing (Fig. 1.2). Words, symbols, lines, and numerals are combined to produce this pattern. The specific pattern of the drawing presents an engineer's ideas in an orderly, meaningful way to someone else.

An IBM card is another type of pattern that does not use sentences and paragraphs (Fig.

FIGURE 1.3 What messages do these illustrations convey?

1.5). Printed information on an IBM card often consists only of words, symbols, numbers, and phrases. Information on the card is arranged in certain subpatterns. A card-punch operator can add other information, thus expanding the information the card can deliver. The total pattern "orders" the computer to respond in specific ways and thus produce other patterns called *printouts*.

For ordinary computer use, information is "punched into" cards. If an optical scanner is used, printed or written information can be taken from one or both sides of the card, in addition to that which is punched in.

Technical software takes the form of both the informal pattern ("Joe, here is what we have cut out for us today") and the formal pattern (the formal letter, the IBM card, the engineering drawing). One of the aims of this book is to help you decide when the formal pattern is appropriate and when the informal pattern is okay.

There are many formal technical software patterns. Some of those you will learn about in this book are:

Specifications and standards
Directions and instructions
Letter reports
Parts lists
Reports of tests, investigations, and experiments
Proposals for action or work
Reports of comparisons
Job application letters
Graphs and tables
Minutes of meetings
Oral reports

The goal of this book, therefore, is to show you how to use the conventional patterns used by technologists in business, industry, and government. These patterns are of two types:

FIGURE 1.4 The man who gets the message ends up "in the driver's seat." (Copyright © 1972, King Features Syndicate, Inc. World rights reserved.)

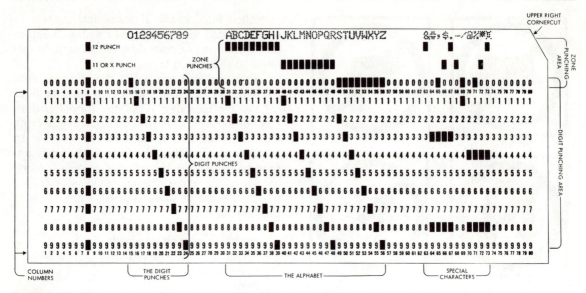

FIGURE 1.5 IBM card. (Courtesy of International Business Machines Corporation.)

a) language patterns, such as sentences and paragraphs, and b) structural patterns, such as letters, reports, proposals, parts lists, and instruction manuals. A secondary goal is to show you how to find the information you will often need.

You will be given the necessary information about the two kinds of patterns. You will also be shown many examples of both kinds of patterns, many of which were produced by students like yourself. You will be shown both good and bad examples—how to do it and how not·to do it. Finally, you will be given opportunities to practice what you have learned.

STUDY QUESTIONS

Bring to class examples of verbatim (word-forword) notes from some of your technical classes. Or, as an alternative, bring examples of technical paragraphs from your textbooks or from technical magazines that you have read.

Take turns reading these to the other students, many of whom will be enrolled in a technical program other than yours. Ask them to tell you what you have read. Or else, explain to them what the paragraphs mean.

If all members of the class are enrolled in the same technical program, practice writing a nontechnical explanation of a technical subject. Assume that you are presenting this nontechnical information to members of a high school group, a Boy Scout or Girl Scout troop, or some other group of young people.

Or, prepare an explanation of a technical subject for a nontechnical father, mother, or grandmother. Or an English teacher!

What techniques do you use in preparing or in giving an explanation? What changes do you make in the language? Is your explanation longer or shorter than your original? If it is either, why?

Are you successful in avoiding condescension (talking down to your audience)? Can you explain without insulting their intelligence? Can you hold your audience's interest?

Are you able to explain easily, or does the work of explaining seem difficult?

2 | The Technical Sentence Pattern

The kind of person you are is the most important consideration to your family and friends—whether you are a decent person, whether you are loyal when loyalty is required, whether you can take over in an emergency. These people are not likely to criticize the way you speak or write, although they may tease you at times about an idiosyncrasy of speech or a bit of slang.

Your personal qualifications will be appraised on the job as well, for human nature always tends to be subjective. But you will also discover that the people you work with will be critical of the language you use when you speak and write, particularly in situations that require formality. Elsewhere in this book, distinctions are made between informal and formal reporting situations, but, in general, any time you put yourself on the record, you should be cautious about the language you use.

As you write, your four basic concerns should be good manners, accuracy and precision, clarity and brevity, and concern for your readers.

These four concerns are discussed in this chapter in terms of the construction of individual sentence patterns. Implicitly, they are matters that must also concern you when you write paragraph patterns (discussed in Chapter 3), as well as the larger patterns of technical software discussed later.

Like all sentences, the technical sentence may sometimes stand by itself and may sometimes function as part of a paragraph. In this chapter, we shall consider only the first function. The second function—the sentence as a building block—is discussed in Chapter 3.

Although a sentence may consist of only one word ("Oh!"), a few, or many hundred, it is ordinarily conceived as a relatively short unit with the following parts:

Subject (one word or several)
Subject modifiers (articles, numbers, adjectives, phrases)
Verbs (simple or compound)
Direct objects of verbs
Indirect objects of verbs
Verb modifiers (adverbs, phrases)
Sentence modifiers

If you are not clear about parts of the sentence, consult a good handbook, such as the *Practical English Handbook* by Floyd C. Watkins,

William B. Dillingham, and Edwin T. Martin (Boston: Houghton Mifflin Company, 1971).

As a matter of good working practice, a handbook such as this should be on your desk next to your engineering handbooks and a good dictionary.

Good Manners

Good manners in speech and writing reflect your respect for the people you work with and your customers. Good manners require that you address yourself to these people in the language they are most accustomed to.

With some people, it may be quite all right to say:

"I ain't gonna do it. It's too much Mickey Mouse. They can go hang, as far as I give a damn."

With others, good manners will dictate this kind of speech:

"I'm not going to do it. It's unnecessary. If they want it done, they'll have to ask someone else."

Good manners in writing demand that you use patterns of usage, spelling, grammar, sentence structure, and paragraph structure that your readers are most familiar with. Patterns such as the following examples are not the kind that most technical readers can read easily:

You will be using the C & D scales all slide-rules hav these scales and a hareline that will be a convenience and that will increes acurasy. The scales our identicle to each other and our placed side by side they are free to move independant from each other.

The sliderule only can multiply diggits you are responsible for giving the product the corect magnetude.

The third type of non preventible acidents were acidents do to the falling of objects in the mine shaff. Such falling objects as rocks dirt sand and ice. there were several acidents do to faling timber which was in some cases avoidable.

IN-CLASS DISCUSSION ASSIGNMENT

Discuss the faults in the sentences above and rewrite them to make them more understandable. If you have trouble recognizing the faults in these sentences, look up the following subjects in your handbook: Spelling, capitalization, run-on or fused sentences, dangling modifiers, and punctuation.

Accuracy and Precision

Many sentences reflect good manners in writing, but they are inaccurately and imprecisely written. As a result, the reader either cannot grasp their meaning or else is forced to do a great deal of unnecessary work to decipher the meaning.

Which of these two sentences is easier to understand?

The car was taken in tow near Mill Mine Junction and transferred to the under Portage Bridge passage where there exists a track having relationships to both the CBRR and the SOO line.

The car was picked up at Mill Mine Junction and transferred to the SOO line at the Portage Bridge Junction.

Clarity and Brevity

Businessmen and engineers prefer short sentences. They think (often rightly) that long sentences help produce confusion. So, when you write, try to use crisp and concise language. Instead of:

It is expressly specified that in entering into the agreement to perform the work herein specified, the Contractor admits that he has read each and every clause of these specifications and the circular of instructions, fully understands the meaning of the same, and that he will comply with all the requirements herein set forth;

Write:

The Contractor agrees to comply with all specifications and with all the terms of this agreement.

Concern for Your Readers

When you write, you must always make as careful an estimate as possible of your audience. Some audiences are technical people, others are not. Some like a nontechnical approach, others do not.

Some readers will understand sentences like these:

In a nonideal section of circular cylindrical waveguide, the circular electric TE_{01} couples to other modes of transmission which are permitted. The gest coupling for bonds is to the TM_{11} mode since it is degenerate in a perfectly conducting straight waveguide.

Just like their OMs, most CBing XYLs buy transceivers with but one thought in mind.

Other readers will not understand such sentences and you must, in effect, translate the sentences into a language they can understand:

Just like their fathers, most Citizen-Band operators who are no longer young ladies will buy their transceivers with but one thought in mind.

The Passive and the Active Voices

The *passive voice* places the object of an action before the verb and the subject of the action after the verb:

The conglomerate vein in the Keweenaw Peninsula was discovered by Ed Hulbert.

Although there are cases where it is necessary to use the passive voice, many writers and readers prefer the *active voice*—a usage that places the subject before the verb and the object of an action after the verb:

Ed Hulbert discovered the conglomerate vein in the Keweenaw Peninsula.

Your best practice is to use the active voice on most occasions. However, two examples follow in which the passive voice is better.

1. When the agent of an action is unimportant, irrelevant, or less important:

The Mackinac Bridge was built by the State of Michigan.

2. When the emphasis is on the object of the verb, the verb itself, or a modifier:

The Latham loop was conceived almost simultaneously in three places.

Some Other Bits of Advice

1. Use punctuation sparingly, but accurately. Do not construct sentences where the addition, omission, or misplacement of punctuation could alter the sense.

For example, apply punctuation to these sentences to give them at least two meanings:

At Atlantic City he saw a man eating fish
What do you have in the tank Ethel
Woman without her man is at a loss as to what to do

2. Minimize the number of pronouns, especially relative pronouns (who, what, where, which) and demonstrative pronouns (this, that, these, those). Don't write sentences that give your reader two or more possible referents for a pronoun. He may choose the wrong one and misconstrue your intentions:

If the Engineer concludes that any employee of the Contractor is lazy or dishonest, he shall be discharged. (*Who shall be discharged—the Engineer, the Contractor, or the employee?*)
In case it is necessary to replace any parts and the supplier is asked to do so by the customer, he shall replace them with as many parts as he thinks necessary, at his expense. (*Who is he? Whose expense?*)

3. To avoid monotonous sentences, try to begin at least one-fourth of your sentences with something other than the subject. As examples, this sentence and the previous one have been deliberately constructed with sentence modifiers. In both sentences, the subject of the sentence does not appear until the sentence modifier has been completed.

4. Always proofread and edit your work carefully. If you don't know what to look for, ask a friend or your teacher.

DISCUSSION OR WRITING ASSIGNMENT

Revise, edit, or punctuate each of the following sentences so that each has a good pattern and a clear meaning. Notice that some sentences will produce more than one meaning, depending upon the punctuation selected.

1. Having completed the tour of the Engineering Museum, our bus left for the Conrepco Corporation.

2. These cards are to be return in sets. With each set clearly indentified.

3. 25 mebers of the class were present absent were Barstow Danielson Gerdeen and Nordeng.

4. John said Fred had drop out of mechanics before the Holidays (*two possibilities*)

5. Transceivers have been bought by young ladies with but one tuning knob

6. Until the 1920s–1930s when mining cos. were forced by law to pay accidint penshuns to injurd minors were minning cos. serius about safty

7. The lifes of the miners while under ground was rested souly upon there awearness and judgments of safty.

8. He was standing waste deep in the cold rushing waters of the trout streem when he felt a fish nibling at his fly.

9. Upstairs in our labortory, it is also acesible by to elevaters.

10. The plans of a labortory should be very compact and not to roomey.

11. The engineer was seen by him as he left the dam.

12. The engineer is 30 year's old with brown hair waying about 175. lbs.

13. The intake faze of the gass terbin takes place thru a annuler chamber. Which leads to a compresor.

14. He spend all his time writting and on his studys.

15. Just as the Bunsen burner was turned on by him, the city heard a loud explosion.

3 | Patterns in the Technical Paragraph

What Is the Paragraph?

Although a paragraph may consist of only an exclamation ("M-m-m-m!") or may continue for several pages, it is generally thought of as a collection of several sentences, all related to a central point or topic, or providing an anecdote or an example. Even though there are many kinds of paragraphs—perhaps some that would be very difficult to classify—some are used over and over again.

The Paragraph That Develops a "Topic Sentence"

In this type of paragraph, the topic sentence is either the first or the last sentence. Like any complete sentence, the topic sentence consists of a *subject* and a *predicate*. The predicate can take any one of several patterns: a verb only; a verb and its modifier; a verb and its complement; a verb and a direct object; or a verb, a direct object, and an indirect object. (For explanations of these terms see your handbook.)

1. All doubts — Subject
   were removed. — Verb
   The problem — Subject
   was solved. — Verb

2. Environmental jobs — Subject
   may double — Verb
   during this decade. — Modifier
   The copper's purity — Subject
   was startling — Verb
   in the beginning. — Modifier

3. Our new technician — Subject
   is — Verb
   a Houghton Institute grad. — Complement
   The principle — Subject
   can be — Verb
   a simple one. — Complement

4. Hodge — Subject
   built — Verb
   a smelting furnace. — Direct object
   Others — Subject
   soon adopted — Verb and modifier
   the Hussey method. — Direct object

5. The Institute — Subject
   paid — Verb
   him — Indirect object
   a fine compliment. — Direct object
   The engineer — Subject
   handed — Verb
   the transit — Direct object
   to his assistant. — Indirect object

The Topic Sentence

The topic sentence usually raises questions that begin with *how, where, when, who, what,* and *why*—the kinds of questions people invariably ask, particularly engineers and technologists.

Let's consider some examples:

Environmental jobs may double during this decade. . . .

1. When we find this statement at the beginning of a paragraph, we ask questions like: *What* are environmental jobs? *Who* says they will double? *How* many people are presently employed? *How* many new jobs will there be? *Why* will they double? *What* are my chances of getting one?

Here is how the balance of the paragraph answered these questions:

. . . With the rising interest in restoration of the environment, says Herbert Bienstock, New York regional director of the U.S. Department of Labor's Bureau of Labor Statistics, the number of people now employed in environmental activities—665,900 —could double to 1.2 million by 1980. He notes the areas of oceanography, geology, meteorology, architecture, and wildlife conservation as fields that are growing rapidly. He expects, too, that 50 percent more people will be engaged in water-quality improvement by 1975.

2. Here is another example:

An ecology research center is under construction at Oak Ridge. . . .

About this statement, we ask: *Who* is building the center? *How* much will it cost? *When* will it be done? *Why* is it being built? And, for what purposes?

This is how the balance of the paragraph answered these questions:

. . . The U.S. Atomic Energy Commission expects the $440,000 facility to be completed by the spring of 1972 at its National Laboratory at Oak Ridge, Tenn. Primary goal of the project is to determine the effects of thermal discharge on aquatic life in lakes and streams surrounding electric power plants discharging heated water. The usual effect has been adverse: Heated water accelerates the growth of undesirable plants and bacteria.

3. Sometimes the topic sentence will appear in one paragraph and the answers to the questions it raises will appear in the following paragraph:

Survey Sub I came to the Gulf last June and immediately encountered two main problems: high temperatures in the submarine's interior and poor visibility [end of paragraph].

Were the problems solved, we ask, and, if so, how?

Modifications of the craft's ventilating apparatus lowered the temperature in the cabin, but not much could be done about the poor visibility. In Gulf waters there is a high density of plankton and fine sediment, such as marl and clay. Stirred up by tides and turbulence, these miniscule particles reflected the submarine's powerful searchlights the way fog reflects an automobile's headlights.

4. Sometimes the questions we ask are only about the subject of the topic sentence:

A new book, *Opportunities in Technology Careers,* has just been published.

The primary question about this sentence would be: What are the opportunities and where are they? In other words, we want to know about the book's contents. Later, we might ask where we could get a copy and the price; we might also want to know something about the author. These questions would be answered in succeeding paragraphs.

5. Sometimes the questions we ask are only about the predicate part of the sentence:

The ranger said the region is a good hunting ground for deer.

The questions about this sentence would deal with the region and the deer. What is the region like? How many deer are there? Where are they most likely to be found?

6. Sometimes the questions are only about the verb:

Last year, General Electric synthesized diamonds.

Here, our questions would concern the process of synthesizing. How was it discovered? How does it work? How successful is it?

We can also see the possibility of topic sentences in which questions are asked about the subject, the verb, and the balance of the predicate, whatever its parts. In such cases, it is a good idea to write the topic sentence and then treat each of the parts of the sentence in succeeding paragraphs.

Comparison Patterns

Fires are A, B, C, or D. An A fire, the most common around the house, is flaming trash, paper, cloth, wood, and so on. The B fire, not unlikely in a workshop or a garage, includes paint, gasoline, oil, tar, and other materials that can set up quite a blaze in a short time. All C fires are electrical, involving motors, switch boxes, and so on. D fires include such combustible metals as magnesium, titanium, and zirconium.

1. This is the simplest kind of comparison paragraph. How does the topic sentence introduce the subject and structure of the paragraph?

2. When more detail is necessary, the topic sentence is followed by a paragraph for each of the subjects being compared. Here is a typical topic sentence:

Two kinds of nuclear power are presently being used by man—fission and fusion. . . .

That sentence sets up the two topics to be compared. The first subject, *fission,* is discussed in the first paragraph; the second subject, *fusion,* is discussed in the second paragraph:

. . . *Fission* involves splitting a single atom into two or more new atoms. The bigger the atom, the better, according to current technology, so the supervised atoms of radioactive uranium and related elements are generally used in nuclear fission reactors and in A-bombs, which derive their energy from fission.

Fusion takes two or more atoms and links them together into a single new atom. At present, lightweight atoms, such as relatives of hydrogen, are used. Fusion is the process used in the H-bomb, by the sun and the stars and, as we shall see, is much more suitable than fission for generating tomorrow's electricity. In both processes, only the nucleus of any atom is of importance, hence the terms *nuclear physics and nuclear reactor.*[1]

3. A third type of comparison pattern focuses on one of the two subjects; the other subject is compared only by implication. In the following example, two paragraphs are required, and the second has its own topic sentence:

The 1-G Trainer was built by General Motors (GM). Outwardly, the principal difference between the trainer and the Lunar Roving Vehicle (LRV) is the wheels. The 1-G has conventional rubber tires for most training purposes, though mesh tires are available for simulations. Because it has been strengthened for earth gravity, it doesn't fold. The LRV folds for storage aboard the LM. The chassis ends fold toward the center. Then, the wheels fold inward over the chassis. All assemblies are snapped open by springs and locked into place as the LRV is lowered from its pod to the moon.

Just about everything else on the 1-G is the same as the LRV: big, dish-shaped, high-gain antenna to start TV pictures back to the earth, the TV camera, a caddy of rock tools, low-gain antenna, lunar dust brush, and other items.[2]

Patterns of Parallelism in the Paragraph

Some paragraphs are developed through the use of sentences that are parallel to each other in structure and in meaning:

Some extinguishers have a squeeze-pump handle that squirts the water. *Some have a pump* that puts air pressure on the water, forcing it out. *Some contain soda and acid,* which create the pressure chemically when the extinguisher is turned upside down. *Some are pressurized* when they are purchased.[3]

[1] Franklynn Peterson, "New Blackout Solution," *Science and Mechanics,* September 1971, p. 68.
[2] From an article by Bruce Wennerstrom, "We Ride the Moon Car," *Mechanix Illustrated,* August 1971, p. 123.
[3] "Consumer's Guide to Fire Extinguishers," *Mechanix Illustrated,* August 1971, p. 96.

The parallel structures are italicized. With one exception (the last one), they are alike in the use of a subject, a verb, and a direct object:

Some extinguishers have a squeeze-pump handle . . .
Some [extinguishers, implied] have a pump . . .
Some [extinguishers] contain soda and acid . . .

The last sentence does not have an object:

Some [extinguishers] are pressurized. . . .

To what extent is this paragraph a comparison paragraph?

In the following paragraph of *instructions* (notice the command voice), verbs are used to establish parallel patterns:

Build the frame first because every other part fits either onto it or into it. *Cut blanks* for the inside ends and center pieces and *nail them* to a fir plywood panel marked off as a routing guide. *Nail through the corner* of the ends that will be cut off later. *Rout mortises* for top, bottom, and shelves. . . . *Remove blanks* from plywood and *trim to size*.[4]

Parallel patterns like these make it easier for you to explain and make it easier for your reader to follow your explanations.

Overwriting: The Elegant Variation

Technical software does not use the style of the newspaper sports section even though the audience for each may be the same. Technical software should stick to the facts, to the situation, and it should use standard English, the language of the technical worker or his audience. Although the technical worker may use slang and cliches, the writer of technical software is more successful if he translates the slang and the cliches into technical language:

The Mazda RX-2 is one of the most unusual buckets I have ever driven. Performancewise it contains not a few surprises. Its looks? The kindest thing I

can say is it's neat but hardly more chic than a pair of long johns in your favorite color. After picking up our little test mouse at Jacksonville, we headed south on Interstate 95. Before going more than 10 mi. I realized this little Mazda was something else again, entirely different from the typical import on wheels.[5]

The style of that paragraph may be fine for the readers of *Mechanix Illustrated,* but it doesn't belong in the kind of technical software you will be asked to write. The following version, while less lively than the style of parajournalism, is more suitable:

The Mazda RX-2 is one of the most unusual small cars I have ever driven. Its performance offers a number of surprises. Its appearance, however, is ordinary. I picked up the test model at Jacksonville and drove south on Interstate 95. Within ten miles, I knew that the RX-2 was entirely unlike other small imported cars.

To understand what the "elegant variation" is, make a list of the synonyms for the Mazda RX-2 in the first paragraph. Slang and cliches include "performancewise," "neat," "chic," "long johns." These usages give life to the magazine article, but in writing technical software it is more effective to use precise, technical language.

The Funnel Principle in Paragraph Patterns

Use the "funnel principle" when you write introductory paragraphs and you will begin to write like the experts.

1. Begin with a sentence that will catch and hold your reader's attention. Don't exaggerate or use tricks, though. Relate your sentence to your subject in a logical way, but try picking an aspect of your subject that is more interesting than other aspects.

2. Follow the lead sentence with two to four sentences that explain the first statement and at

[4] Thomas H. Jones, "Mini Chest for Jewelry," *Mechanix Illustrated,* August 1971, p. 102.

[5] Tom McCahill, "We Test the Hot Wankel-Engine Mazda RX-2," *Mechanix Illustrated,* August 1971, p. 61.

the same time lead to the final sentence in your paragraph. This final sentence will be your *thesis sentence*—a statement of the main point your paragraph will make:

Three examples will illustrate the technique:

Row after row, those shiny, nearly-new cars on used-car lots represent a lot of mileage at a reasonable price. . . .

This introductory sentence begins with an overall view of a used-car lot. Then, the last two words of the first sentence are picked up and expanded upon. The funnel principle is at work:

. . . A two-year-old model usually sells for about 50 percent of the new-car price. . . .

As the funnel principle continues to work, the next sentence picks up the middle part of the first sentence and enlarges on the subject of mileage:

. . . Some used cars may have as much as 30,000 miles on the odometer, but with a little care they can be run for double or triple that mileage. . . .

Now, having made the point that used cars can be a bargain, the paper produces its *thesis sentence,* which is the theme of the ensuing technical paper:

. . . To buy such a bargain, you have to give a little time and a lot of thought to how used cars are sold.[6]

Here is a second example of the funnel principle:

In less than 50 years, no place on Earth will be more than an hour's flying time away by passenger-carrying rocket. Today's "jet set" will be tomorrow's "rocket set." On antipodal flights (between opposite points on the globe), passengers will be offered a 90-minute trip around the world. Aboard such a rocket ship, 21st-century travelers will fly up as high as 500,000 feet and at speeds approaching Mach 25. That's more than ten times as fast as the new Anglo-French Concorde SST and Russia's Tupolev Tu-144 . . Science fiction fantasizing? Not at all. *Current space shuttle studies and advances in nuclear propulsion would seem to indicate that the nuclear-powered hypersonic concept is feasible.*[7]

In that paragraph, what is the function of the first three sentences? In which ways are these sentences parallel to each other? In which ways are they not parallel? How is the fourth sentence related to the first three? What is the purpose of the fifth sentence? What purpose is served by the sixth and seventh sentences together? How does the thesis sentence tie the first seven sentences together?

This is a third example of the funnel principle:

Running over Aramco's widespread area of operations in eastern Saudi Arabia are more than 1,500 miles of pipelines, ranging from 10 to 42 inches in diameter, which transport oil from source to delivery points. The oil inside the pipelines gets so warm during the lengthy hot weather season that it tends to foam. Foam in oil not only occupies unwanted space inside a pipeline but it has a deleterious effect when the crude is stored in huge floating-roof tanks. Oilmen long ago discovered that the heat problem can be minimized by covering pipelines with whitewash that deflects some of the heat from the scorching sunlight.[8]

What are the key words in that paragraph? How are these words and the concepts they represent developed in the first two sentences? How are they brought together in the thesis sentence?

IN-CLASS WRITING ASSIGNMENT

Using one of these sentences as a *thesis sentence,* write two, three, or four sentences that lead up to it to complete a first, or introductory, paragraph:

[6] From Bert Davis, "A Lot of Transportation for a Little Money," *Mechanix Illustrated,* August 1971, p. 48.

[7] Paul Wahl, "Around the World in 90 Minutes," *Science and Mechanics,* September 1971, p. 48.

[8] "Another Kind of Whitewash Job," *Aramco World Magazine,* September–October 1971, p. 26.

1. An automobile is a useful machine powered by a gasoline engine.

2. If you intend to buy a bicycle this year—any kind of bicycle—you had better buy early.

3. There will be a shortage of engineering technologists and technicians by 1980.

4. More and more uses are being found for the amazing (you supply the name of the item).

5. Sooner than we think, we will be making manned voyages to Mars.

6. We will not be able to survive unless we find new, long-range sources for our energy needs.

The Inverted-Funnel Ending

The funnel principle for writing introductory paragraphs can be used as well in ending a paper. How? Simply invert the funnel. Begin the closing paragraph with a broad statement that summarizes the closing situation. Then, in a sentence or two or three, add the details that are necessary to make the summary clear and acceptable.

This is the beginning of the paragraph that closed the article about used cars. You saw the first paragraph earlier in this chapter:

Now that you've learned to thread your way through used-car displays and to find a good value, don't stop. . . .

Summary sentences often begin with a phrase like: "Now that . . ."; "We may yet see the day . . ."; "It will be some time yet . . ."; "In conclusion . . . ," and so on.

The paragraph concluded:

. . . On the way home have the car serviced—oil change, lube job, new filter, new air cleaner. Check the plugs and points. From there on all you have to do is keep up the payments and enjoy the savings. Happy motoring.

This final paragraph repeated several points made in the body of the article: the purchase of the used car, the payments to be made on it, and the savings made through the purchase of a used car. Closing paragraphs often restate some of the main points of a paper.

Finally, this paragraph ended on an optimistic "Happy motoring." What better way to end an article than to leave the reader in a good mood?

Here is the "inverted-funnel" conclusion to the article on the rocket flight:

But whether [militant environmentalists] and their friends in Congress like it or not, air transport's Supersonic Era is here. It arrived New Year's Eve, 1968, when the USSR's Tu-144 became the first supersonic airplane to fly. The HST age may be only thirty years away. Don't be surprised if the first hypersonic transport is made in Japan.

This paragraph also restates a number of points made in the article: the objections to supersonic flight, the Tu-144, the probability of the high-speed transportation era (HST), and the reference to Japan. The final three words echo a label found on many products—"Made in Japan."

Here is the inverted-funnel conclusion on whitewashing Aramco pipelines:

The main challenge has been finding some means of providing sufficient amounts of whitewash to keep up with the speed of the machine putting it on. But when that problem is licked Norton figures that the same thirty-mile stretch of KRT line which has been requiring so many man-hours to cover can be whitewashed by two men in about two weeks. Putting it another way, a smoothly functioning spider-sprayer has the potential of saving 99 percent in manpower and cutting the time required to accomplish its objective by 83 percent.

This paragraph restates problems discussed in the article. It also ends on a note intended to make the reader happy—the tremendous savings in manpower (money) and time (money) achieved through the use of a whitewashing machine described in the article.

4 | Person to Person: The Letter

In our everyday lives and in our work, we are constantly in touch with people—friends, relatives, fellow students or workers, teachers or employers, customers, and so on. We meet some of these people face to face and others only through the media of the telephone, the letter, or the printed page.

In Chapter 5, "Retrieving Technical Information," you will learn about face-to-face contacts, similar to the kind you will make on the job. In Chapter 10, "The Routine Technical Report," you will learn about some kinds of telephone contacts. This chapter deals with the kinds of letters that are written as part of your work. They represent the most common and most frequent writing task.

Letters vs. the Telephone

Today it is possible to pick up a telephone and, within a few seconds, talk to anyone we have business with. Soon, perhaps, we'll be able to look at the person we are talking to, possibly thousands of miles away.

As telephone technology improves, the cost of telephone service drops. Meanwhile, the cost of writing letters continues to increase, and the time lag between writing a letter, its receipt, writing an answer, and the receipt of the answer does not decrease much, even with airmail.

Yet we continue to rely on letters. Why? There are a number of reasons.

1. In business, letter-writing can be turned over to less experienced people, perhaps a bright beginner.

2. The letter provides a permanent record If it is microfilmed, it takes up little storage space. A letter is an acceptable legal document. The oral equivalent of the letter—the recording of a telephone conversation—is not an acceptable legal record because alterations may sometimes be made in it without leaving a trace. Moreover, for various reasons, many people are wary of recordings made in this way.

3. If telephone calls are not planned in advance, the discussions are usually improvised. At the end, a speaker may not be certain what he has said, whether he said all that he intended, or whether he has emphasized his main points. A letter, on the other hand, can be revised after the initial writing. The structure or pattern of a letter makes it easy to emphasize main points.

4. The letter reader can review the contents quickly and easily. He can compare the information in one paragraph with the information in another. He can compare the letter he wrote and

the reply he received. Or, he can compare a file of letters that represents a continuing correspondence on a subject over a period of time.

5. Telephone calls must be made during the working day, and the caller must take into account time-zone differentials. A letter can be read at leisure. A telephone call must compete with other demands on the time of the caller or the receiver. The potential receiver may be out of his office for hours or days. When he returns, the letter is waiting.

6. During a telephone call, ideas and responses must be formulated quickly. The letter writer has more time to think about what he wants to say and how he wants to say it.

7. Letters attract the attention of people who are very busy or of people we do not know well enough to call on the telephone.

8. Copies of letters can be made easily by either the sender or the receiver for distribution to interested people.

Purposes for Writing Letters

We write letters for many purposes:

1. To ask for and to furnish information
2. To make appointments, such as for an interview with a potential employer
3. To make or to answer complaints
4. To persuade people to our point of view
5. To report about work in progress—a shipment being made, a study underway, tests being conducted
6. To report delays and reasons for delays
7. To serve as letters of transmittal for a report, a book, or a package of parts
8. To recommend and to refer
9. To answer other letters
10. To conduct business and engineering affairs when the parties are not in the same place
11. To furnish routine information through form letters, bulletins, memoranda, notices, and so on, when the same information must be sent to many people

In this chapter and in other chapters, you will find examples of letters. In particular, the letter report and the letter of transmittal are discussed in detail in Chapter 11.

Letter Patterns

Letters take many patterns or forms. In the following sections, we'll discuss the ones you will use most often.

The Interoffice Memorandum

The interoffice memorandum exists to get information on the record and to show responsibility. Within an office or organization, there are many opportunities for casual conversations in which a decision is made. The interoffice memorandum records these decisions. People forget, evade, deny, and regret. The interoffice memorandum records who said what.

These memoranda usually take one of two patterns—a short pattern (Fig. 4.1) or a longer pattern, which is usually machine-written (Fig. 4.2). The choice of patterns will be based on (a) the length of the memorandum copy and (b) the degree of formality required.

STUDY QUESTIONS

Study the two patterns in Figs. 4.1 and 4.2, then answer these questions:

1. How many subjects does either memorandum deal with?
2. Is there cross-referencing between these two memoranda?
3. What two purposes does the short example serve?
4. A virtue of memoranda is their brevity. Can you rewrite either memorandum to make it shorter?
5. Do both memoranda specify clearly and exactly what is required?
6. In the longer memorandum, what is the reason for numbering the parts? Suppose that Mr. Irvine calls Mr. Brown for an account number for charges. What purpose would the numbering serve?

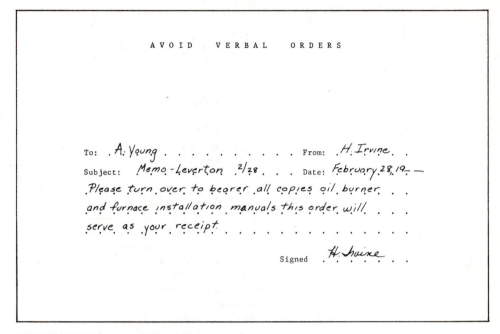

FIGURE 4.1 Short interoffice memorandum.

7. How many copies were made of the "Avoid Verbal Orders" memorandum? Who has a copy? How many copies were made of the memorandum in Fig. 4.2? Who has these copies? How do you know?

8. The longer memorandum deals with a problem. What is the problem and where does it appear in the memorandum? What is the solution to the problem? Why are sections (a) and (b) of paragraph 2 (Fig. 4.2) lettered in that fashion?

9. In what ways has Mr. Leverton tried to foresee all the problems that his memorandum may cause? Can you tell if he has overlooked anything?

In Chapter 11, "The Technical Report," you will discover that the pattern of the memorandum in Fig. 4.2 resembles the pattern of the technical report in many ways.

10. Whenever an order for work is issued in an organization, the matter of priorities arises:

What must be done first? How does Mr. Leverton's memorandum take care of this matter? How will Mr. Irvine's department respond?

11. Why weren't these matters handled in a telephone call?

12. What indications of informality are there in the two memoranda in Figs. 4.1 and 4.2?

There is a lesson for you in these two memoranda. Often you will be called upon to prepare memoranda for your supervisor's signature. Learn to prepare good memoranda so that your supervisor will be able to review them quickly and initial them for early transmittal.

WRITING ASSIGNMENT

1. Write a short memorandum to I. Leverton (see Fig. 4.2) telling him that compliance with his memorandum is complete. Sign your own name as an agent for Mr. Irvine. Be sure

```
                    I N T E R O F F I C E   M E M O R A N D U M


        Date:   Ferbuary 28, 19__
        To:     H. Irvine                       Dept:  Publications
        From:   I. Leverton                     Dept:  Engineering
                                  J.L.

        Subject: Inclusion of required notice in Oil Burner Installation Manuals
                1.  Under date of February 22, 1975, the local representative of
        the National Board of Fire Underwriters has called to our attention the
        requirement for including the following paragraph in all of our Oil
        Burner and Oil Furnace Installation Manuals:
                    Oil burners shall be installed in accordance with the
                Regulations of the National Board of Fire Underwriters for the
                class, which Regulations should be carefully followed in all
                cases.  Authorities having jurisdiction should be consulted
                before installations are made.
                2.  ACTION:  (a)  Please add this paragraph to all instruction
        manuals which are packaged with our oil burners and oil furnaces.  Use
        whatever procedures are feasible.
                            (b)  Pick up all manuals in the possession of Produc-
        tion, Shipping, and Parts Stores.  Make necessary additions or corrections
        and return manuals as soon as possible.  No further shipments of
        oil burners or oil furnaces will be made unless instruction manuals
        carry this paragraph.  No delays of production, shipment, or replacement
        of parts will be permitted.
                3.  If it is necessary to destroy any present inventory of manuals,
        please check with H. Brown, Accounting, for responsibility procedures.
                4.  Overtime as necessary is approved.  H. Brown, Accounting, will
        assign an account number for charges.
                5.  All other costs will be charged to usual account numbers for
        oil burner and furnace manual preparation.
                6.  Report when compliance has been achieved.
                7.  Compliance date:  upon receipt of this memo.


        CC:     H. Brown, Accounting
                C. Nelson, Shipping
                P. Johnson, Parts Stores
```

FIGURE 4.2 Long interoffice memorandum pattern.

that your memorandum is clear about what is being reported.

2. Figs 4.3 a-d are examples of interoffice memoranda written as student exercises. Using the patterns of the examples, write answers to as many of these as your teacher may direct.

3. Can you simplify the two sentences in paragraph 1 of Fig. 4.3d?

The External Letter

The memoranda patterns discussed are used only within an organization. When a letter must go outside an organization, the circumstances are changed, and other patterns are used.

Some of the changes are the use of better quality stationery; all letters are machine-written; use of the U.S. Postal Service rather than internal messenger service; more concern for formality and good manners; greater concern for the language used; possible review by, and perhaps even the signature of, a supervisor.

Most organizations stress the fact that a letter *is* the company to many people—the only representative of the organization that many people will see. Executives, therefore, demand that letters represent the organization as favorably as possible. Many organizations spend a great deal of time and money training their employees to write better letters.

The following list contains some guidelines for writing letters:

1. When you have to write a letter, take nothing for granted. Sit down with a secretary and find out what the rules are. Find out what stationery to use, how many copies to make, to whom copies are sent, whether you are allowed to sign letters, how much of the letter you have to prepare, and how much you can rely on a secretary.

2. Be careful of what you say in a letter. Spoken words can often be withdrawn; politicians, for example, have a tendency to claim they were misquoted or misunderstood. Printed words are on the record. The written language seems colder and stiffer, and the witty remark may become trivial or even facetious.

3. Answer all letters within twenty-four hours. If you cannot furnish the information in that time, at least be courteous to your correspondent by letting him know that you are working on an answer. In such cases, try to let him know when he can expect complete details.

4. Be brief. Be clear. Be yourself. Remember, however, that you speak for your employer. To your reader, you are the organization.

5. Restrict each letter to one main subject. If the subject has several parts, discuss each part in a separate paragraph.

6. *Always* proofread your letters for errors in spelling, grammar, mechanics, and factual accuracy. Be sure that each sentence says exactly what you want it to say. If you are in doubt, rewrite the sentence or ask someone to paraphrase the sentence.

7. Once you have signed a letter, it is your letter and not the typist's. Once you have put a letter in the mail, it is probably irretrievable.

The Parts of the Letter

1. *The letterhead.* Letterhead designs vary greatly. But a good letterhead will have the complete name of the organization; the complete address, including the Zip code; the complete telephone number, including the area code and, if appropriate, the extension number of the writer; and the overseas cable address, if the company has one. Omission of any of this information may force your correspondent to do some unnecessary and irritating leg work.

2. *The date.* Always date every letter with the name of the month spelled out; the date in numerals; and the year in numerals. Although you may write a date as 6/9/75 (for June 9, 1975), there are many people who would write this date as 9/6/75 (for June 9, 1975). Moreover, some letters contain code numbers designed to help filing and finding, and some of these may be confused with a shortened date.

On this point, *always* date every letter, every

```
                    GREDE FOUNDRIES, INC.

                    INTEROFFICE MEMORANDUM


    TO:  Ralph Andeen              FROM:  Gary Mainville

         Plant Manager             DATE:  April 11, 19__

    SUBJECT:  New safety requirements

         Due to numerous recent injuries to workmen's feet, the

    President has ordered that effective Monday April 23 all plant

    personnel shall be required to wear safety shoes on the job.

         By taking this precautionary measure, we hope to cut

    down on the number of injuries and thereby lower our insurance

    costs.

         Please use standard procedures to inform employees of

    the requirement.
```

FIGURES 4.3a-d Student-written interoffice memoranda.

```
                    AVOID VERBAL ORDERS




    TO:  Joe Leff                  FROM:  Randall Simonson

    SUBJECT:  Job 246-L            DATE:  April 12, 19__

         Please cast 12 concrete cylinders, each 12 in. high,

    6 in. dia., for the testing of the concrete mixture to be used

    on Job 246-L.  Strength must be in the range 50,000 to 60,000

    psi.  Cylinders must be ready by Saturday, April 21.
```

IN-PLANT MEMO

TO: P. Moss   FROM: R. Hector

SUBJECT: Boiler at Northwestern   DATE: April 12, 19_

          Elementary School

     Please check all water pipe connections to the boiler

in the janitorial office at the east end of the Northwestern

Elementary School. Leakage has been reported. It should be

stopped at once.

     Please report as soon as the situation has been taken

care of.

INTEROFFICE MEMORANDUM

April 13, 19_   DENTON CONSTRUCTION CO.

To: James Tendon   DEPT: Maintenance

From: Thomas Sera   DEPT: Paving Group 3

SUBJECT: Hydraulic Pump Replacement

     1.   It has been found that the main hydraulic pump

          on CMI SLIPFORM PAVER model SF-500, number

          68-13, has not been functioning properly.

          I am having it sent to the shop by 12:30 p.m.

          today.

     2.   ACTION: Repair pump at once and return it to

          job site by tomorrow morning. We cannot hold

          up paving work.

BETTER TECHNICAL LETTERS
Box 1010
Holton, Michigan
49932

Logorrheans, Inc.   February 1, 19__

Clinton and Washington Streets

Tucson, Arizona

85716

                          Attn: Robert Sutherlin

Gentlemen:

1. When you ask a favor by letter, make it easy for your reader to say yes.

2. Make your reader want to answer. Show him that he or his knowledge is
    important to you. Ask questions that show you understand his general
    interests. Show respect for his privacy or his desire to limit the
    use of information he may give to you. Give him all the details you
    may have that will hwlp him with any decision, but do not burden him
    with excessive commentary. You may have to tell him a little about
    yourself.

3. Make it possible for your reader to answer. If you do ask questions,
    be specific. Know what you want to know, for he cannot be expected
    to respond to "Tell me all you know about ...." If you have several
    points, tabulate them and number them. If you want an appointment,
    tell him how long you'll need. If you want to invite him to speak
    to your group, tell him where, when, how long, about what, to whom,
    why, and whatever else you think will help him decide to come. In
    short, be complete, but precise, in stating exactly what you want.

4. Make your reader feel appreciated by the tone you use. Thanking him
    in advance merely shows that you value your thanks very lightly. A
    pleasant, courteous manner encourages cooperation.

                          Yours very truly,
                          BETTER TECHNICAL LETTERS

                          R. L. Jones
                          by: R. L. Jones
                             Consultant

rt

cc: H. Arnold Wilson

FIGURE 4.4 The parts of a formal letter. For examples of the use of item 5 (the letter subject line) and item 6 (references to other correspondents), see Figs. 4.5 and 4.6.

memorandum, every set of notes you take of a meeting, a telephone call or a visit, every sketch or drawing, every photograph. Otherwise, you risk ending up confused, at best, or sorry, at worst.

3. *The address.* Put the *complete address* of the recipient, including the Zip Code, on every letter. For all the tender care of the U.S. Postal Service, letters sometimes end up outside the envelope they were mailed in.

4. *The salutation.* The use of the form "Dear Mr. . . ." is standard. If you are writing to a woman, substitute "Dear Miss," "Dear Ms.," or "Dear Mrs." "Dear Sir" is too reserved.

If you are addressing a corporation or an institution, substitute "Gentlemen" for "Dear Mr. . . ." If you are addressing a doctor, a clergyman, an elected official, a member of the armed forces, a university professor, or some member of a similar class, use the given title. (Only "Doctor" is abbreviated.) If you don't know your correspondent's title, get it from a telephone directory, *Who's Who*, or some similar directory.

5. *The subject.* You should make the subject of the letter clear at once. In Fig. 4.5, two ways are shown.

6. *References to previous correspondence.* Whenever your letter answers a letter, refers to another letter, or refers to a body of correspondence, mention the subject or referenced correspondence in one of the ways shown in Fig. 4.6—either in a line placed distinctly between the *address* and the *salutation,* or in the first line of the letter *body.*

7. *The formal close.* The most common phrases used to close a letter, "Yours truly" and "Sincerely yours," are meaningless, although there is some degree of closeness in phrases such as "Cordially yours" or "With best wishes." Some writers omit the formal close from letters, but the device is so conventional that many recipients would notice its absence.

8. *The signature.* This is followed by the typed name (in the style used by the writer) and the title. You may be writing to someone you know and therefore sign your name "Corky,"

```
1.    Mr. Morris A. Huit
      603 Rouge Boulevard
      Detroit, Michigan
      48807
                 Subject: Formal technical letters
      Dear Mr. Huit:

2.    Mr. Richard Hootman
      2375 Rundell Street
      Iowa City, Iowa
      52241
      Dear Mr. Hootman:
                 The formal technical letter is ...
```

FIGURE 4.5 Two ways of indicating the subject of a letter.

```
1.    Mr. Thomas T. Thomas
      Box 733
      Oberlin, Ohio
      43301
                 Ref:  Your letter of February 28, 19_
      Dear Mr. Thomas:

2.    Ms. Dale F. Morgan
      201 Selden Avenue
      Minneapolis, Minnesota
      60501
                 Ref:  602/12/4/19_
      Dear Ms. Morgan:

3.    Dr. Lippincott B. Morgenstern
      Suite 6811
      John Hancock Building
      Chicago, Illinois
      60209
      Dear Dr. Morgenstern:
                 In your letter of March 21, 19_, you asked if...
```

(Reference is in the first line of the letter. The subject could be announced in the balance of the line, or it could be placed in a subject line between the address and the salutation.)

FIGURE 4.6 Three ways of referencing previous correspondence.

but Corky's secretary will appreciate knowing that your official name is Mortimer Ballingbrooke Corcoran III.

If you are a woman, be sure to indicate that you are, feminist movements to the contrary. You may avoid some possible embarrassments because your male correspondents may assume from a name such as "M. Utley" that you are a male.

9. *Other information.* The lower left-hand corner of letters is reserved for this kind of information:

The initials of the writer in capital letters and of the typist in lower case letters. A colon separates the initials.

References to enclosures in the letter.

Names of persons to whom copies of the letter are being sent (see the long memorandum form, Fig. 4.2, for an example).

10. *The body.* You will find more discussion of this in Figs. 4.7 through 4.13.

STUDY QUESTIONS

1. How is neatness achieved in the sample formal letter?

2. Is the letter cool in tone? If so, what makes it cool? Can you rewrite the letter to give it a warmer tone?

3. Under what circumstances is the short formal letter likely to be used? Be as specific as you can in your answer. If you were writing a letter of application for a job interview, would it be formal or informal? Why?

The Informal or Simplified Letter

Not all of the letters you write need to be formal. when you are trying to be gently persuasive, or when the subject matter does not involve a com-
when the subject matter does not involve a complaint or a claim, a less formal letter may be in order. Such a letter is shown in Fig. 4.7. You can use this model if you wish, or you can develop your own model. Just remember that the kind of letter you write depends on your correspondent and the circumstances.

Informality, however, does not mean triviality or frivolity. Your letters must be to the point, however informally you write, and they must be businesslike.

STUDY QUESTIONS

1. Are all the parts of the letter (as listed in Fig. 4.4) in Fig. 4.7? If so, where are they?

2. How does the pattern of this letter differ from the patterns of Fig. 1.1? of Fig. 4.4?

3. This letter has an informal, warmer tone than the letter in Fig. 4.6. How was the informality achieved?

4. Rewrite the letter as a formal letter, cool in tone. Which letter serves the writer's purpose better?

5. What is the point of this letter? Where is the point made?

6. Were any enclosures sent with the letter? How do you know?

7. There are at least two reasons why the writer has chosen to be informal. What are they? Do you think the writer knows the recipient?

8. In what ways might advances in technology have influenced the pattern of this letter?

The Salutation for the Informal Letter

A widely used pattern for the salutation of the informal, simplified letter is as follows:

Mr. Morris A. Huit
603 Rouge Boulevard
Detroit, Michigan
48807
The simplified letter, Mr. Huit, is used by many technical people . . .

The formal close is often omitted in this pattern:

Your secretary will like the efficient form and the ease of typing; your clients will like the pleasant approach; they'll know that a person—not a machine—wrote the letter; you'll like the simplified letter, Mr. Huit, because they will.

R. L. Jones

R. L. Jones

rt

Another Pattern for the Technical Letter

Fig. 4.8 shows a useful model for technical letters. Notice the variant pattern of the heading and the salutation, which may also be used on the formal letter. However, if you have a subject line or reference line, this pattern is not advisable.

Before you write this pattern, make a simple outline. If you are answering a letter, number the points on that letter in the order in which you will answer them. Use these numbers as keys to paragraphs in your letter. If you are initiating the correspondence, jot down a list of the points you intend to make and number them in the order in which you will discuss them.

The Letter of Inquiry

Occasionally, you will find it necessary to write letters seeking information, advice, or assistance. Fig. 4.9 shows such a letter—the letter Thomas Zarnke might have written when he was seeking information from Die-Draulic, Inc.

When you write for information, advice, or assistance, keep these circumstances in mind:

1. The people you are writing to are probably under no obligation, real or implied, to help you. Therefore, make your case as convincing as you can, remembering that facts are often your best persuasive device. Do not overstate your case either pleasantly or unpleasantly.

2. The people you are writing to are busy. Keep your inquiry brief and easy to answer. Always enclose a self-addressed, stamped envelope for the anticipated reply.

3. Don't ask for the impossible. If answering your request will cost too much, take too much time, or cause other strains, your letter may go unanswered.

4. Don't ask someone else to do what you can do for yourself. For example, don't ask for information that you can find in your local library.

5. Be as clear and as specific as you can about what you want. Don't ask for "any information you have about your firm." Ask for a brochure about a specific product.

6. If necessary, state your reasons for seeking information. Don't imply that you are a potential customer if you are not.

7. Don't be profuse in your thanks. Don't promise to repay the favor on some later occasion. Most people feel good about requests for assistance or information.

8. Unless the response is something that obviously took a great deal of time or cost a good deal of money, don't write a thank-you note. Most people get too much unnecessary mail already.

9. Read the letter in Fig. 4.8 for further advice.

STUDY QUESTIONS FOR FIG. 4.9

1. Is Zarnke's letter too long? Can you think of any valid reason for his lengthy explanation?
2. Will Zarnke get his requested information?

The Letter Packet

Some organizations use a letter packet, consisting of three or more sheets of paper interleaved with one-time carbon paper and all joined together at the top. After the letter has been typed, one carbon copy is detached from the packet and retained by the sender, and the balance of the packet is forwarded. The addressee's answer is typed in a "Reply" section of the packet. Then, his carbon copy is detached, and the original (containing both letter and answer) is returned to the first writer.

THE TECHNICAL MONTHLY
Industrial Park
Pennsylvania 21681

October 24, 19_

Dear Professor Andrews:

May we take the liberty of bringing to your attention. . . . Sounds
stuffy, doesn't it? According to this October Technical Monthly
article, most of us could write much more clearly and convincingly
if we could write the way we talk. Author Christian Kringle explains
that learning to "talk on paper" is really pretty simple. His advice
may be of interest to you--and useful to your students.

If you agree, I'll be happy to send you a supply of reprints of "Write
It the Way You Say It," with our compliments.

Sincerely,

Orville R. Yetter

Orville R. Yetter

ORY:mew

Professor Clarence A. Andrews, Head
Communications and Technical Writing
Michigan Technological University
Houghton, Michigan 49931

Orville R. Yetter — Vice President
138 Freeway Drive • Telephone 861-5973

FIGURE 4.7 Simplified, informal letter.

BETTER TECHNICAL LETTERS
Box 1010
Holton, Michigan
49932
(1)-907-333-1313

1 February, 19—   (1)

(3)   Mr. Morris A. Huit

603 Rouge Boulevard

Detroit, Michigan

48807

(4)   Dear Mr. Huit:

(10)   The formal letter is neat in appearance and rather cool   (2)
in tone. Its pattern is conventional in industry and business. A
letter following this conservative pattern will always be acceptable.

      Brevity is desirable. Limit the letter to one subject.
It will be easier for the recipient either to file it, answer it, or
forward your ideas to others. If additional matters require consideration, write a second letter. Explanation beyond what can be included
on a single page is often better presented in an enclosure.

Yours very truly,   (7)

R. L. Jones

R. L. Jones   (8)

Consultant

(9)   Enclosures: 3

RLJ:rt

FIGURE 4.8 Pattern for a technical letter.

Thomas R. Zarnke

623 North Woolworth Hall

Michigan Technological University

Houghton, Michigan 49931

January 2, 19_

Die-Draulic, Inc.

1440 Front Avenue, N. W.

Grand Rapids, Michigan

49504

Gentlemen:

Would you please send me one or two brochures that illustrate the "Die-Draulic" process and one or two of your "Die-Draulic" press brochures?

Recently in a metalworking class, Professor Irving Herman mentioned that your equipment had some advantages over more conventional stamping presses. He did not, however, go into detail.

In my technical writing class, I am required to write a long research paper. It occurred to me that I might do my paper on your process and its advantages. However, I could find no information on the "Die-Draulic" process in our learning materials center. In a magazine I did find an advertisement in which you offered to send further information.

I enclose a self-addressed stamped envelope for your reply.

Thank you.

Thomas R. Zarnke

Thomas R. Zarnke

FIGURE 4.9 Letter of inquiry.

You can create your own version of the packet. When you receive a letter, copy it on an office copier. Place a sheet of carbon between the original and the copy and type your response at the bottom of the page, or even on the back side. Return the original and keep the copy.

STUDY QUESTIONS

What advantages do you see in the use of the letter packet? What disadvantages? What objections might be raised to the use of the letter packet?

The Letter of Application

Even after you accept your first job, you will probably have to write a very important letter. Fig. 4.10 is an example of a letter you will write when you apply for a job or ask for an interview to discuss your employment.

Usually when you apply for a job, you do one of two things: (a) respond to an advertisement or other notice about the availability of a specific job; or (b) inquire of an organization because you know or have heard that it hires people with your qualifications.

Answering an Advertisement

1. If the address from which you write is a temporary address such as a dormitory or a lodging house, give a permanent address as well. This can be placed at the lower corner of the letter.

2. Refer to the advertisement or whatever notice you have seen:

I am applying for the position of technical report writer advertised in the Detroit *Clarion* on Sunday, January 31, 1975 . . .

Mr. O. D. Batholow, Placement Director of the Robinson Technical Institute, Robinson, Idaho, has told me that you are looking for an engineer with a second-class license . . .

3. If the advertisement lists a box number rather than an organization name, write the address as follows:

Box J-2807
Detroit *Clarion*
Detroit, Michigan
48807

It is a good idea to attach a copy of the advertisement you are responding to. Some companies place several advertisements at a time and in a great many places. Moreover, some organizations entrust the initial solicitation to an agency, which may be screening for hundreds of jobs and thousands of applications daily.

4. When you write a letter of application, you are actually trying to get a personal interview. Your letter, therefore, must convince the reader that he should spend his time and money interviewing you rather than others who may have applied.

So be brief, direct, and businesslike. Stick to the point. Avoid attempts at cleverness or elegant variations. Omit references to mutual friends or to the fact that the organization has already employed one of your best friends.

5. Your education and your relevant work experience are your most obvious assets. Get this information down at once. But don't toot your own horn with statements such as "I was rated the best xologist in my class." It is better to write, "All my work in the X program, which is designed to train xologists, was B or better."

At the same time, don't apologize. There is no point in calling attention to your limitations with statements such as: "Please excuse speling in this leter I was never any good at english."

6. Keep your letter brief. Supply pertinent data on a biographical data sheet (resume, vita sheet) which you attach. Most organizations expect data to come in on a form similar to that in Fig. 4.11.

7. Be sure to furnish significant details: when you are available for employment, when you can come for an interview, where and when you can be reached by telephone, what other reasons there might be for an interest in you.

                                                    Charles Marlow
(Address where you can be reached, ————————→ 401 Noir Street
and date of letter)
                                                    Slippery Rock,
                                                    Pennsylvania
                                                    12345
                                                    June 16, 19___

Communications Consultants
Box 616 ←————————————————————— (Addressee — complete address)
Mesa, Arizona
85317
                          Subject:←——————— (Advertisement you are answering
                                                    or title of job you are applying for)

Gentlemen:
        In applying for a position by letter, you will be wise to ask
for an interview to present your qualifications in detail. Unless you
know a great deal about the firm or the job opening, it is wise not
to be too enthusiastic in the first letter.
        The second paragraph should offer key reasons why the potential
employer should take the time and trouble to interview you. Present
summary statements about your education and work experience. Details
will be on the accompanying resume. (see Figure 4.11)
        The third paragraph should offer reasons for your interest in
the job. Avoid such statements as your need for money or your desire to
locate in a particular area. It is better to concentrate on your interests
and immediate or lifetime goals.
        Your final paragraph should indicate when and where you are
available for interview, and when you can reprot for work.
        Usually your interest in the position offered can be suggested
naturally in the course of your letter.

                                                    Charles Marlow
                                                    Charles Marlow

Enclosure: Vita sheet
           Photograph   (optional)

           (If you are a student at the time of writing,
           put your permanent (parents') address here and identify it
           as such.)

FIGURE 4.10 Pattern for an application and information suggested for inclusion.

DATA SHEET FOR (YOUR NAME)

Name:

Address: (Both temporary and permanent, each identified)

Telephone number where you can be called:

Date of availability:

Birth Date:

Marital status:

Height:

Weight:

Health:

Previous Experience: (In general, list most recent first in each of the following.)

  Education:

    List institutions and degrees or diplomas.
    List courses and programs that specifically fit you
    for this job, and describe content briefly.
    State grades received for courses, grade-point
    average, and rank in class.

  Armed Services: (optional)

    If any military experience qualifies you for this job,
    describe it.

  Former Jobs: (List last job first)

    State firm, address, position held. If not obvious
    from the title of the position, describe what you did.

  Social Activities:

    Extracurricular activities in school_
    Memberships in organizations
    Hobbies   (especially if relevant to the work)

  Salary desired: (optional)

  References:

    Give name, position and address. Make relationship
    to you clear. List from three to five names. Be sure
    to tell your references what you have done.

FIGURE 4.11 Skeleton vita sheet (or data sheet or resume). Your school may also be able to suggest a format.

```
          Wilson B. David

          1204 East Washington Avenue                    August 21, 19 _

          Iowa City, Iowa


          Mr. Lockwood Hammer

          Employment Office

          Mainstee Std. Lime & Refractories

          East Lake, Mich.
                                      In reference to the add in the

                                      Mainstee News Advocate about the

                                      job opening in your packing div.

          Dear Mr. Hammer

          I'm writing in reference to the add I read in the Manistee News

          Advocate about the job opening in your packing div.  I am presently

          attending Houghton Technical Institute and in the Electrical

          Engineering Technology Program.

          In previous summers I have worked for two different construction cos.

          hauling brick & concrete.  I would like the oppertunity to meet with

          you and discuss the job, and pay should we decide I am the right

          person for the job.

                                          Sincerely

                                          Wilson B. David
                                          Wilson B. David
```

FIGURE 4.12 Letter of application. If you were Mr. Lockwood Hammer, how would you react to this letter?

```
Name :  WILSON  S.  DAVID

address:  1204  East  Washington

Birthday:  December  28,  1955

Height:     5'  11"

Weight:    160  lbs

Health :   GOOD

Experience:

  1  Summer   DOBB TRUCK & CRANE

  1  Summer   PART OF MAINTENANCE
              CREW FOR APARTMENT PROJ.

  3  Summer   TEACHING PRIVATE AND
              GROUP SWIMMING

  1  Summer   VANDUNCLER CONSTRUCTION

School Attended :  HOTON INSTITUTE

             ( ELECTRICAL ENGINEERING
               TECHNOLOGY )
```

FIGURE 4.13 Vita sheet accompanying letter of application in Fig. 4.12.

Examples of Good and Bad Application Letters

Figs. 4.12, 4.13, 4.14, and 4.15 show student-written letters of application and vita sheets. One is a poor example, the other is a good example. You should have no problems deciding which is which.

STUDY QUESTIONS

1. What are the specific faults of the bad application letter? What are the specific virtues of the good application letter?

2. Do you find any good points in the bad example? If so, what are they?

3. Do you find any bad points in the good example? If so, what are they?

4. Rewrite the bad example. Your goal is to produce an application letter that will best represent the writer.

5. Rewrite the good example, improving it if you can. What directions will your editing take? Why?

6. Dr. Rudolph Flesch suggests that we should learn to write the way we talk. Is this good advice for an application letter? Is this good advice for you? Why or why not?

Dictating Memoranda, Letters, and Reports

Because some people are intimidated by the idea of dictating but cannot type or write legibly, the following rules for dictating are furnished.

BETTER TECHNICAL LETTERS
IntraOffice Message
TO: H. Arnold Wilson
DATE: 15 February 1975

FROM: R. L. Jones,
Consultant

RE: Dictation Rules

A number of your supervisors have asked for advice about dictating. I propose that you duplicate and distribute the following list:

Steven Clark

415 Seventh Street

Calumet, Michigan

49933

Box X-178

Register and Tribune

Chicago, Illinois

60606

Gentlemen:

     In your advertisement for a technician, you indicated that
you require the services of a person with knowledge of both electrical
and mechanical maintenance. Please consider me an applicant for this
position. Here are my reasons for believing I am qualified for this
work.

     I shall graduate in June from the two-year Electromechanical
Program offered by Michigan Technological University. I have a good
background in both the design and testing of AC and DC circuits,
mechanical drives and linkages, and automatic control systems.

     Last summer I worked for Coon Electric as an electrician's
assistant. I gained much practical experience from this work.

     I would be available for an interview at any time that is
convenient for you. I can be reached at the above address or by
telephone at 905-338-1940.

Steven J. Clark

Steven J. Clark

Enclosures: 2

FIGURE 4.14 Letter of application for an interview about a potential job. The writer attached a copy of the advertisement to his letter. How do you think Box X-178 will respond
to this letter?

```
                         PERSONAL DATA



        Name-  Clark, Steven John
        Address- 415 Seventeenth Street, Calumet, Michigan,  49933
        Birthdate- July 13, 1954  Birthplace- Calumet, Michigan
        Height- 6' 3"  Weight- 162
        Date of availability- Any time after June 16, 1975
        EDUCATION
               Institution              Degree                Date
        Calumet High School        Diploma                    1971
        Michigan Technological     Associate in Applied       1975
           University              Science in Electromechanical
                                     Engineering Technology
               Applicable Courses and Description            Grade
        DC Circuits:  A study of resistance networks under the influence   B
                      of direct current
        AC Circuits:  a study of electrical networks in the sinusoidal     B
                      steady state
        Automatic Control Systems:   an introduction to the theory and     B
                      analysis of servomechanisms
        Mechanical Drives:  a study of basic mechanical components such as  A
        and Linkages        gears, pulleys, belts, chains, sprockets, cams,
                            levers, and their related applications
            Grade-Point Average: 2.85 on a 4-point scale
            Class Rank- Fifth in a class of 12
        MILITARY EXPERIENCE-  None
        WORK EXPERIENCE
            One summer for Coon Electric, Inc., 424 Hancock Street, Hancock,
            Michigan, 49930
            Title- Electrician's Assistant
            Supervisor-  J. B. Coon
        HOBBIES
            Electronics
            Mechanical Drawing
```

FIGURE 4.15 Personal data (vita sheet, data sheet, resume) accompanying letter of application in Fig. 4.14.

1. Before you dictate, make notes. You can use the margin of the letter you are answering. Small file cards are good too (Figure 4.16). The whole letter should be organized and in your mind before you say the first word.

2. Have any necessary data at hand, or instruct the stenographer to get it before beginning to type.

3. Whether you dictate to a person or to a machine, give all the mechanical details first. How many copies on which letterheads, with what layouts, to go to whom? Remember the order in which the typist needs the information.

4. Speak clearly. Monotony is allowable, but fuzziness isn't.

5. Spell unusual names or words. Dictate the punctuation, even if it is just ordinary. Even if your typist does know punctuation, she is typing, not trying to make sense.

6. If you dictate in person, keep your eyes on the pen or pencil. If you dictate to a machine, stop it while you think about the next idea or phrase. Long silences worry transcriptionists.

7. Remember that the person who takes dictation is not only human, but is getting paid. Don't waste time and money by making the typist wait, or by making it necessary to type everything twice.

1. Make notes
2. Data
3. Mechanical Details
4. Speak clearly
5. Spelling, punctuation
6. Dictating speed
7. Concern for secretary

FIGURE 4.16 A note card prepared before dictation. This card was used as an outline for the memorandum on dictation.

WRITING ASSIGNMENTS

1. Write the following letters: a letter in which Hospital Electronics, Inc., 1218 Keosaqua Way, Chicago, Illinois, 60606, offers a job to Steven J. Clark (see Fig. 4.14), and a letter in which Clark rejects the position. Attach your note outline cards.

2. Write a letter of application for a job you have seen advertised either in a newspaper or at your school's placement service. Or, write a letter of application for a job for which you think you are qualified. Prepare and attach your own data sheet. Attach note outline cards.

3. Write a letter of complaint about some product or service that has been unsatisfactory. Choose one of the appropriate letter patterns described in this chapter. As you write, ask yourself "What kind of letter of complaint would I respond most readily to if the letter were being written to me?" Then having written the letter, assume the role of the person receiving the letter and write a reply. Attach note outline cards for both letters.

4. Write a letter soliciting an interview with someone who can give you information about a project you are working on. Attach note outline card.

5. Write a letter asking someone to serve as a reference for a job you are applying for. In your letter, be sure to give your potential sup-porter all the information he or she needs. Attach note outline card.

6. Write a letter to someone asking him or her to speak at a meeting of an organization you belong to. Give your reader all the information he will need, including a description of the audience. Attach your note outline card.

5 | Retrieving Technical Information

Sooner or later each of us realizes the extent of our dependence upon others. This situation, of course, is reversible since others depend upon us as well.

We depend upon others particularly for technical information, which is the basis for all technology. We cannot possibly know everything, even in our limited areas of expertise. Even if we did, it would not be advisable to trust our memories. And there is a certain feeling of security in knowing we can rely on an expert.

For these and many other reasons, it has been found useful to store information for future use.

Our information storehouses are called libraries or, more and more commonly, learning materials centers. The latter term has developed to refer to those centers which store not only books, but other learning material as well.

Whatever the center is called, the information is preserved in one of these forms:

The print media—books, newspapers, magazines, journals, file cards
The sound media—records, tapes
The visual media—pictures, films, videotapes
"Micro" forms—microfilms, microfiches

Many of these centers also have facilities for retrieving materials stored elsewhere, either through the mail or through electronic means such as the computer.

Retrieving Information from Printed Sources

Books

Books serve many information-storage purposes. Among them are the following:

Catalogues contain lists of materials and descriptions.
Directories list names of people and organizations.
Handbooks, manuals, and guides have basic information about specific technologies and subjects.
Dictionaries and thesauruses compile lists of words, terms, and symbols.
Encyclopedias contain short generalized articles on numerous subjects, usually alphabetically arranged by subject.
Yearbooks present an annual record of a subject, for example, a college class.
Indexes are directories of information of

specific kinds, arranged to make information finding easier.

Abstract periodicals compile abstracts of articles written by experts in specific subject areas.

Bibliographies are lists of books about specific subjects, people, or books. There are also bibliographies of bibliographies.

Biographies narrate the life history of people, industries, or disciplines.

Histories are narrative records of a series of events over a given time period.

There are books "about" many technical and scientific subjects: the building of a bridge; the nature of the universe around us; the works of man, such as architecture, dams, and so on.

Reference books are all of the above and many others as well.

Textbooks are designed to help us develop certain skills at specified levels of learning.

Newspapers

Newspapers furnish a daily, semiweekly, weekly, biweekly, or monthly record of the ongoing life around us. They are usually a primary source of current events, but they also record opinions, reviews, editorials, columns, and so on.

The New York Times should be in every school library. It is the national newspaper of record—which means it carries complete news stories and records of daily happenings.

The Wall Street Journal, which is the newspaper of record for news about money, business, and economics, should also be received by school libraries.

On the West Coast, the *Los Angeles Times* is another major newspaper of record. Libraries should also carry the state newspaper of record (the *Des Moines Register,* the *Milwaukee Journal,* the *Chicago Tribune,* the *Detroit Free Press* and so on). Such newspapers are useful for current information about developments in technology.

Most school libraries have the Index for *The New York Times.* It is useful because it indexes subjects such as engineering, automobiles, and construction. Even though *The Times* may not be available, the Index helps locate stories in available local newspapers.

Magazines

Magazines are published at regular intervals—weekly, monthly, biweekly, or quarterly.

Time, Newsweek, and *U. S. News and World Report* report and summarize news. They also present opinions in editorials and reviews. All three focus on technology and science in news stories and in longer essays.

Business Week and *Fortune* focus on the world of commerce and industry and carry many articles about technology, its uses, and new developments.

Technological magazines are highly specialized. Some, such as *Ford Times* or *Westinghouse Engineer,* are published by an industrial firm. Others, such as *Buildings, Datamation,* or *Power Engineering,* focus on a particular aspect of engineering.

There are also the so-called house organs, of which there are thousands. They are published either for internal distribution among employees or for external distribution. Some are published for both audiences.

Each of the technological specialties (aerospace, air-conditioning, automobiles, and so on) probably has at least one magazine.

STUDY QUESTIONS

What magazines are published in the area of technology in which you are interested? Which ones does your learning materials center receive?

Does your learning materials center publish a catalogue of periodicals received? Is there a posted list of these periodicals in the center?

Journals

Journals are periodical publications of special groups. They usually contain reports of research by engineers and scientists, and thus are primary sources of information about the "state of the art" in the discipline which the journal focuses on. There are several journals in some fields of interest.

Some typical journal titles are: *Journal of Industrial Engineering; Journal of Materials; Journal of Metals*; *Journal of Nuclear Materials*; *Journal of Petroleum Technology.*

STUDY QUESTIONS

Does your learning materials center receive any journals? Are any of them in areas you are interested in? If so, look at them. Does the subject matter of any of the journal articles look interesting to you? Why or why not?

"Advances," "Reviews," "Proceedings," and "Transactions"

Other publications update the state of the art in various technological areas. They may or may not be published on a regular basis, or the periods may be a year apart. Such publications are called by one of the above titles.

There are many publications whose titles begin with the word "Advances." One you may find in your center is *Advances in nuclear science and technology*, published annually since 1962.

Similarly, there are many publications that have the word "Review" in their titles. Some of these are: *Review of American Chemical Research*; *A. S. M. Review of Metal Literature*; *Review of Scientific Instruments*. The titles indicate the subject matter and purpose of each.

"Transactions" and "Proceedings" are publications that reprint papers and reports presented at meetings and conferences. Here are four which you may find in your center:

Encyclopedia Britannica Conference on the Technological Order, Santa Barbara, California, 1962. *The technological order: proceedings.* Ed. Carl F. Stover. Detroit, Wayne State University, 1963.

International Powder Metallurgy Conference, New York, 1960. *Powder metallurgy: proceedings.* Ed. Werner Leszynski. New York, Interscience, 1961.

International Symposium on Basic Environmental Problems of Man in Space, 2d, Paris, 1965. *Proceedings.* Ed. Hilding Bjurstedt. Vienna, Springer, 1967.

International Symposium on the Physics and Medicine of the Atmosphere and Space. 2d, San Antonio, 1958. *Physics and medicine of the atmosphere and space: proceedings.* Ed. Otis O. Benson, Jr. and Hubertus Strughold. New York, Wiley, 1960.

STUDY QUESTIONS

Notations, such as those above, are printed in certain styles to save effort and space. The various stylistic devices in the notation are used to give us more information than the bare words and phrases furnish.

1. In each of the four notations, what was the official name of the meeting or conference? How do you know?

2. If you were to go to your center to find any one of these, what title would you look for? How do you know what the title is?

3. When and where were each of these "Proceedings" published? Who was the publisher?

4. What connection with the proceedings did Messrs. Benson, Strughold, Bjurstedt, Leszynski, and Stover have? Clue: Look up the abbreviation "ed." in a standard dictionary. Or, look at the title page of a typical "Proceedings."

Where to Look for Periodicals Outside Your Center

You may want to look at magazines or journals that your center doesn't have, or you may want to obtain an article published in one. The reference librarian or interlibrary loan librarian can help you.

The titles of magazines, which are available in libraries or centers other than your own, are catalogued in *Ayer's Directory of Newspapers and Periodicals.* Every center has this publication.

Titles of magazines and house organs will be found in:

Ulrich's Periodicals Directory (R. R. Bowker Co., New York, New York)

Writer's Market (*Writer's Digest*, Cincinnati, Ohio, 45210. This yearbook lists some newspapers as well.)

Gebbie Press House Magazine Directory (Gebbie Press, New York, New York)

Titles of journals are listed in guides or handbooks published in the several knowledge areas or disciplines, or in abstract indexes for the several disciplines.

Microfilm and Microfiche

To save space in storage centers, to save money, and to insure permanence of materials as well, many books, newspapers, magazines, journals, and other materials are recorded and stored on microfilm or microfiche. *Microfilm* is 35-mm film in rolls, each frame of which reproduces in "micro" or miniature a page, part of a page, or more than one page of a publication. *Microfiche* is a method for storing a number of greatly reduced pages on one card. Both methods use microphotography and both must be read with special reading machines available at your center. Many centers have equipment for making normal-size reproductions of materials stored by one of these processes.

Microfilm and microfiche are more easily shipped than are larger volumes and are therefore usually easy to borrow from other centers. Consult your reference librarian.

Retrieving Information in the Learning Materials Center

Suppose you are interested in a topic or subject, but you have no idea if any information is available about that topic, whether information can be found in your center, or how to go about looking for information.

Experienced information finders will tell you that the best place to start is with an encyclopedia since all centers have them. These five are your best sources:

Encyclopedia Americana and its annual supplement or yearbook, the *Americana Annual*

Encyclopedia Britannica and its annual supplement or yearbook, the *Britannica Book of the Year*

McGraw-Hill Encyclopaedia of Science and Technology, and its annual supplement or yearbook (see Fig. 5.1)

The Harper Encyclopedia of Science

Van Nostrand's Scientific Encyclopedia

Subjects are listed in alphabetical order in encyclopedias; however, you should also consult the main index because it often cross-references subjects, showing where other information on the subject can be found.

Encyclopedia articles are not comprehensive; they furnish only an overview of the subject. In addition, bibliographies (lists of books or articles) list additional sources for information. The author of the encyclopedia article is usually an expert in his field, and you may find other materials indexed under his name in the center's card catalogues.

Your center should also have the following *specialized* encyclopedias and dictionaries:

American Dictionary of Culinary Terms: a Comprehensive Guide to the Vocabulary of the Kitchen. 1962.

Audio Cyclopedia. 1959.

Aviation and space dictionary. Los Angeles, 1940–.

Chamber's Technical Dictionary. Rev. with supplement, 1958. A good, general purpose, technical dictionary.

Chemical Trade Names and Commercial Synonyms: A Dictionary of American Usage. 2d ed., rev. and enl., 1955.

Complete Encyclopedia of Homemaking Ideas. Meredith, 1968.

428   TECHNETIUM

attention to its progress is required. Approximately $3\frac{1}{2}$ hr are needed for the rolling and fermentation operations.

Firing or drying of fermented tea leaf conventionally is carried out by passing it through heated ovenlike chambers. Temperatures of 170–180°F arrest fermentation and develop the familiar blackish color. Drying is practically completed in one pass, but further heat is applied to produce the "case hardening" that protects quality. The leaf is sieved, graded, and packed into chests lined with aluminum foil. Each chest contains about 100 lb of finished tea.

Green tea. Green tea manufacture requires that the plucked leaves be steamed as quickly as possible. Such processing at 160°F makes them soft and pliable and, by inactivating the natural enzymes, prevents fermentation. After steaming, the leaf is alternately rolled and dried until it becomes too stiff for further manipulation. For export, green tea is refired in pans with mechanical stirring to produce a luster.

Oolong teas. Oolong teas are midway between black and green teas in that they are semifermented. After a short sun-withering in the garden, the leaf is gently rolled in the plucker's hands, whereupon a slight fermentation is initiated. After a short period this leaf is sent to the factory to be fired and packed for shipment.

Instant tea. This type of tea is obtained by spray-drying of a black tea extract, with or without the admixture of maltodextrins. The technology is patterned closely after that followed in manufacturing of instant coffee. Concentrated tea extract also may be combined with a heavy sugar syrup and marketed as a liquid. Solubility of instant tea powder can be varied widely by manipulations in processing. *See* FOOD ENGINEERING.

[JOHN H. NAIR]

Technetium

A chemical element, Tc, atomic number 43, discovered by C. Perrier and E. G. Segrè in 1937 as a result of cyclotron bombardment of molybdenum by deuterons. The element was the first made artificially, thus the name technetium, from the

Greek for "artificial." It is also produced as a major constituent of nuclear reactor fission products or, alternatively, by action of neutrons on Mo^{98}, as in Eq. (1). The isotope Tc^{99} is most suitable for

$$Mo^{98}(n,\gamma)Mo^{99} \xrightarrow[67\ hr]{\beta^-} Tc^{99} \tag{1}$$

chemical investigation because of its long half-life, 2×10^5 years. The chemistry of technetium is very similar to that of rhenium, and corresponding compounds have been prepared in many cases. The metal can be prepared by reduction of the sulfide with hydrogen at temperatures of 1000–1100°C, and its crystal structure has been found to be isomorphous with that of rhenium, osmium, and ruthenium.

Technetium metal reacts with oxygen at elevated temperatures to form the volatile oxide Tc_2O_7, which is analogous to Re_2O_7. Another oxide, TcO_2, is formed by the decomposition of NH_4TcO_4 at elevated temperatures in vacuum according to Eq. (2). Reactions which produce the compounds Ag-

$$NH_4TcO_4 \rightarrow TcO_2 + 2H_2O + \frac{1}{2}N_2 \tag{2}$$

TcO_4, $KTcO_4$, NH_4TcO_4, K_2TcCl_6, and TcS_2 are analogous to those used to form the corresponding rhenium compounds. *See* NUCLEAR REACTION: RHENIUM; TRANSITION ELEMENTS.

[SHERMAN FRIED]

Bibliography: R. Colton, *The Chemistry of Rhenium and Technetium*, 1965; S. Tribalat, *Rhenium et Technetium*, 1957.

FIGURE 5.1 Page from an encyclopedia. (From the **McGraw-Hill Encyclopedia of Science and Technology.** Copyright 1960 by McGraw-Hill Book Company. Used with permission of McGraw-Hill Book Company.)

Detergents: A Glossary of Terms Used in the Detergents Industry in English. 1960.

Dictionary of Automatic Control. 1960.

Dictionary of Commercial Chemicals. 3d ed., 1962.

Dictionary of Electronic Terms. 1965.

Dictionary of Gems and Gemology, Including Ornamental, Decorative, and Curio Stones. 5th ed., 1951.

Dictionary of Industrial Technics, Including Related Fields of Science and Civil Engineering. 1965.

A Dictionary of Metallurgy. 1959.

Dictionary of Nutrition and Food Technology. 2d ed., 1965.

Dictionary of Plastics. 2d ed., 1966.

Dictionary of Technical Terms. Rev. ed., 1964.

Dictionary of Terms Used in the Theory and Practice of Mechanical Engineering. 8th ed., rev. and enl., 1960.

Drake's Radio-Television Electronic Dictionary. 1960.

Electronics and Nucleonics Dictionary. 1960.

Encyclopedia of Chemical Technology. 2d ed., 1963.

The Encyclopedia of Electronics. 1962.

The Encyclopedia of Engineering Materials and Processes. 1963.

Encyclopedia of Modern Firearms, Parts, and Assembly. 1959.

Encyclopedic Dictionary of Electronics and Nuclear Engineering. 1959.

Encyclopedic Dictionary of Production and Production Control. 1964.

Engineering Encyclopedia: A Condensed Encyclopedia and Mechanical Dictionary. 3d ed., 1963.

The Fashion Dictionary: Fabric, Sewing, and Dress as expressed in the Language of Fashion. 1957.

Jane's All the World's Aircraft. 1909.

The Man-in-Space Dictionary, a Modern Glossary. 1963.

The McGraw-Hill Encyclopedia of Space. 1968.

Pistols: A Modern Encyclopedia. 1961.

The Practical Dictionary of Electricity and Electronics. 1959.

Rifles, a Modern Encyclopedia. 1958.

The SPACE Encyclopedia: A Guide to Astronomy and Space Research. 2d, rev. ed., 1960.

A Syllabus of Stage Lighting. 8th ed., 1953.

THE WAY THINGS WORK: An Illustrated Encyclopedia of Technology. 1967.

Wine: A Brief Encyclopedia. 1960.

STUDY QUESTIONS

With the advice of your instructor, choose one of the above titles, either in your area of interest or in an area of general interest. Answer the following questions in class for the benefit of your fellow students:

1. Is the book available in the learning materials center? If not, did the reference librarian suggest a substitute?

2. Is an older or newer edition of the book available, if this edition is not?

3. What do the abbreviations "ed.," "rev.," and "enl." mean?

4. Who is/are the editor(s) or writer(s)?

5. Where and by whom is the book published?

6. Read the preface or introduction. Look carefully at some sample items. Then decide what the purpose and range of the book is. Is it specific or general?

7. If the book is several years old, where could you look for updated information?

8. Approximately how many words or topics does the book treat?

9. Can you find mention of the compiler(s) in a biographical dictionary such as *Who's Who, American Men of Science,* or *Dictionary of Scientific Biography?* What does the book tell you about the compiler(s)?

Guides, Handbooks, and Manuals

Assume that you are still searching for information on a topic and that you have looked at encyclopedias and dictionaries. Your next stop might be in the reference section of your center, where guides, handbooks, and manuals are kept. These books generally furnish extensive overviews of their respective fields. However, guides, handbooks, and manuals are not uniformly alike. Their formats and subject matter treatments depend on the judgment of their authors or on the disciplines they describe.

These are some guides your center should have:

A Concise Guide to Plastics. 2d ed., 1963.

Earth Manual: A Guide to the Use of Soils as Foundations and as Construction Materials for Hydraulic Structures. Rev. reprint, 1963.

Food Standards and Definitions in the United States: A Guidebook. 1963.

Guide to Audio-Visual Presentations. 1963.

Guide to Microreproduction Equipment. 1959.

Human Engineering Guide for Equipment Designers. 2d ed., 1964.

Industrial Data Guide. 1962.

Materials for Architecture: An Encyclopedic Guide. 1961.

Solvents Guide. 2d ed., rev. and extended, 1963.

The Space Guidebook. New rev. ed., 1963.

These are some handbooks and manuals your center should have:

The Amateur Photographer's Handbook. 1925.

American Electricians' Handbook: A Reference Book for Practical Electrical Workers. 8th ed., 1961.

ASME Handbook. 2d ed., 1965.

Chemical Engineers' Handbook. 4th ed., 1963.

Civil Engineering Handbook. 4th ed., 1959.

Electrical Engineers' Handbook. 4th ed., Wiley.

Electronic Test Equipment Handbook. 1962.

The Engineer's Companion: A Concise Handbook of Engineering Fundamentals. 1966.

FAA Statistical Handbook of Aviation. 1944.

Gliding: A Handbook on Soaring Flight. 2d ed., 1967.

Handbook for Observing the Satellites. 1958.

Handbook of Adhesives. 1962.

Handbook of Applied Hydraulics. 1969.

Handbook of Applied Instrumentation. 1964.

Handbook of Basic Motion Picture Techniques. 1950.

Handbook of Chemistry: A Reference Volume for All Requiring Ready Access to Chemical and Physical Data in Laboratory Work and Manufacturing. 1934.

Handbook of Electronic Tables and Formulas. 3d ed., 1968.

Handbook of Engineering Fundamentals. 2d ed., 1952.

Handbook of Engineering Mechanics. 1962.

A Handbook of English in Engineering Usage. 2d ed., 1940.

Handbook of Hydraulics for the Solution of Hydrostatic and Fluid-Flow Problems. 5th ed., 1963.

Handbook of Instrumentation and Controls: A Practical Design and Applications Manual for the Mechanical Services. 1961.

Handbook of Machine Shop and Drafting-Room: A Reference Book. 1914.

Handbook of Semi-conductor Electronics: A Practical Manual Covering the Physics, Technology, and Circuit Applications of Transistors, Diodes, and Photocells. 2d ed., 1962.

Handbook of Structural Design. 1963.

Handbook of Textile Fibres. 1959.

Handbook of the Engineering Sciences. 1967.

Industrial Electronics Handbook. 1958.

Industrial Engineering Handbook. 1956.

Kidder-Parker Architects' and Builders' Handbook: Data for Architects, Structural Engineers, Contractors, and Draughtsmen. 1958.

Machinery's Handbook: A Reference Book for the Mechanical Engineer, Draftsman, Toolmaker, and Machinist. 18th ed., 1968.

Materials Handbook: An Encyclopedia for Purchasing Agents, Engineers, Executives, and Foremen. 1929.

Mechanical Engineers' Handbook. 12th ed., 1950.

Metals Handbook. 1927.

National Electrical Code Handbook. 1932.

The New American Machinist's Handbook. 1955.

New Space Handbook: Astronautics and its Applications. 1963.

Nondestructive Testing Handbook. 1959.

Nuclear Engineering Handbook. 1958.

Production Handbook. 2d ed., 1959.

The Radio Amateur's Handbook. 11th ed., 1960.

Radio Engineering Handbook. 5th ed., 1959.

Rare Metals Handbook. 2d ed., 1961.

Standard Handbook for Electrical Engineers. 1956.

Standard Handbook for Mechanical Engineers. 7th ed.

STUDY QUESTIONS

With the advice of your instructor, choose one of the titles listed and answer the same questions listed on page 45. Bring your answers to class for the benefit of your classmates.

There are other guides you should know about:

A Guide to the Literature of Chemistry lists abstract journals (see below) and annual reviews in specific branches of chemistry. Chapter 10 has some good advice on how to conduct systematic literature searches.

Guide to the Literature of Mathematics and Physics, in Part II under subject headings, offers suggestions for starting a search for information on a subject. Part I discusses ways to make effective use of learning materials centers.

Guide to the Literature of the Zoological Sciences (1962) has a good general section on the preparation of technical papers.

Biographies of People in Technology

Many biographies have been written about people who have worked in technology. Here are four you might find in your library:

Boyd, Thomas Alvin. *Professional Amateur: The Biography of Charles Franklin Kettering.* New York: Dutton, 1957. 242 pp.

Frankenberg, Richard Alexander. *Freiherr Von Porsche: The Man and His Cars.* Cambridge: Bentley, 1961. 223 pp.

Stewart, Robert Ernest, and Mary Frances Stewart. *Adolph Sutro, a Biography.* Berkeley, Calif.: Howell-North, 1962. 243 pp.

Walters, Helen B. *Herman Oberth: Father of Space Travel.* New York: Macmillan, 1962. 169 pp.

Brief biographies are found in the following books: *Chemical Who's Who*; *Who's Who in America*; *American Men of Science*; *Who's Who in Science*; *Dictionary of American Biography*; *Who's Who in Engineering*; *A Biographical Dictionary of the Engineering Profession.*

STUDY QUESTIONS

Who were Adolph Sutro, Herman Oberth, Charles Franklin Kettering? Where was Freiherr Von Porsche born? Where did you find the answers to these questions?

Yearbooks

You have already seen a reference to the yearbooks published as supplements to three major encyclopedias. There are six others that should be in your learning materials center:

Minerals Yearbook. U.S. Government Printing Office, from 1932–33 on.

The Agricultural Yearbook

Facts on File

New International Yearbook
World Almanac
Book of Facts

STUDY QUESTIONS

Three of the world's largest bridges are in the United States—the Verrazano Narrows Bridge, the Mackinac Straits Bridge, and the Golden Gate Bridge. When was each of these bridges built and how do they compare in size? How much did each cost? Where did you get your answers?

Books

Suppose that in your search for information you have decided to look for some books on your subject. If the book is in your learning materials center, the place to begin is in the card catalogue, where you will find a card for each book in the center, filed alphabetically in at least two or three ways. All titles by one author will be found where the author's name appears in its alphabetical position. Each book title will be filed alphabetically ("a," "an," and "the" appearing as first words in a title are not considered). Each book title will also be filed alphabetically in a subject file. The subjects are also filed alphabetically. Thus, Courtlandt Canby's *A History of Rockets and Space* will be filed in the "C" section (for "Canby"), in the "H" section (*History of Rockets and Space, A*), in the "S" section (under "Space"), and in the "R" section (under "Rockets") (see Fig. 5.2).

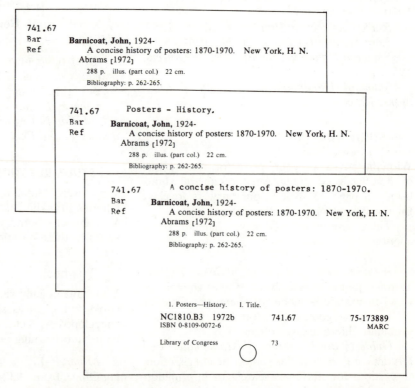

FIGURE 5.2 Book cards from a library card catalogue. The first is filed by author, the second by subject, and the third by title.

If you want a book that is not in your local center, it can probably be borrowed by mail—from the library of the State University, from the library of a nearby large city, or from the Library of Congress in Washington.

To find the titles of such books, consult the numerous bound volumes that have facsimile reproductions of all the cards of the books in the Library of Congress. (So far, only books catalogued before 1950 are catalogued by subject; but all are catalogued by title and by author.) If you find a book listed there, the interlibrary loan librarian will help you get a copy of the book (see Fig. 5.3).

But suppose you don't know the title. Then you turn to *bibliographies*, which are lists of books in a given area or by a given author. (Guides, handbooks, and manuals often contain bibliographies.) One useful bibliography is the *Cumulative Book Index* (CBI), which lists thousands of books by subjects on a year-to-year basis.

STUDY QUESTION

Find out if your learning materials center has a book on a history of technology, a biography of either Henry Ford or Thomas A. Edison, a history of oil in America, or a history of photography. If your learning materials center has none of these books, see if you can find the title of any of these, the name of the author, and the year of publication. Report back to the class.

Abstracts and Indexes

Technical publications today produce a flood of paper, which is enough to drown the unsuspecting information seeker in a sea of frustration. Not only are these published in English; they are also published in Russian, Chinese, Japanese, French, German, and other languages. If it were not for technical translators, a reader would have to know several languages to keep up-to-date.

To find information published in journals, turn first to either an *abstract* or an *index* jour-

United Nations. General Assembly. Delegation from Saudi Arabia
  see Shukairy, Ahmad, 1908-   Statements made during the 13th Session of the United Nations general assembly. New York, 1959.

United Nations. General Assembly. Delegation from Saudi Arabia
  see Shukairy, Ahmad, 1908-   Statements made during the 15th Session of the United Nations general assembly... New York, 1961.

United Nations. General Assembly. Delegation from Saudi Arabia
  see Shukairy, Ahmad, 1908-   Statements made during the 16th session of the United Nations General Assembly. New York, 1962.

United Nations. General Assembly. 14th sess., 1959
  see Shukairy, Ahmad, 1908-   The Palestine refugees. New York [Saudi-Arabian Mission to the United Nations] 1960.

United Nations. General Asesmbly. 14th sess., 1959
  see Shukairy, Ahmad, 1908-   Statements during the 14th session of the United Nations General Assembly. New York, Saudi Arabian Mission to the United Nations, 1960.

United Nations. General Assembly. Special Committee on the Question of Defining Aggression.
  Report, 1 February–5 March 1971. New York, United Nations, 1971.
  iv, 46 p. 28 cm. (United Nations. General Assembly. Official records, 26th session, suppl. no. 19) ([United Nations. Document] A/8419) $1.50
  1. Aggression (International law)   I. Series. II. Series: United Nations. Document A/8419.
JX1977.A2 A/8419   341.5'8   72–179418
[JX4471]   MARC

United Nations. Industrial Development Organization.
  Guide to industrial directories. Guide des répertoires de matériel industriel. Guia de anuarios industriales. New York, United Nations, 1970.
  xvi, 137 p. 28 cm. ([United Nations. Document] ID/53) $2.50
  In English, French, and Spanish.
  "United Nations publication sales no.: E.F.S.71.11.B.5."
  1. Commerce—Directories—Bibliography.   I. Title. II. Title: Guide des répertoires de matériel industriel. III. Title: Guia de anuarios industriales. IV. Series.
JX1977.A2 ID/53   72–178800
           341'.23'08 s [380.1'25]
[Z7164.C8]   MARC

United Nations. Industrial Development Organization
  see Expert Working Group Meeting on Fibrocement Composites, Vienna, 1969. Fibrocement composites... New York, United Nations, 1970-

FIGURE 5.3 Page from the **Library of Congress Catalogue—Name Headings with References.**

nal, which indexes publications of less than book length and many book-length publications as well.

Either type of periodical publishes abstracts (also called "briefs," précis," "summaries," "resumés," "synopses") of technical and scientific articles. However, not all abstracts are alike in form. Some abstracts digest or summarize the whole article. Others summarize only the results and conclusions or perhaps other important features. Abstracts are listed by subjects.

You will find the titles of abstract periodicals and indexes in appropriate handbooks, guides, and manuals. Some of these periodicals attempt to cover a whole area of knowledge; some attempt to cover only part of an area.

Some sample abstract periodical titles are:

Biological Abstracts
Chemical Abstracts
International Aerospace Abstracts
Mathematical Reviews
Meteorological and Geastrophysical Abstracts
Nuclear Science Abstracts

Some sample index titles are:

Applied Science and Technology Index
Engineering Index

Because it sponsors a vast amount of research in all areas, the Federal Government publishes its own indexes. The major titles are:

Government-Wide Index to Federal Research and Development Reports
Monthly Catalogue of U.S. Government Publications
NASA Index of Technical Publications
Technical Abstract Bulletin (referred to as "TAB")
U.S. Government Research Reports
U.S. Government Research and Development Reports

The Federal Government also publishes one combination abstracting-indexing publication, *Scientific and Technical Aerospace Reports* (STAR—formerly called *Technical Publications Announcements*). STAR indexes and abstracts world-wide literature.

These government publications may or may not be in your learning materials center. However, the government maintains document storehouses at many locations (such as the library of your state university) across the nation.

STUDY QUESTIONS

Where is the nearest government document storage center? Which government documents are in your learning materials center?

The words TAB and STAR, as used just above, represent common ways of forming words and names today. The technical term for words formed as these are is *acronym*. What is an acronym?

Periodical Indexes

Suppose that your search for information has led you to the magazine section of the center. Is there an easy way to find information, or must you waste your time flipping pages or reading tables of contents?

The key to many general periodicals is the *Reader's Guide to Periodical Literature*. This index, available in nearly every learning materials center, lists by subject and by author all articles and essays appearing in a selected list of general periodicals. The articles indexed in this set of volumes tend to be more popular treatments of technical subjects.

In the sample of two *Reader's Guide* pages, notice the treatment of the subject "Engineering" (see Fig. 5.4).

STUDY QUESTIONS

1. If you wanted to find discussions of problems facing engineering educators, how many articles would be available to you?

2. When do these subjects first appear in the *Reader's Guide to Periodical Literature*: Wankel engines; astronautics; the Tagus River Bridge; laser beams; plant and animal ecology; paramedicine; biomathematics?

Other Sources of Information

The American Society for Testing and Materials periodically publishes a *Book of ASTM Standards and Related Materials* together with supplements and an index. Some 4,000 standards applicable to industry are included. This book and other printed materials pertaining to properties, standards, and specifications are discussed in Chapter 6.

The *Thomas Register of American Manufacturers* and *Sweet's Engineering Catalogues* (*Sweet's Files*) are sources of information about manufacturers and manufactured products (see Chapter 6). Both may be used as a source from which to request *catalogues* and *brochures* describing products. (Thomas Zarnke used this method to secure information for "Progress of the Progressive Die," Appendix 6.)

Three books of interest to everyone who owns an automobile are: *Glenn's Auto Repair Manual* by Harold T. Glenn or, for later models, *Chilton Auto Repair Manual; Motor's Auto Repair Manual*, published in 1969 by the Motor Book Division of Hearst Magazine; and Guy F. Wetzel's *Automotive Diagnosis and Tune-Up*. Your center may also have *Motor's Truck and Diesel Repair Manual* and *Glenn's Foreign Car Repair Manual*.

ENGINEERING
Engineering sciences. See occasional issues of Science news
   See also
Automobile engineering
Biomedical engineering
Environmental engineering
Petroleum engineering
Technology
            Study and teaching
Education for innovation: address, December 29, 1969, M. Tribus. Vital Speeches 36:279-82 F 15 '70
ENGINEERING, Hydraulic.
See Hydraulic engineering
ENGINEERING colleges
   See also names of engineering colleges, e.g. Massachusetts institute of technology, Cambridge
ENGINEERING education
   See also
Engineering—Study and teaching
ENGINEERING offices.
   See Offices
ENGINEERING research
   See also
Highway research
ENGINEERING societies

   See also
National academy of engineering
ENGINEERS
Ph.D. holders in private industry. M. F. Crowley. il Mo Labor R 93:65-6 Ag '70
   See also
Civil engineers
            Supply and demand
Cuts threaten industry capabilities. Aviation W 93:12-14 Ag 31 '70
Down and out along route 128. R. Rice. il N Y Times Mag p28-9+ N 1 '70 Discussion. p48+ N 22 '70
Engineering jobs. Sci N 97:480 My 16 '70
   Projected requirements for technicians in 1980. M. F. Crowley. bibliog f il Mo Labor R 93:13-17 My '70
ENGINES
   See also
Automobile engines
Automobile engines
Diesel engines
Flywheels
Gas and oil engines
Marine engines
Motorcycle engines
Rocket engines

FIGURE 5.4 Sample of a section of the **Reader's Guide.** (Reprinted by permission from the **Reader's Guide to Periodical Literature**, p. 528. Copyright © 1970 by The H. W. Wilson Company.)

Retrieving Information from the General Public

Sampling and Polling

We live in a democracy and, therefore, the opinions of citizens play an important part in the government. But people's opinions are also important in technology. We have seen, for example, the upsurge of the ecology movement and the impact that environmentalists have had on government *and* industry. Paper mills have been forced to make enormous expenditures of time and money to cut down odor emission and the discharge of toxic wastes into streams. Atomic reactor plants for generating power have been restrained until they could demonstrate that they would not be sources of dangerous radiation in case of accident or of unnatural heating of adjacent streams. The automobile manufacturers have been ordered to redesign engines and exhaust systems to reduce or eliminate certain kinds of emissions. All these actions have come about because of people's opinions.

STUDY QUESTIONS FOR FIG. 5.5

1. What are the sources for the predetermined answers in Fig. 5.5?

2. Would a computer have any difficulties in handling the six choices in question 7? If not, why not?

3. Do you think product sampling of this kind is a good idea? Why?

Consumers' opinions play important roles in the design and manufacture of products. Manufacturers conduct test marketing campaigns to determine if a clientele can be built up for a new product. Motion picture companies try out several endings for a film before settling on the one that pleases the most members of preview audiences. Among advertising agencies, a common expression is, "Let's run this up a flagpole and see who salutes it."

Formal research into the opinions held by a constituency (a group limited by boundaries, such as city limits or state lines) is done through

1. Do you want a vinyl-covered roof?
   □ Yes   □ No
2. Do you want an exterior appearance trim group?
   □ Yes   □ No
3. Do you want an exterior protection trim group?
   □ Yes   □ No
4. Do you want wheel covers, if not standard equipment?
   □ Yes   □ No
5. If wheel covers are standard, do you want a special kind of wheel covers instead?
   □ Yes   □ No
6. Do you want special wheels?
   □ Yes   □ No
7. What kind of tires do you want?
   □ Standard-equipment tires
   □ Bias-ply, belted (if optional)
   □ Radial-ply, belted (if optional)
   □ Wider tires
   □ Whitewall or other special-appearance tires.
   □ Snow tires
8. Do you want a luggage rack?
   □ Yes   □ Permanent type   □ Temporary type
   □ No

FIGURE 5.5 Questionnaire used by an automobile company.

polling or sampling. In a *poll*, every member of a constituency is given the opportunity to vote. In a *sample*, only carefully chosen members of a sample population vote. This sample must be as precisely proportionate to the whole constituency as it can be. In polling, the results of the poll are accepted, even though only a fraction of eligible voters may go to the polls. In sampling, there must be a response from every member of the sample, or the results may be invalid.

STUDY QUESTIONS

How many Americans were eligible to vote in the last general election? How many voted? What percentage of eligible voters voted for the

President? What proportion of those who voted chose the winning candidate for President?

In a national poll, such as the Gallup or Harris polls, how many people's opinions are sampled? How is it possible for the opinions of such a few people to be truly representative of the total population of the country or of the total of eligible voters? How can the national television news services predict early in the evening of a national election just who the eventual winner will be?

Designing the Questionnaire

The design of the sampling questionnaire is critical. Although write-in-votes are allowed in polling, they are usually not allowed in sampling. For one thing, questionnaires are ordinarily processed by computer, and it is difficult to program the computer for random responses.

In sampling, therefore, the answers are predetermined. The questionnaires must deal with matters that are suitable for predetermined answers. This means a careful analysis of the subject matter to select questions that are relevant and pertinent to the subject. The next job is to design the questions in such a way that they can be processed on the computer and at the same time give the needed information.

Start with choices or answers, which can be of the following types:

1. For a proposal—opposed to it; no opinion

2. Opposed to a program—mostly opposed; neutral or no opinion; mostly for the program; entirely for

3. A specific quantity—16 feet; 18 feet; 20 feet; 22 feet; 24 feet; or $10,000; $20,000, $30,000; $40,000; $50,000

The first set of answers allows the respondent to be either for or against a program, or undecided or neutral. The second set allows him to take any *one* of five positions—two are polar opposites (*yes* or *no*); two are moderately opposed (maybe yes, maybe no); and one is neu-

tral or undecided. The third set of answers gives the respondent a choice of one of five possibilities. Three to five choices fall within the computer's range; at the same time, that number of choices doesn't inhibit a respondent too much.

If the problem is more complex, the questions are broken down into more detail:

Should Pottsville hire a town electrician?
Yes ( )   No ( )   No opinion ( )
If you favor hiring a town electrician, how much education or experience should he have?

Work experience ( )   Degree from a 2-year college ( )   Degrees from a 4-year college ( ) Combination of a 2-year degree and work experience ( )   No opinion ( )

If an electrician were hired, how much should he be paid?

$5,000 to $10,000 ( ) $10,000 to $15,000 ( )   The going wage in towns the size of Pottsville ( ) Let the Town Council decide ( ) No opinion ( )

In any case, questions are framed to fit the above three types of answers:

Where do you stand on the proposed city ordinance to require everyone to ride to work on a bus or in a car pool?

What is your opinion of the company's proposal to go to a three-day work week of twelve hours a day?

What should be the width of the proposed driveway through the new company grounds?

STUDY QUESTIONS

You have heard students complain about inequalities in the operations of the numerous sections of the Freshman English program in your school or institute. How would you determine if inequalities exist, what the inequalities are, and what students think should be done about them? Be specific in your answers.

WRITING ASSIGNMENT

Prepare a questionnaire on a subject of real interest to you or your fellow students: provisions for student parking; effectiveness of teaching; the school's athletic or concert programs; disbursement of student fees; dormitory regulations; and so on. Prepare five questions that might go on a questionnaire and give your respondents three to five choices for each of the five questions. Then bring your questionnaire to class for review by your classmates.

Prepare a list of characteristics of students at your school. Describe a typical student or several students who seem typical. How many students would constitute a sample group on your campus?

Retrieving Information from Individuals

The Interview

Sampling and polling are methods of learning the attitudes or opinions of a large number of people. The *interview* is used to learn one individual's attitudes and opinions or else to get factual information from an individual.

For instance, you may have to interview a project manager to find out some things about the project in order to do a better job. You may have to interview the project engineer to get information from him. You may have to interview someone in personnel, sales, production, or accounting. You may have to interview a client or a customer.

The sampling questionnaire asks questions to which only a limited number of responses are possible. The interviewer, however, asks *open-ended* questions which allow the respondent to furnish as much information as he wishes. The interviewer may also, on occasion, ask *close-ended* questions when he needs specific answers. An open-ended question might be: What are the relative merits of American-made and Japanese-made television sets? A close-ended question might be: If you were to buy a new television set, would you buy a Sony or a Zenith?

Whenever you interview, prepare yourself in advance. First, learn as much as possible about the subject of your interview (the topic on which you are seeking information). Don't ask the person you are interviewing to give you data that is already accessible in an encyclopedia, a newspaper, or a magazine article. Then, if possible, find out something about the person you are interviewing and, if he is an executive of an organization, something about the organization. If the person is the author of magazine or journal articles, read them.

Second, prepare the key questions you will ask and list them in a logical order, with the most important questions first. Then, as each question is answered, check it off.

Have a note pad and a supply of pencils or pens. If you have access to a cassette-type tape recorder, use it. Otherwise, take ample notes.

If you can, assure your respondent in advance about the length of the interview and then stick to that time. Move through your questions efficiently and quickly. Don't, however, interrupt your respondent while he is talking. If there is time left over, you can ask additional questions (the unimportant ones at the end of your list), or you can ask your respondent to comment in general.

If you can't finish asking your questions before your time runs out, ask for permission to leave one or two questions to be answered at his or her leisure.

If your respondent seems uneasy about the use you may make of the information, offer to call and read your completed paper. Experienced reporters advise against turning a copy of your paper over for corrections or editing.

STUDY QUESTIONS

Assume that you have been called in to be interviewed in response to a job application.

1. Make a list of questions the interviewer is likely to ask you. Then prepare the answers to each question. For example, a question frequently asked is: What are your salary expectations? How will you answer that question?

2. Prepare a list of questions you will ask when the interviewer turns to you and says: Now, what questions do you have?

6 | Standards, Properties, and Specifications

The success of modern technology depends on a thorough knowledge of the materials being used, on interchangeability of parts, on the repetition of processes, and on total agreement about measurements and quantities.

Here are some examples:

1. If an expressway or a county highway is to be built, there must be agreement about what constitutes a good roadway and what materials must be used in its construction. There must also be a means for determining that proper materials are used in the proper way.

2. If an automobile owner needs a new part for his automobile or a certain grade of lubricating oil, he must be able to purchase a part that will exactly replace the worn part as it was when it was new, or he must be able to purchase lubricating oil with the required SAE rating.

3. If a person wishes to build a building or a house, the contractor and the contractor's workmen must understand exactly what is to be built—the type of building, the size, the location, the cost, the materials and fittings to be used, and the date of completion.

To insure successful completion of any technological project, technologists, and engineers, and others rely on *standards*, *properties*, and *specifications*. In your educational experience and in your work experience you will have to utilize and know about these three subjects.

Standards

A standard is a unit which under specified conditions (temperature or altitude above sea level) defines a quantity or quality (a unit of measurement or a color), represents these (a yardstick or a ruler), or describes or records either. Formerly, for instance, a platinum rod approximately 39.37 inches long defined the unit of measurement called the meter. Exact duplicates in length, if not necessarily in materials, were used all over the world. Until 1960, the basis for the length of this rod was one ten-millionth (10^{-7}) of the earth's quadrant passing through Paris. In 1960, the basis was redefined as the length equal to 1,650,763.73 wavelengths in a vacuum of the orange-red radiation of krypton 86.

Similarly, the kilogram is defined as the mass of a platinum brick, called the International Prototype Kilogram, kept, like the standard meter, at the International Bureau of Weights and Measures in Sèvres, France.

Standards do not occur naturally. They are created by man to insure accuracy. Formerly,

ROUTINE TEST PROCEDURES

SEPTEMBER 1973

1. DIMENSIONS

The increase in dimensions due to the insulation shall be determined in the following manner:

1.1 Round Wire

1.1.1 Film Coated. The film-coated wire shall be measured at four points, spaced approximately 45 degrees apart, around the circumference. The largest and smallest readings shall be recorded, and the average of these two readings shall be taken as the overall diameter. The insulation shall then be removed at approximately the same position on the wire by means not injurious to the bare wire and the measurements repeated around the bare wire. The average of the largest and smallest readings shall be taken as the diameter of the bare wire. The increase in diameter due to the insulation shall be calculated in accordance with the following:

$$\left(\begin{matrix} \text{Overall} \\ \text{diameter} \end{matrix} \right) - \left(\begin{matrix} \text{Diameter of} \\ \text{bare wire} \end{matrix} \right)$$

1.1.1.1 Self Bonding Film Coated. The increase in diameter due to the thermoplastic outer coating shall be determined in the following manner.

The overall diameter shall be measured in accordance with 1.1.1. The thermoplastic outer coating shall then be removed by immersing the wire for 2 minutes in a solvent which will remove the outer coating without swelling or softening the underlying film coating and then wiping the wire with a cheesecloth pad dampened with solvent. The dimension of the wire over the underlying film coating shall be measured at four points, spaced approximately 45 degrees apart, around the circumference of the wire. The average of the largest and smallest readings shall be taken as the diameter over the underlying-film-coated wire. The increase in the diameter due to the thermoplastic outer coating shall be calculated in accordance with the following:

$$\left(\begin{matrix} \text{Diameter} \\ \text{over} \\ \text{thermoplastic} \\ \text{outer} \\ \text{coating} \end{matrix} \right) - \left(\begin{matrix} \text{Diameter} \\ \text{over} \\ \text{underlying-} \\ \text{film-coated} \\ \text{wire} \end{matrix} \right)$$

The increase in diameter due to the underlying film coating shall be determined in accordance with 1.1.1.

1.1.2 Fibrous Covered. The fibrous-covered wire shall be measured at three points, spaced approximately 1 foot (300 mm) apart. The average of these readings shall be taken as the overall diameter. The insulation shall then be removed at approximately the same positions on the wire by means not injurious to the bare wire and the measurements† repeated around the bare wire. In the case of glass-fiber or polyester-glass-fiber covering over film-coated wire, the film coating as well as the glass fibers shall be removed and the measurements† repeated around the bare wire. The increase in diameter due to the insulation shall be calculated in accordance with the following:

$$\left(\begin{matrix} \text{Overall} \\ \text{diameter} \end{matrix} \right) - \left(\begin{matrix} \text{Diameter of} \\ \text{bare wire} \end{matrix} \right)$$

†In each set of measurements, the diameter shall be measured at two points on the circumference, approximately 90 degrees apart.

FIGURE 6.1 Sample test procedures. (From the NEMA **Standards Publication for Magnet Wire MW 1000–1973.** Copyright © 1973 by National Electrical Manufacturers Association. Reprinted by permission.)

there were no standards for the width between railroad tracks and, as a result, it was necessary to unload and reload merchandise every time it passed from one rail line to another. Similarly, there were no standards for fire hydrants, and more than one building burned to the ground while firemen stood by helplessly, unable to attach their hoses to a nearby water supply.

STUDY QUESTIONS

What can you find out about the original basis for the units of measurement known as the inch, the foot, the yard, and the mile? What is the present basis for these standards? Why is it important that this country ultimately convert to the metric system?

Properties

Properties are the natural or inherent qualities of materials under given conditions. For example, the specific gravity of water is a property of water. The flash point of a combustible fluid is a property of the fluid. Men do not create properties, although they can control them. For instance, humidity and temperature are properties of the atmosphere that man has learned to control.

In your work, you will often have to measure or ascertain properties. If you are in civil engineering, you will have to determine the properties of soils, water, aggregates, and concrete. If you work with metals, you will have to determine such properties as Rockwell hardness, Charpy V-notch strength, and tensile strength. If you work with electrical energy, you will have to determine such properties as resistance, voltage, and wattage.

In making these several determinations, you will follow predetermined methods and processes and you will record what you discover.

Fig. 6.1 illustrates a partial set of test procedures for determining certain properties of insulated magnet wire. There are similar test procedures in every area of technology.

Fig. 6.2 illustrates one way of recording (*tabulation*) the test results for determining properties of wire steel used in building a suspension bridge. Such tests are made to insure that the wire or other material to be used has the properties specified by the designer. In Chapter 8, you will find procedures for making your own forms for reporting such tests.

Sources of Information About Specific Properties

Properties of materials may be found in *manuals* or *handbooks* (see Chapter 5). Some of these are:

Timber Construction Manual, American Institute of Timber Construction, Washington, D.C. (New York: John Wiley and Sons, Inc., 1966).

Wood Handbook, USDA Handbook No. 72, published by the United States Department of Agriculture, Washington, D.C.

ACI Standards, American Concrete Institute, Detroit, Michigan.

Other manuals and handbooks are published by such organizations as the National Electrical Manufacturers Association, New York City, and the American Society for Testing and Materials, Philadelphia.

STUDY QUESTIONS

1. Can you find the one instance in Fig. 6.2 where the maximum (max.) property exceeds the specification?

2. What are the properties at ambient temperatures (the temperatures to be found in a laboratory) of iron, copper, lead, aluminum, and carbon?

3. Where would you look to find the properties of any one element or of a compound such as carbon tetrafluoride or zinc oxide?

4. What are the properties of iron at 1,535° C and 3,000° C? What are the properties of copper at 1,083° C and 2,595° C?

Average Chemical Properties of the Wire Steel—Determined From Ladle and Check Analyses

MATE-RIAL	NO. OF MELTS		LADLE					CHECK				
			C	MN	P	S	SI	C	MN	P	S	SI
Cable Wire	735 (1)	Specified ...	0.85	—	0.04	0.04	—	0.935	—	0.05	0.05	—
		Max.	0.85	0.79	0.035	0.037	0.36	0.93	0.78	0.035	0.039	0.39
		Ave.	0.81	0.66	0.026	0.028	0.24	0.82	0.64	0.025	0.029	0.24
		Min.	0.78	0.54	0.020	0.023	0.15	0.73	0.51	0.014	0.020	0.14
Sus-pender Rope Wire	44	Specified ...	0.85	—	0.04	0.04	—	0.935	—	0.05	0.05	—
		Max.	0.84	0.75	0.039	0.034	0.28	0.89	0.76	0.041	0.035	0.27
		Ave.	0.81	0.67	0.025	0.027	0.23	0.82	0.66	0.025	0.030	0.22
		Min.	0.78	0.57	0.020	0.024	0.18	0.76	0.56	0.019	0.024	0.16
Hold-Down Rope Wire	4	Specified ...	0.85	—	0.04	0.04	—	0.935	—	0.05	0.05	—
		Max.	0.82	0.76	0.028	0.031	0.28	0.85	0.69	0.029	0.041	0.25
		Ave.	0.81	0.68	0.026	0.028	0.23	0.81	0.64	0.025	0.034	0.22
		Min.	0.79	0.61	0.023	0.025	0.18	0.78	0.56	0.021	0.027	0.17
Hand Rope Wire	3	Specified ...	0.85	—	0.04	0.04	—	0.935	—	0.05	0.05	—
		Max.	0.83	0.72	0.033	0.031	0.28	0.88	0.69	0.034	0.031	0.27
		Ave.	0.80	0.68	0.028	0.029	0.23	0.83	0.68	0.026	0.027	0.23
		Min.	0.78	0.66	0.024	0.026	0.19	0.78	0.65	0.021	0.024	0.20
Wrap-ping Wire	11	Specified	0.50-0.55	—	0.04	0.04	—	0.50-0.55	—	0.05	0.05	—
		Max.	0.52	0.63	0.028	0.030	0.28	0.57	0.63	0.030	0.037	0.29
		Ave.	0.51	0.57	0.024	0.028	0.23	0.53	0.56	0.025	0.031	0.21
		Min.	0.49	0.54	0.020	0.027	0.20	0.50	0.53	0.020	0.025	0.16

FIGURE 6.2 Table from **The Golden Gate Bridge** (San Francisco, 1937) showing **properties** of the wire steel used on the bridge, as determined from analyses.

5. In Fig. 6.2, what chemical properties of wire steel were reported? What do "Max.," "Ave.'" and "Min." mean?

6. Where would you look in your learning materials center for the properties of materials or of specific phenomena that are pertinent to your area of study?

Specifications

In Fig. 6.2, the word "specified" was used several times. This means that the designer of the Golden Gate Bridge specified that the wire steel used in various parts of the bridge had to have certain properties—certain percentages of the several elements that go into making certain kinds of steel.

The designer determined what these *specifications* were from his knowledge of the estimated loads the bridge would carry, the estimated stresses placed on material by these loads, and by other forces such as wind and temperature changes.

Specifications are the exact requirements of quantities or qualities established for specific situations where something is to be built, manufactured, operated, maintained, or repaired.

Standards are often general specifications, designed to apply broadly to an industry or a work area or even to all industries and work areas. Many standards are international in scope.

Some specifications are broad in scope. An example is the set of specifications for the construction of steel tanks for fluid storage written by the American Petroleum Institute or the American Water Works Association. Other specifications are written for specific situations.

Specifications may be written, tabulated, or illustrated, or combinations of these may be used.

STUDY QUESTIONS

1. Fig. 6.2 contains a number of specifications as well as the properties identified. What are the specifications?

2. Are the specifications in Figs. 6.1 and 6.2 broad or limited in scope?

3. Underscore at least three of the specifications you find in Fig. 6.2.

4. What are the relationships between *properties* and *standards* in Fig. 6.2?

Specifications for Naming

In the world of your family and friends, there are many popular names for objects. Popular names tend to be nontechnical and nonprecise. For example, in common usage, a *weed* is any plant that is either unattractive, seems to have no practical use, or interferes with the growth of attractive and useful plants. *Work* is the word popularly applied to what one does on the job. A *nail* is an object, usually made of metal, with a point at one end and a head at the other.

In the world of technology, names must be more precise. A plant is not called a *weed;* it is given a specific name, such as *Taraxacum officinale* (the common dandelion). In technology, *work* refers to the transfer of energy from one object to another. The word *nail* is replaced by such specific terms as *nail, anchor* and *nail, sinker.*

Precise terms are used because they mean the same to everyone everywhere in a particular or general area, as the case may require. To insure that technical words have the same meaning for everyone, *dictionaries,* or *glossaries,* of technical terms are written and distributed to those concerned. In these dictionaries or glossaries, specific definitions or meanings are given for each term listed. The group for whom the dictionary or glossary is published emphasizes the need to use those terms according to the published meaning, especially in letters, reports, catalogues, and other documents of record.

An excerpt from a glossary of packaging terms is shown in Fig. 6.3. The glossary names and describes nineteen different types of nails, thirteen of which are listed here.

N

nail, anchor—A cement-coated nail designed for use with anchor strapping and doorway-protection retaining strips.

nail, anchor plate—A ringed nail for use with anchor plates, mechanical brakemen plates, and hold-fast cleats.

nail, blunt point—Nail with blunt point and minimum taper at point.

nail, box—Nail with a large, flat head. Usually made of lighter gauge wire than a sinker nail.

nail, cement coated—Nail to which a coating has been applied to increase its holding power.

nail, checkered head—Nail with checkered indentations in top of head.

nail, cooler—Same as sinker except that the head is flat underneath and of slightly greater diameter than a sinker of the same penny-size.

nail, corker—Nail with flat counter-sunk head.

nail, diamond point—A nail with a point having four facades, the most common point used.

nail, double headed—Nail with double heads to provide easy removal at destination, for use generally with retaining doors and grain doors.

nail, drive—Common nail. An all-around nail for general construction purposes and usually made of wire of greater diameter than sinkers, coolers, corkers, etc.

nail, duckbill point—Nail having a thin, flat point to facilitate clinching.

nail, etched—Nail with surface roughened by etching in acid bath. Has more holding power than cement-coated nails.

FIGURE 6.3 Example of specific definitions of terms. These meanings are standard for everyone in the packaging industry. Can you find even more specific meanings for such terms as "nail," "box"? (Reprinted by permission from the **Glossary of Packaging Terms,** 4th ed., The Packaging Institute, U.S.A., New York, 1967, p. 24.)

STUDY QUESTION

For each of the following popular words, write an alternative specific word. The popular word must be applicable to the specific word, but the specific word (or term consisting of two or three words) must be applicable to only one specific object:

bulb (electric), car, truck, hammer, pliers, screwdriver, stereo, TV, gas, oil, alcohol, battery, wire, switch, dirt, cement, dam

IN-CLASS DISCUSSION

Ask a local city inspector or consulting engineer to visit your class and talk about local codes (specifications). Be sure to ask about such matters as plumbing, heating, electricity, fire safety, buildings, highways and sidewalks, bridges, sewerages. Ask what the sources are for the local codes. Find out how the codes are enforced.

Sources for Specifications and Standards

Three of the largest sources of standards and specifications are:

The Federal Government and the U.S. Bureau of Standards, The Department of Defense, The American Society of Mechanical Engineers (ASME).

The American Society for Testing and Materials (ASTM) produces an *Annual Book of ASTM Standards.* The Society of Automotive Engineers, Inc. (SAE) produces the *SAE Automotive Handbook* containing many standards and specifications for the automotive industry.

STUDY QUESTION

Does your learning materials center have a handbook or manual of standards and specifications for your area of study or future work? What is its title and who publishes it? When was it last published and how recent is the information?

The Kinds of Specifications You Will Be Called on to Write

As you may have surmised, most of the specifications we have looked at are prepared by engineers or groups of engineers. Some of them are prepared by lawyers working with engineers, especially the specifications that are included in contracts.

How to Write the Production Parts List or the Bill of Materials

There are some specifications that you will quite likely be called on to write. One of the more common of these is the production parts list or bill of materials (see Figs. 6.4a&b and 6.5).

1. Procure an engineering drawing or architect's drawing or plan. The engineering drawing in Fig. 1.2 is a good example. So is Fig. 6.4a, although it is technically an exploded drawing. It is useful here because it shows all parts and assemblies clearly.

2. List every part and assembly in order, working systematically through the drawing (clockwise, top to bottom, or left to right). As you list each item by its exact title, check it off on the drawing. Make sure that you overlook no parts.

3. As you list each part, write the part number and name. Bolts, lockwashers, nuts, screws, wires, and so on should be described as well as named and numbered. (See Fig. 6.4a, items 3, 8, 16, 19, 20–23.) The same practice is used for electrical component parts—capacitors, resistors, transistors and so on.

4. When all parts are listed, correlate identical items. That is, for every item listed more than once, combine all the listings into one and note the number of items required (see right-hand column, Fig. 6.4b).

5. Double check to make sure that each item is listed.

6. Now list the items in a logical order. For example, the items in Fig. 6.4b are listed according to their order in the drawing in Fig. 6.4a.

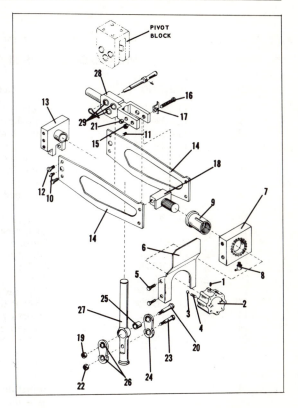

FIGURE 6.4a Exploded drawing accompanying the production parts list in Fig. 6.4b. (Reprinted by permission of Cherry-Burrell Company, a division of Cherry-Burrell Corporation.)

Two other logical orders are possible; if the production parts list is to be detached or used separately from the drawing, you will need to use one of these two orders. One of them would list the items in numerical order according to the part number, beginning with the lowest number and proceeding *in sequence* to the highest (you may not use every sequential number, of course). The other system would be to list the parts in alphabetical order.

Logical order may mean listing parts according to the assemblies and subassemblies in which they are used.

PIVOT BLOCK ADJUSTING ASSEMBLY, LL-2389-244

REF.	PART NO.	DESCRIPTION PIVOT BLOCK ADJUSTING ASSEMBLY	REQ'D. REF.
1	LL-2389-102	Lockscrew	1
2	LL-2389-28	Adjusting knob	1
3	LL-2389-231	Ball, steel, 1/8"	1
4	LL-2389-232	Spring, retaining	1
5	LL-2389-195	Capscrew	4
6	LL-2389-248	Adjusting block end bracket	1
7	LL-2389-244	Adjusting knob bearing block	1
8	LL-2389-36	Bolt, hex head, 5/16-18 x 1/4"	2
9	LL-2389-113	Adjusting clutch	1
10	LL-2389-3	Lubricating pin	2
11	LL-2389-102	Lockscrew	1
12	LL-2389-195A	Capscrew	4
13	LL-2389-87	Adjusting clutch retaining block	1
14	LL-2389-263	Adjusting assembly retaining plate	2
15	LL-2389-110	Nut	1
16	LL-2389-189	Bolt, hex head, 5/26-18 x 2"	1
17	LL-2389-204	Bracket washer	1
18	LL-2389-5	Adjusting clutch differential block	1
19	LL-2389-19	Washer, copperlined, 1/4"	1
20	LL-2389-177	Screw, shoulder, 5/26-18, 1 1/2"	1
21	LL-2389-77	Setscrew, 3/16"	2
22	LL-2389-50	Washer, steel lined, 1/4"	1
23	LL-2389-47	Screw, shoulder, 5/26-18, 1 1/4"	1
24	LL-2389-84	Adjusting assembly transmission lever plate, right hand	1
25	LL-2389-9	Adjusting assembly transmission lever bearing	1
26	LL-2389-10	Adjusting assembly transmission lever plate, left hand	1
27	LL-2389-15	Adjusting assembly transmission lever	1
28	LL-2389-23	Pivot block	1
29	LL-2389-99	Pivot block bearing and retaining spring (in sets only)	3

FIGURE 6.4b Production parts list accompanying the exploded drawing in Fig. 6.4a. (Reprinted by permission of Cherry-Burrell Company, a division of Cherry-Burrell Corporation.)

7. Notice that in naming parts, the name of the part comes first, followed by the description (in Fig. 6.4b, the names of the parts are printed in capital letters and the descriptions are printed in a combination of capitals and lower case). Follow local style procedures in naming.

Fig. 6.5 shows a bill of materials for an item of furniture.

Engineering Change Orders

Once specifications or standards are established for any object or procedure, they may not be changed except on authorization; often the person who established the "specs" must authorize changes. Because specifications and standards are always put into written, tabulated, or illustrated

FLEETWOOD FURNITURE CO.
BILL OF MATERIALS

Order #			Finish	*SEE ORDER*	Quantity	
Date *MAY 10, 19—*			Revised	*MAY 30, 19—*	Written by *WEENER*	

	Q	Description	Part #	Size	Notes
1	1	INTERIOR PANEL, (WOOD)	30461	93 5/16 × 47 3/4 × 3/4	
2	1	FILLER PANEL, VINYL G-2-S	30458	93 1/2 × 15 9/16 × 3/4	
3	2	END PANEL, VINYL G-2-S	30459	15 3/4 × 19 3/4 × 3/4	
4	1	FRAME, 1 1/4 ⌀ TUBE	10485	96 × 66	
5	2	FRAME, END 1 1/4 ⌀ TUBE	10478	19 3/4 × 15 3/4	
6	2	CHANNEL, TRIM, STEEL	10482	46 11/16 × 16 GA.	
7	2	CHANNEL, TRIM, STEEL	10484	47 1/8 × 16 GA.	
8	2	GUSSET PLATE, STEEL	10554	20 GA.	REVISION
9	2	BRACKET, STEEL	10480		
10	2	CHALK TROUGH, ALUMINUM	10481	93 7/16 × 4 1/8 × 16 GA.	
11	2	SHIPPING CLIP, 1/8 STEEL	10556	1 1/2 × 3/4 × 1/8	
12	4	CASTERS W/ BRAKE	70044	5	
13	4	CASTER INSERT	10021		
14	4	TUBE CAPS	70078		
15	2	TUBE CAPS	70108		
16	22	SCREWS O.H.		3 × #10	
17	6	SCREWS O.H.		2 × #10	
18	6	SCREWS F.H.		1 1/2 × #10	
19	12	SCREWS P.H.		5/8 × #8	
20	8	SCREWS P.H.		3/4 × #10	
21	1	CARTON MATERIAL			

WIDE 96	HIGH 72	DEEP 22	MOUNT
		MODEL 1631	

FIGURE 6.5 Sample bill of materials form. Notice such details as order number, finish, quantity, item number (left-hand column), quantity ("Q"), description, part number, and size. The "Notes" column is used primarily to refer to revisions or changes from an original bill of materials. You should always be certain that you are working with the most recent list or engineering drawing. (Reprinted by permission of Jack Weener.)

No. 3024

REQUEST FOR ENGINEERING CHANGE

NOTE: Design changes affecting major parts or functional performance must be approved by Mr. E.J. Murphy.

Request By	Approved By	Date Rec'd. By Eng. Dept.	Recorded By	Date Complete And Released to Shop
Date	Date			

Machine affected:_____ Model No._____

Drawing No's.:_____

Bills of Material:_____

Reason for change:_____

_____

Change:_____

_____

_____

Remarks by Engineering Dept.:_____

_____

_____

Note: White and Pink Copy Go to Engineering Dept.
      Yellow Copy is Retained by Requester.
      Pink Copy Will Be Returned to Requester When Work is Finished.

FIGURE 6.6 Sample of a form used to request an engineering change.

form, the authorization to change them must be in writing.

Fig. 6.6 illustrates a typical "Request for Engineering Change." Once this form is approved, it could become the change order, or the change order could be written on another form.

STUDY QUESTIONS FOR FIG. 6.6

1. In Fig. 6.6, who must authorize changes? Can anyone else authorize changes? Under what conditions?

2. The Engineering Department makes the changes. Who can request them?

3. What provisions are made for cross-referencing this engineering change request to other records of the company?

4. What distribution is made of this change request?

Why Written Specifications?

At this point, you may be asking why specifications can't be presented through a blueprint, a design sketch, an engineering drawing, or a

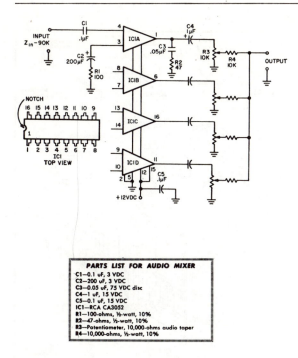

PARTS LIST FOR AUDIO MIXER
C1—0.1 uF, 3 VDC
C2—200 uF, 3 VDC
C3—0.05 uF, 75 VDC disc
C4—1 uF, 15 VDC
C5—0.1 uF, 15 VDC
IC1—RCA CA3052
R1—100-ohms, ½-watt, 10%
R2—47-ohms, ½-watt, 10%
R3—Potentiometer, 10,000-ohms audio taper
R4—10,000-ohms, ½-watt, 10%

FIGURE 6.7 Schematic and specifications (bill of materials) for a four-channel microphone mixer. (Reproduced by permission from **Elementary Electronics**, September-October 1971, p. 73.)

For example, in the case of a simple tool such as a hammer, the drawing would show its dimensions and its appearance—the relation of the head to the handle and the shape of both. But the list of specifications would prescribe variations in material, sizes, or finishes, the methods of manufacture, methods for testing or insuring quality, details about the sales features of the model, and so on.

Plans for a bridge would show the various elevations and cross-sections, each properly dimensioned. The specifications would list materials, the quantities of each, and necessary details about pouring, mixing, welding, riveting, and finishing.

Examine Figs. 6.7 and 6.8. Fig. 6.7 shows a schematic for a four-channel microphone mixer. The bill of materials (parts list) for this mike mixer is also given. One item is not listed in the parts list. Which is it?

Fig. 6.8 shows a three-dimensional outline drawing for a gazebo. This building would need the following kinds of materials:

A poured concrete slab
Sill and post anchors
2 × 4 dimension lumber for sills, wall studs, rafters, and plates
Cedar posts for roof supports
Lag bolts and washers
Dowels and handrails
Masonite bayside lap siding
Shingles, certigrade red cedar
$\frac{3}{8}$" plywood sheathing for sidewalls of gazebo and roof
Rustproof nails and wood preservative
30 lb felt for underlay between siding and walls and between shingles and roof sheathing
1" × 6" lumber for fascia
8-ft sectional door, rollers, and track
1 × 3 strips (2 for finishing each corner).

Fig. 6.9 shows an exploded drawing for a chest.

photograph. In fact, these kinds of illustrations are important as a part of specifications or as a part of any communications that take place in a technology. They help to show matters such as proportions and relative positions. In a general way, they also indicate the materials to be used and some of the specifications. However, there is usually not enough space on the plan to add all the necessary details, to account for all the variables, to allow for later changes or additions, or to explain all the necessary workmanship. Moreover, even if there were space, the addition of so much information might make the plan overloaded and confusing. In any case, much of the detail has to be written.

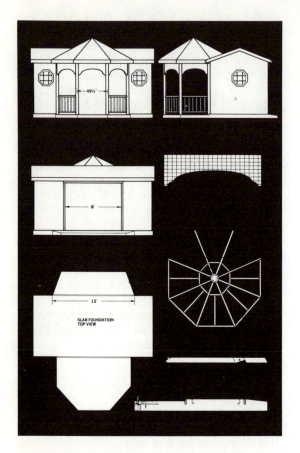

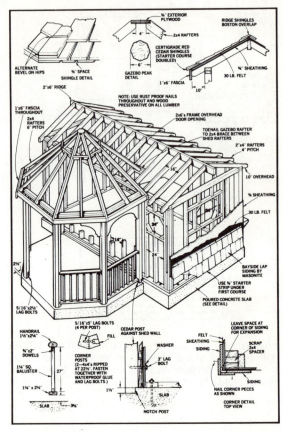

FIGURE 6.8 Plans for a gazebo. (Reprinted by permission of **Mechanix Illustrated**, copyright © 1971 by Fawcett Publications, Inc.)

WRITING ASSIGNMENTS

1. Complete the bill of materials for the gazebo in Fig. 6.8, specifying the amounts of each item needed. Use the list of materials as the basis of your bill.

2. Write the bill of materials for the chest in Fig. 6.9. Choose mahogany, cherry, or walnut for facing materials (those that show when the chest is backed against a wall).

3. Write the bill of materials for the intercom and the stereo phono preamplifier in Fig. 6.10.

4. Assume that you are planning to refurbish your car. You intend to put in a new carburetor, new dual exhausts, a new timing system, a supercharger, new wheels and tires, and new springs. You also plan to add a tape deck and an amplifier and to repaint the car. Write the specifications for the equipment you will need, making sure the specifications fit both the car and the new equipment. Include the tools needed and an exact description of the paint.

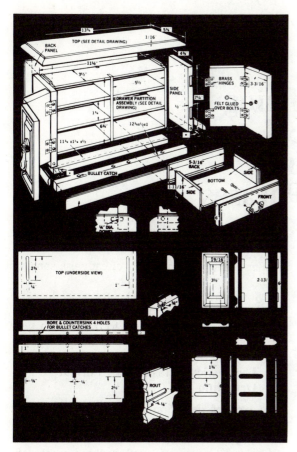

FIGURE 6.9 Plan and exploded drawing for a chest. (Reprinted by permission of **Mechanix Illustrated,** copyright © 1971 by Fawcett Publications, Inc.)

Stereo Phono Preamplifier

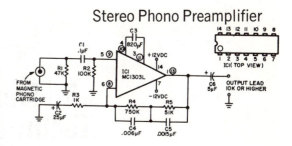

Home Intercom

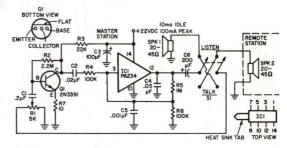

FIGURE 6.10 Schematics for a stereo phono pre-amplifier (top) and a home intercom (bottom). (Reproduced by permission from **Elementary Electronics,** September-October 1971, p. 75.)

7 | Defining Technical Words and Phrases

If you were to examine two dictionaries, one published in 1958, the other, only fifteen years later, you would notice a difference between them. The newer dictionary has many technical terms and phrases that are not in the older one: laser, maser, pulsar, quasar, spinoff, jet stream, and freeway. Also in the newer dictionary are words that are in the older dictionary but with new meanings: Saturn, Mercury, Gemini, tube, Apollo, mace, and salt.

In Fig. 6.3 we saw another type of dictionary, a glossary, which gave specific meanings for certain words and phrases: anchor nail, corker nail, spiral nail, drive nail, and duckbill point nail.

During your career, thousands of new words will come into existence (you may even be responsible for some); old words will take on new meanings; and words or phrases will take on specific, limited meanings. All of these words will require definitions so that everyone concerned can understand what the words or phrase means.

Moreover, as you write about your work, you will often have to tell your reader what you mean by a certain word or phrase. You will need to know the various ways to define words and phrases. They are not hard to learn and, as a matter of fact, you probably already use some of them.

Some methods are brief, others are lengthy. Each method serves a different purpose or need. You will need to know how to frame each type of definition and when to use it.

The Logical, Classical, or Formal Definition

The type of definition that is usually, but not always, found in a dictionary is variously called the logical, the classical, or the formal definition. For simplicity we will call it the *formal definition*.

Here are two examples:

nail: a slim, pointed piece of metal hammered into wood or other materials as a fastener.
technology: the application of a science, especially to industrial or commercial objectives.

In dictionary definitions, the colon (:) is used to replace the word *is* or *are*. However, when you write the formal definition you will use these verbs:

The stabilizer *is* a hinged damper, free to swing in the space provided, admitting air into the smoke pipe to relieve chimney drafts in excess of the stabilizer setting.

STUDY QUESTIONS

1. In the above definition, what word is being defined?

2. What *class* of objects or concepts is the word put into? (In the definition of *nail* above, *nail* is put into the class *metal*. *Technology* is put into the class *application*.)

3. In what way is the defined word differentiated from all other members of its class? For instance, how is *nail* differentiated from all other members of the class *metal*? How is *technology* differentiated from all other members of the class *application*?

4. Before you continue with the text, can you define the formal definition?

A Definition of the Formal Definition

The formula for the formal definition is as follows:

A _____ is a _____
(concept to be defined)   (member of a class)

which _____
(method by which concept differs from all

_____
other members of the same class).

There are several precautions to observe when you write this type of definition:

1. Be sure that your reader is familiar with the class of objects. We have to ask, for instance, how much is gained by defining the Siberian tiger as a member of *panthera tigris longipilis* subspecies.

2. Don't define words with similar words derived from the same roots or stems:

A water meter is a device for metering water.

A thermometer is a device for measuring thermal variations.

If your reader doesn't recognize a word in one form, he will hardly recognize it in another.

However, there is one circumstance in which it is all right to repeat a word from the left side of the equation:

A ring thread *nail* is a small *nail* that has circumferential rings along the shank to provide increased holding power.

In a definition such as this one, you are not interested in defining the specific word *nail* (which in this case also happens to be the name of a class), but in defining how *ring thread nails* are unlike other nails. You assume, in a case such as this, that your reader knows what a *nail* is.

WRITING ASSIGNMENT

Write formal definitions of: a ball-point pen or a lead pencil that is yours. Write the definition in such a way as to define your pen or pencil and no other. Or, write a definition of any one of your textbooks or something similar that belongs to you. In any case, treat the object as unique and only one of a kind.

Partial Definitions

In many cases you will find it useful to define only partially, usually to refresh your reader's memory or to make a useful comparison. There are several types of *partial definitions*.

Definition by Synonym

A synonym is a word that has the same meaning as another word:

A smokepipe is a chimney.
A nail-finder is a wooden rake.

When you use the partial definition, you must be sure that the right-hand member of your equation (chimney, wooden rake) is familiar to your reader. It does no good to tell him, for example, that a *tectrix* is one of the *coverts* of a bird's wing, unless he knows what a covert is.

You must also keep in mind that no two words are exactly synonymous or have identical meanings. Moreover, although the left-hand member of the equation may equal the right-hand member, the right-hand member may not be equal *only* to the left-hand member. In the second example above, a nail finder may be a wooden rake, but a wooden rake is not necessarily only a nail finder. In other words $2 + 2$ may equal 4, but 4 is also equal to such sets as $8 - 4$ and $1 + 3$, or even 2×2!

Definition by Antonym

An antonym is a word meaning exactly the opposite of another word. For instance, *antonym* is the *antonym* of *synonym*! When you define by antonym, you usually do so by indicating that one side of your equation is not equal to the other:

The right-hand lane of a freeway is not a two-way street.
Dynamite is not a toy.

Definition by Appositive

The fountain pen, *a pen containing a tube of fluid ink,* was widely used before the invention of the ball-point pen.

Snopake, *a white correction fluid for blotting out unwanted words or lines on a page,* may be purchased in bottles of several sizes.

The arch has a critical point of equilibrium (*the keystone*), the precise point where weight is divided.

Anything new—*a department, a program, a service*—needs meticulous spadework, *a carefully worked-up plan.*

In the above examples, the appositive is italicized to call your attention to it.

STUDY QUESTIONS

1. In each of the definitions by appositive, what word or phrase is being defined? In each case, convert the appositive definition to a formal definition. What problems do you have?

2. If you look at the four examples carefully, you will observe that the appositive definition may be punctuated in several different ways. What are they? Rewrite the four sentences, changing the punctuation in each to another form and using all of the exemplified forms of punctuation. What problems did you have?

Definition by Etymology

Sometimes it is useful or appropriate to define a word or term by exploring its etymology—its history in terms of its several parts:

Television comes from two very old words: the Greek word *tele,* meaning "distance," and the Latin word *visio,* meaning "sight." *Meter* comes from the Latin *metrum,* meaning "measure." What, then, should the word *telemetry* mean?

Most dictionaries supply the etymology (from the Greek *etymos,* meaning "true," plus the Greek *logos,* meaning "word") of words.

Write formal definitions of teleology and etymology. Then compare your definitions with the ones you find in a dictionary. What are your conclusions?

Definition by Example

Perhaps the simplest form of definition is to point at something:

That animal over there is a duck-billed platypus. . . . That's a 1974 Mustang.

Next to displaying the actual object (which may or may not produce the *understanding* you are hoping for), the exhibition of a picture, a drawing, or a schematic is the most direct way of defining by example. Many of the illustrations in this book represent attempts at definition by example. See Fig. 7.1, "Modern Telephone Service." You can compare the purposes of definition by example with a more formal definition by comparing the information given in Fig. 7.1 with this dictionary definition of the word *telephone*:

telephone: An instrument that directly modulates carrier waves with voice or other acoustic source signals to be transmitted to remote locations and that directly reconverts received waves into audible signals; especially, such an instrument connected to others by wire (*The American Heritage Dictionary,* p. 1323).

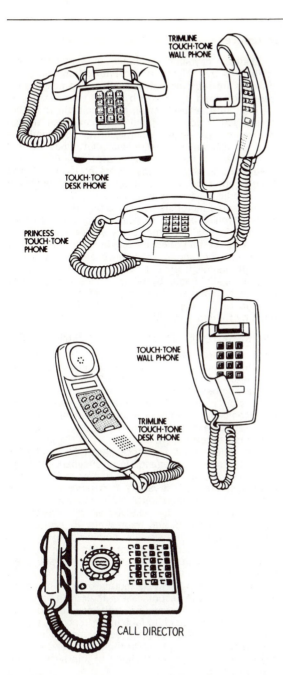

TRIMLINE
TOUCH-TONE
WALL PHONE

TOUCH-TONE
DESK PHONE

PRINCESS
TOUCH-TONE
PHONE

TOUCH-TONE
WALL PHONE

TRIMLINE
TOUCH-TONE
DESK PHONE

CALL DIRECTOR

FIGURE 7.1 Definition by example. (Reproduced by permission of Northwestern Bell Telephone Company, Des Moines, Iowa.)

STUDY QUESTIONS

1. What does Fig. 7.1 tell you about the process of telephoning?

2. What does the definition of the telephone tell you about the word it defines?

3. Can you suggest a picture or drawing that might define the telephone process?

4. Write a formal definition of the telephone instrument. Be sure that your definition covers all the instruments in Fig. 7.1.

5. Write a formal definition of the phrase *partial definition*.

The Operational Definition

If you are trying to help someone understand a process such as telephoning, you need to use something more than the formal or partial definition. Because you are defining an operation, you need a definition that will work for your purpose—a broader form than either of those discussed so far. Such a definition is the *operational definition*.

An operational definition will take into account such items as these:

Materials used in an operation and the changes that may take place in them (carrier waves, for instance)

People employed in an operation and the tasks they perform (all the parties to a telephone call, for example)

Machines used in an operation and the tasks they do (the telephones and the switching and amplifying apparatuses, for example)

Stages in an operation, in a machine's operation, in processing materials, in people's tasks (looking up a telephone number, dialing the number, talking with the called party, replacing a receiver on the instrument)

Processes employed in an operation and the changes they make in machines, materials or men (dialing, switching, talking)

Time consumed, either as a whole or in parts (how much time can be saved by dialing direct rather than asking an operator to complete a call?)

Costs, either per stage or for a whole operation

The ongoing relationships among all of these

Automobile Insurance

The basic kinds of automobile insurance available include:

Liability
Collision
Comprehensive
Medical payment
Uninsured motorists

Of all the above, the most important is liability insurance. This is the insurance that is compulsory in states having compulsory insurance laws.

Liability insurance does not cover injury to you or damage to your own car and property. It covers only those you injure and the property of others. On your behalf, liability insurance pays any claims of bodily injury or property damage for which you are held responsible. Some states are changing their auto insurance procedures to a "no-fault" basis; the person from whom you buy insurance will know the situation in your state.

Liability claims could arise, for example, if you erred in driving and collided with someone else's car, struck a pedestrian, or damaged a neighbor's fence.

Your insurance company would then handle the claim, defend you in court if necessary, and pay the settlement or award in any amount up to the dollar limit of your policy.

Collision insurance covers damage to your own car, even if the accident is your fault. Collision insurance policies are commonly the deductible type. Deductibles are available at several levels, $50—$100—$250, etc., and the premiums you pay decline as the deductible amount becomes higher. The most commonly used deductible is $100. If you choose to purchase $100 deductible, that means you pay the first $100 worth of repairs to your car in the event of a collision. If the repair costs are only $100, you pay that $100, and the insurance company pays nothing. If the repair costs are more than $100, you pay the first $100 and the insurance company pays the remaining cost.

Comprehensive insurance gives you financial protection against damage to your car for such hazards as fire, theft, vandalism, riots, and natural-cause losses (hail, flood, windstorms). Comprehensive policies may or may not be the deductible type. As with collision insurance, comprehensive premiums decrease as deductibles increase and the deductible amount, if one is applicable, is paid by you.

When a new car is financed, the lending institution usually requires that the car be covered by collision and comprehensive insurance to protect its interest.

Medical payment insurance is sometimes described as the "Motorists' Hospitalization Policy." It provides for the payment of medical and hospital expenses incurred by you—or by any of your passengers—which are the result of an auto accident. It further covers you if you're injured by a car, even though you're not a passenger. Whether or not you need this kind of insurance depends on what kinds of and how much hospitalization or medical coverage insurance you and your car passengers now carry. If you have no other medical protection, you probably should have medical payment insurance.

Uninsured motorists insurance provides protection in case you're injured or your property is damaged by an uninsured motorist, or by a hit-and-run driver who is never identified or caught; but **only** if that driver can be shown to have been legally liable through his negligence in driving. Once he's been proved legally liable by reason of negligence, your uninsured motorists insurance company pays your loss up to the liability limits required as the minimum by the state in which your loss occurred.

FROM WHOM DO YOU BUY INSURANCE?

There are three principal sources for car insurance:

1. Independent insurance agents, including agents associated with automobile dealers, who may represent a number of insurance companies.

2. Salaried agents who represent a single insurance company or group of associated companies.

3. Special associations, including auto clubs, that offer insurance to their members.

The independent insurance agent, frequently referred to as a "local agent," is an independent business man. He usually represents several insurance companies and sells a variety of coverages including auto, fire, home-owners', etc., on a commission basis.

The salaried agent is actually an employe of one particular company and represents it exclusively. Salaried agents are usually employed by "direct writers," that is, companies that utilize their own employes rather than independent agents to sell their insurance.

Associations may have a mutual or interinsurance exchange to write insurance for their members. For example, such a company will sell insurance only to members of an auto club, farmers' or teachers association, etc. These are specialized companies offering particular attractive plans for their members. (It may pay you to see if you're qualified to join such a specialized group.)

FIGURE 7.2 An extended definition of automobile insurance. (From **Car Buying Made Easier,** 2nd ed. A publication of the Ford Motor Company, 1972. Reprinted by permission of the Ford Customer Service Division.)

When checking out car insurance policies and costs, you should investigate the performance of the companies you're considering. For example:

Are they patient and clear in explaining what the various policies cover and do not cover?

Do they have special rates for good driving records, or for not drinking alcoholic beverages?

Do they offer a lower premium rate for younger drivers in the family, if those younger drivers have successfully completed a formal, certified driver-training course or program?

Are their prices competitive with, lower than, or higher than other companies offering the same kinds of insurance?

Do they offer "around-the-clock" nationwide claim service?

Most, if not all, of the above questions can be answered by shopping around and asking various agents or company representatives for the answers. Armed with this information, you can compare coverages, prices, and service before you buy insurance. This will place you in a better position to get adequate coverage at a fair price from a company that renders good service.

The amount of premium you pay is decided by a number of factors, including:

make, model, special equipment, and age of car,
how you use the car (pleasure, business, etc.),
where you live geographically,
who drives the car, how often, how far, and for what purposes,
ages, sex, and marital status of all drivers, and driving records of all drivers.

HIGH-RISK INSURANCE

High-risk drivers—those who most often get involved in accidents—find it difficult to get any kind of insurance unless they pay extremely high prices for coverage.

Because most insurance companies wish to avoid covering these poor risks, most states have formed separate insurance plans (commonly called "assigned risk pools") to insure them. In these pools, all companies writing the type of insurance desired by high-risk drivers agree to insure their proportionate share of such policies. The cost of such insurance coverage is far above the cost to the careful, safe driver. This fact alone should be sufficient to make you drive safely at all times.

Not all of these items will necessarily appear in an operational definition. You will use only such items as are appropriate. What makes an item appropriate? Thomas Zarnke's essay on "Die-Draulic," Appendix 6, is an example in part, at least, of an operational definition.

WRITING ASSIGNMENT

Write an operational definition of an automobile, motorbike, or ten-speed bicycle changing its route from a level surface to a steep grade; the act of walking, either up- or downhill; a powerplant or waterplant; the process of making beer, wine, or bread; or some other process that you know of. Begin with a formal definition of your subject: an automobile is . . . walking is . . . wine is . . . .

The Extended Definition

Operational definitions are used to define operations or processes that are essential parts of modern technology. Another essential part of modern technology is the *concept* or basic set of ideas. An operational definition will not work for abstract notions. Nor is a formal definition complete enough. Consider, for example, the following *American Heritage Dictionary* definition of *measurement*:

measurement: 1. The act of measuring or the process of being measured. 2. A system of measuring. 3. The dimension, quantity, or capacity determined by measuring (p. 811).

This set of formal definitions is only a beginning on the subject of measurement. A person could spend a lifetime studying the concept and still not learn everything there is to know about it. But you must get on with your daily work, and somewhere between the bareness of the formal definition and the fullness of the maximum possible knowledge, you must construct a suitable mean. That suitable mean is the *extended definition*.

There is no set pattern for the extended definition. Just as the pattern for the operational definition will depend on what is being defined, so will the extended definition depend on what is being defined and on what information is available. In both the operational and the extended definition, the techniques will also depend on the purposes you have for defining and on your audience.

An extended definition can use logical definition and any of the forms of partial definition. It uses illustrations, formulas, and statistics if they will help. It uses classification, analysis, comparison and contrast, and description.

Fig. 7.2 is an extended definition of automobile insurance. Read it and answer the questions below.

STUDY QUESTIONS FOR FIG. 7.2

1. What formal definitions are used in the extended definition of automobile insurance? What partial definitions are used?
2. What definitions are made by example?
3. How are comparison and contrast used?
4. What unfamiliar terms are defined? How?

WRITING ASSIGNMENT

Write an extended definition of electrical, civil, mechanical, automotive, or aeronautical technology, as the concept will apply to you after you leave school. Or, write an extended definition of your school or of the department in which you are enrolled. Or, write an extended definition of the phrase *educated person* as it will apply to you when you get your degree.

When to Use Technical Definitions

1. Never define a word or phrase that you will find in current editions of standard desk or technical dictionaries.

2. Don't define standard technical terms if you are sure that your work will be read only by technical people in your own field. However, if your readers are likely to come from any other group, define any technical terms not usually found in standard dictionaries. If the members of your audience are nontechnical (sales department people, for instance), they may not have access to technical dictionaries.

3. If you have many terms to define, define them in a glossary of technical terms (see Fig. 6.3, for example) placed either at the beginning or the end of the report. If the glossary is at the end of the report, include it in the table of contents.

4. Use logical definitions in the glossary; partial definitions belong in the text. Extended or operational definitions may appear as part of the report if they are necessary for all your readers. Otherwise, place them in an appendix, and footnote them in the text.

5. If you don't have enough terms for a separate glossary, define them in footnotes placed at the bottom of the page where they are used for the first time. Use an asterisk (*) to signal that the footnote is there.

However, if you do use a new word infrequently throughout a long report, you run the risk that your readers will forget the meaning after its first appearance or that they will be reading only the latter part of the report and not know that the word is defined earlier. In such cases, it is better to put the word in a glossary.

6. If you use a familiar word but give it some new or special meaning, be sure to define it.

8 | What is Description?

On the job, your responsibilities will occasionally take several directions. You will *report* to others about work you have done. You will make *decisions* and report them. You will be asked to *propose* a course of action, *persuade* others to accept your ideas, or *defend* a position you have taken. Sometimes you will *direct* or *instruct* others. And you will have to *inform* others.

Each of these information processes requires a different pattern or form. But all of them will probably require that you *describe* something, such as hardware, skills, layouts, or systems. The purpose of this chapter is to show you the skills required in preparing technical descriptions. Although we discuss the skills of technical description in this chapter, examples will be found in other chapters as well.

What Is Description?

Description is an information process that enables others to see and understand what you see and understand. Description provides a "picture," or means of identification. It also furnishes a means for understanding.

There are many kinds of description:
1. Description in words alone,
2. Description through illustrations: photo-graphs, maps, drawings, motion pictures, schematics, tables, graphs, models, and so on,
3. Description by means of numerical quantities,
4. Description through combinations of these.

There are other types of description that we avoid in technical work:
1. Description that results in a feeling or mood, such as sadness or laughter,
2. Psychological description of abnormal or atypical behavior,
3. Description that presents subjective points of view. Such description does not focus on the object; it describes attitudes of the writer—prejudices, narrow-mindedness, overenthusiasm, pessimism, optimism, or other extreme views. It is sometimes an attempt to be funny or satirical.

When you write technical description, you should be objective, and focus on your subject. You should be fair-minded, impersonal, and thoughtful. You should consider and weigh all the facts and evidence.

You must look at the object in the way necessary to give your reader the picture he wants. You must keep your own objective purpose in mind. But organize the description for the reader's convenience, not for your own.

Here is an excerpt by a writer who let his subjective point of view interfere with technical description:

First let's find a pack that fits you. It need not be expensive to serve its purpose. Find one that can hold a maximum of 45 pounds, with straps that fit comfortably on your shoulders. This is your first opportunity to cheat and if you do, you can expect your arms to fall to the ground because your straps will saw through your shoulders within the first mile.

Inspect the sewing and stitch work done on the pack. This I would look very close at because there is nothing more hilarious than seeing your pack literally falling apart with your pink underwear a-flying.

In the above example the writer has attempted to inject his sense of humor into a situation where a reader expects information. Compare that description with this one:

You will need a pack frame and waterproof pack bag to insure an enjoyable backpacking experience. The frame should be of welded tubular aluminum, about one inch in diameter and contoured to body design. It should be equipped with approximately 5-inch-wide back bands; these, in turn, should be fitted with T-bar and nylon cord for tension adjustment. These prevent the frame from touching the wearer and allow air circulation between the frame and the back. The best straps are of nylon and are padded with foam. They should have a buckle that permits strap adjustment while the frame is placed on your back.

The pack should be strong, yet lightweight. Waterproofed 7-ounce duck weave nylon is recommended. The pockets should be bellows-type with sturdy zippers. The pack should have a lightweight inside frame to hold the top open for easier forming and packing of load. Yet, it should fold flat for storage.

Total weight of frame and pack should not be more than 5 pounds. The price of the combination in this quality will be approximately $35.00.

The Purposes of Description

You will write description when:

1. you define new products, new skills, new tools, new processes (*definition,* discussed in Chapter 7, is a special kind of description).

2. you inform people in brochures, catalogues, specifications, and other kinds of technical publications.

3. you give basic technical information in writing about operations, experiments, tests, or job skills.

4. you write reports of work done or of decisions made. Some parts of these reports may include description. The description may be incorporated in the body of the report or it may be appended. Report writing is covered in Chapters 10 and 11.

5. you direct or instruct people in operations, maintenance, assembly, or sales manuals, and it is necessary for the reader to know about equipment, skills, and processes. Writing instructions is a special skill, which is covered in Chapter 9.

On the job, you may be asked to give either oral or written descriptions of tools, machines, equipment, skills, layouts, and systems. Some of these descriptions may be general, others may be specific. In any case, you must realize that different cases and purposes call for different kinds of description.

General and Specific Description

Description is either *general* or *specific*. A *general* description is one that can be applied to all examples of a kind or to all members of a class. A general description of a telephone would apply to all of the telephones shown in Fig. 7.1. A *specific* description is one that helps your reader see a specific object, process, skill, or system. It describes something that, in some way or another, is unlike any specimen of its kind. A specific description of a telephone would apply to only one of the telephones shown in Fig. 7.1 or, precisely, to the telephone in your room. Specific description *can* be applied to more than one object if all those objects are identical. The 1964 Touch-Tone, shown in Fig. 7.1, was manufactured by the millions, but they are all identical, except, perhaps, for color.

Here, in a description of a hammer from *The American Heritage Dictionary*, is an example of general description:

A hand tool used to exert an impulsive force by striking; especially such a tool consisting of a handle with a perpendicularly attached head of a relatively heavy, rigid material, such as iron or hard rubber, used to drive nails or shape construction materials.

Job descriptions, such as those found in classified advertising pages, are usually intentionally general. They limit the applicant to a specific set of skills, but at the same time they may anticipate variations in individuals or in applications of skills:

Electronics technician—Must be able to read blueprints and schematics and to trace electrical impulses. Basic knowledge of solid- and vacuum-state systems. Must be able to solder. Knowledge of oscilloscope, potentiometer, and other testing devices required. At least an associate of science or technology degree.

The advertisement is a general description, but if you were to apply for this job, you would be asked to furnish a specific description of your skills.

Because general descriptions describe *classes* or *types*, class and type words are used in writing them:

tool, device, instrument, system, process, materials, fabricate, metal, assemble, wood, plastic, method, object, machine, technique, artifact, skill, fluid

Here, in a description of a hammer taken from a catalogue, is a specific description:

A Craftsman Hammer, Catalogue no. 9W3820, has a 14-in. Fiberglas handle and a 16-oz. steel head. Its claws are strengthened by a steel rib forged under each claw. The left-hand claw has an exclusive "third claw" specially designed for pulling nails in tight places.

The hollow core in the handle compresses fiber glass strands and resin in the neck. The hammer is rustproof and nonconductive. It has curved claws and a neoprene grip and weighs 1 lb., 13 oz.

For a different audience, this description might be made even more specific. For example, in describing the process of manufacturing this hammer, the steel would be described more specifically: the kind of steel (bar, tool, hot-rolled), the elements in it (manganese, cobalt, chromium, nickel), its Rockwell hardness, and its tensile properties. On the other hand, a carpenter who was reporting the theft of such a hammer might note that his name was stenciled on the handle.

Specific descriptions use specific terms:

14-in., 16-oz., steel rib, hollow core, curved claws, Fiberglas handle, 1 lb., 13 oz., neoprene grip.

WRITING ASSIGNMENT

From a dictionary, copy the description of a stereo set, a motorbike, an automobile, or a snowmobile. Then, working from this general description, write a specific description of the same machine. Follow the pattern of the general description as closely as possible.

The Technique of Writing Description

In the preceding writing assignment, you were asked to model one pattern of description on another. That specification was made to help you organize or pattern your own work. It is good practice to study relevant models of good description before beginning your own, but good models may not always be available. So, here is some practical advice based on a study of many patterns of description.

The Information Block

There is a well-known anecdote about a successful teacher who was asked the secret of his teaching method. He replied, "First, I tell my students what I am going to tell them, then I tell them, and finally I tell them what I have told them."

Here is that method diagrammed in the pattern of an *information block*:

a. Predict what you are going to write
b. Develop your prediction point by point
c. Summarize what you have written

Prediction

The first of the three blocks *begins* the description. It *introduces* the topics of the description and it presents an *overview*—it predicts what the description will be about.

Here is an example of a typical introductory paragraph, from a report that describes how a group of scientists and technicians are studying wildlife from the sky:

Using the Nimbus satellite and computer equipment at the Goddard Space Flight Center, Karen and John Craighead are *collecting information* about animal behavior in Yellowstone Park and in Alaska, *relaying the data* to a ground station at Fairbanks, Alaska, and then *processing the data* to learn how animals' bodies react to changing conditions.

This *prediction*, or *overview*, tells in brief the *who*, the *what*, the *where*, the *when*, the *how*, and the *why* of this story. It helps you anticipate what is coming. It makes your understanding easier. You know that later sections of the report will elaborate on each of these six points.

Development

The initial paragraph also predicts the organization of the *body* of the report and looks to the final part where you will be told some of the results of the study.

The body of the report (the middle part, or *discussion*) will follow the outline implied by the italicized phrases in the first paragraph:

COLLECTING INFORMATION
The Craigheads attach sensors to drugged animals. These will record temperatures, heartbeats, breathing rate, and so on. The Craigheads also attach an electronic package to each animal. For a free-roaming elk, for instance, the research team used an in-strument collar consisting of a miniaturized antenna and a transmitter-receiver.

Twice a day, as Nimbus passes 700 miles above the animals' habitats, it signals the electronics package to transmit the data which the package has received from the sensors.

RELAYING DATA
Nimbus transmits its signals to a ground station at Fairbanks, Alaska. The satellite then receives a fresh set of instructions for its next orbit. Nimbus can carry equipment capable of monitoring more than one hundred weather buoys, balloons, migrating animals, or bear dens.

END PRODUCT
The ground station transmits its signals to a computer center at Goddard Space Flight Center in Maryland. After processing, the data emerges as a computer printout. From Goddard, team member Charles Cote sends the information to the Craigheads.

Summary

The *conclusion* summarizes what has been said and repeats, but in a more concise way, what has been predicted and discussed:

Thus, using some of man's newest technological discoveries, Karen and John Craighead are attempting to learn some of nature's oldest and most carefully kept secrets. If they are successful, we will someday know what happens to bears when they hibernate and how moose and elk react to temperature extremes.

Expanding a Report to Greater Length

A long report may still only discuss three or four main topics; however, it gives more detailed information about and discussion for each topic. In such reports, the main parts are broken into smaller blocks. Here is an outline of a moderately detailed treatment of the wildlife study mentioned above.

I. Collecting information
  A. Trapping and drugging animals
  B. Attaching sensing devices
  C. Monitoring sensing devices from the Nimbus

A lengthier, even more detailed description would produce more division and, perhaps, this outline:

I. Collecting information
  A. The ground crew—who are they
    1. Trapping and drugging animals
      a. Description of equipment
    2. Attaching sensing devices
      a. Description of devices
  B. The Nimbus
    1. Description of the satellite and its operation
    2. How Nimbus monitors sensing devices

A more detailed section might read as follows:

Paradoxically, while the ground crew must slog over deep snows, through dense underbrush, and up steep, rocky slopes in search of the animals, the Nimbus floats effortlessly overhead, passing seven hundred miles above the Yellowstone National Park twice a day.

On snowshoes, and bearing their gear on their backs, the two scientists, an electronics engineer, and two technicians approach the den of a black bear. Just ahead, a pair of black ears rise up above a drift and then the bear's face comes into view. As he rises to a half-standing position, an arrow containing a tranquilizer is fired into his shoulder.

While the bear is tranquilized, one of the technicians checks its respiration. At the same time, to protect the bear, another technician wraps him in a tarpaulin. While a rectal probe, designed to check the bear's temperature is inserted, the electronics engineer installs light and air-temperature sensors in the den. Wires from these sensors are attached to a 25-pound radio package on a ledge above the den. When all of these preparations are completed, the bear is slid back into his den.

Twice a day, for the next thirty days, as Nimbus passes overhead . . .

The Block Pattern in Technical Description

The discussion of printing presses in Fig. 8.1 illustrates the application of the block pattern to technical description. Read the description and then prepare answers to the study questions for in-class discussion.

STUDY QUESTIONS FOR FIG. 8.1

1. The description of printing presses is divided into two main parts. What are they? How are they divided?

2. What function does the first main part serve in relation to the second part?

3. Which are the overview sentences in each part?

4. How, specifically, is the overview sentence in the first part expanded?

5. How, specifically, is the overview sentence in the second part expanded?

6. Is the order of subjects given in each overview sentence maintained in the following description?

7. In the first part of the description, four processes are compared; in the second part, three types of presses are compared. Study the comparisons carefully. Do the comparisons in the first part parallel each other? Do the comparisons in the second part parallel each other? (Look for kinds of information and ordering of kinds of information.)

The Block Pattern and Specific Description

When the block pattern is applied to the description of a specific object such as a tool, the division of the description must be found in the tool or in its uses:

The Mech-An-Eze metalworker's vise weighs about 50 pounds. It has *three major* steel parts: a combination base and fixed jaw that can be fastened to a work bench; a movable jaw set at one end of a 2-inch-square by 15-inch-long metal bar; and a long screw with a slip handle attached perpendicularly to it.

In this description, the writer assumes that the reader has a general idea of a vise, and so the overview (the first sentence) names the tool and describes its size. The second sentence predicts the body of the description by naming the three basic parts of the vise. Later, as these individual

Printing Presses

The history of printing, as has already been noted, is no longer the story of a single process. Through advances in printing technology it has now been expanded to include four highly successful processes, each based on a different principle: letterpress (relief), lithography (plane surface), intaglio (sunken surface), and silk screen (stencil). In **letterpress,** or relief printing, an image is obtained by direct contact of the paper with the inked, raised surfaces of type, line engravings, halftone plates, or any combination of these. **Lithography,** or planographic printing, is based on the chemical principle that grease and water repel each other. The major planographic method is offset lithography, in which a metal plate is treated to hold a greasy image. A felt roller deposits water on all of the plate except the greasy image. Inking rollers deposit ink only on the image, being repelled by water on the other portions. The inked plate then deposits its image on a rubber blanket, from which it is transferred or "offset" to paper. In **intaglio** printing, the plate transfers ink from below-the-surface areas to paper by capillary attraction. The principal example is rotogravure. **Stencil** printing is the process of forcing ink through the openings in a stencil onto paper. Mimeographing and silk screen printing are the two major stencil processes. Of these four processes, letterpress is by far the oldest and the most used. It utilizes a wide variety of press equipment to produce printed matter ranging in size and quantity from one hundred calling cards to five million daily copies of the nation's largest newspaper. The layman, who normally has a very limited acquaintance with the printing industry, is most likely to have come into contact with the letterpress process, since the printed matter with which he is familiar derives in large extent from this type of printing. This section, therefore, in the main is concerned with the various kinds of letterpress printing processes. The presses used in other types of printing are discussed at length in separate articles on their related processes.

TYPES OF PRESS

Each of the many different presses used in letterpress may be classified as one of three types: platen, cylinder, or rotary. Generally, platens are used for short runs of relatively small sheet sizes, such as tickets, stationery, and office forms. Cylinders are used for medium-length runs of all sheet sizes, and are especially valuable for use where the highest quality is demanded. Rotaries are used largely by newspapers and magazines for producing huge quantities of pages quickly.

Platen presses are the simplest; they may be found in almost every small printing plant in the country. It has been estimated that more platen presses are in use than all other types combined, including the presses of all other processes. The bed of the platen press holds a printing surface, consisting of type and relief plates, in a vertical position. A flat metal impression surface (the platen, which gives the press its name) holds the paper for printing. While the platen is opened into a horizontal position, a sheet of paper is presented to the guides upon it. The platen closes to a vertical position and the bed moves forward to press the inked printing surface against the paper and make a print. After the impression is made, the bed recedes to permit inking rollers to pass down and up over the printing surface, and the platen opens to permit removal of the printed sheet and placement of the next sheet to be printed.

Cylinder presses have a flat inked printing surface, similar to that used in the platen, but its impression surface, which holds the sheets for printing, is cylindrical. The printing surface rests on a bed that moves back and forth under the inking rollers. The cylinder rotates in exact time with the movement of the bed. During one direction of the movement of the bed, the cylinder and printing surface come into contact to produce a print; during the opposite direction of movement, the cylinder is held clear of the bed, the printed sheet is removed, and an unprinted sheet is placed in position for the next print.

Rotary presses use both a cylindrical impression surface and a cylindrical printing surface. They cannot print from type or flat plates, but must have one-piece plates made with the proper curvature to fit the cylinder. (The plates are made by either the stereotyping process or the electrotyping process.) The printing surface and impression cylinders rotate in contact with each other; the paper passes between to produce the print. Inking rollers are banked on each side of the printing surface cylinder to apply ink as the cylinder rotates.

FIGURE 8.1 The block pattern in technical description. (Reprinted with permission of **The Encyclopedia Americana,** copyright 1972 The Americana Corporation.)

parts are discussed, the reader can visualize them in terms of the overall view.

STUDY QUESTIONS

1. If the discussion that follows the above description is limited to three paragraphs, what will be the topic of each paragraph?

2. In what order will these topics be discussed in the description? Why?

3. How would you decide in which order the parts of a tool or the divisions of a subject should be listed in the prediction?

WRITING ASSIGNMENT

Select a simple object that you are familiar with: a slide rule, a Tensor desk lamp, a pencil sharpener, a stapling machine, a Skilsaw or electric drill, a desk, a globe, or the like.

Select the main assemblies of the object that together form the whole. It is a good idea never to go beyond five units; if there are more than five, try to combine some of them. It is better to note that an automobile consists of chassis, body, and driving assembly than it is to list wheels, brakes, chassis, engine, radiator, steering apparatus, carburetor, engine hood, doors, seats, and so on. The three major assemblies should be approximately equal in importance. Each can be subdivided within the description.

Try to select a number of assemblies or divisions that can be ticked off on three to five fingers of one hand. Do the same with subdivisions of the main parts.

Write an introductory paragraph that introduces the subject and lists the main assemblies. Think carefully about the order of this listing. Complete the assignment with an outline for the body of the description and a brief summary statement.

The Process Paper

Where description of hardware, a job or skill, a layout, a system, or a process is your goal, you write what is called in the trade a *process paper*. Process papers stand on their own.

At other times, you will write descriptions that are part of a report, a technical manual, a catalogue, a brochure, and so on. On these occasions, the description must be integrated into the longer paper by appropriate transitions. If necessary, cross-reference the parts of the description to parts of the larger paper.

One Object Described in Several Ways

The requirements of a special purpose, a special audience, or a special need necessitate the ability to use various kinds of description. To illustrate, here are several descriptions of a vise.

Technical Definition

vise: A clamping device of metal or wood, usually consisting of two jaws closed or opened by a screw or lever, used in carpentry or metalworking to hold a piece in position.

Because the emphasis in dictionaries must be on brevity, compactness, and completeness in a general sense, the definitions are of limited practical use. A dictionary definition can, however, serve as an overview or introduction.

Description for an Uninformed Audience

In a description for an uninformed audience, a picture must be supplied at the beginning. This picture will use words, but it can be accompanied by a drawing or a photograph:

A vise is a clamping device made of metal or wood. It usually has two jaws that can be opened or closed by a screw or lever. In the closed position, the jaws hold a piece of metal, wood, or other material firmly in place so that a carpenter, metalworker, or craftsman may make some alteration in or addition to the piece.

The second paragraph of this description would begin with a sentence to serve as a *transition* or word *bridge* from the general opening to the specific description:

Vises come in many designs and sizes. A carpenter, for instance, will use a heavy-duty woodworker's vise . . .

Description Concerned with Use

If your purpose was to tell your reader how to use the vise, the introductory paragraph might read like this:

The Plumber-Aid vise has curved serrated jaws that firmly clamp any size pipe from 3 cm. o.d. to 175 mm. o.d. The vise rotates on its base so that the pipe may be held at any angle from horizontal to vertical.

Description Concerned with Identification

In a description of this kind, the purpose is to single out items that may look alike. Such descriptions focus on appearance—size, shape, color, weight, labels, and so on:

Resistors are made in a great many sizes and shapes. For easy identification, each one has printed on it a color code that identifies the amount of resistance and tolerance . . .

In succeeding paragraphs, this description would focus first on sizes, then on shapes, then on the color codes. The color codes would be discussed in two paragraphs. The first one would discuss the code showing the resistances:

Three color bands, in various combinations, indicate resistance. The colors used and their numerical values are: . . .

The second color paragraph would discuss the color codes for tolerances:

A fourth ring, to the right of the three color bands, is either silver or gold . . .

Catalogue Description

The catalogue description has unique features of its own:

1. The description is often intended to persuade or sell to a potential buyer.

2. The description usually assumes that the buyer knows what the product is like. However, if the product is entirely new, such assumptions cannot be made.

3. The style is telegraphic, that is, to save printing costs and economize on space, it leaves out many words, such as names of objects, verbs, pronouns, and noun-determiners (*a, an, the, one*).

4. The style is adapted to the audience. If the audience is a nontechnical one, the style will be nontechnical. For a technical audience, the style will be technical.

Here is an example of a catalogue description:

One of the best heavy-duty bench vises available in this price range. Vise is strong, made from high-tensile gray iron. Large anvil surface and forming horn. Permanently lubricated screw is dust-resistant and protected by a heavy steel channel. Improved, replaceable, serrated steel-face jaw inserts raised for precision work. Swivels 200°. Serrated base for more positive locking in any position. Case-hardened pipe jaw inserts. Handles have a soft end for more comfortable grip.

Other Forms of Technical Description

Description of a Work Process

In the following description of a work process, the three processes are outlined in the first paragraph. In the balance of the description, the title of each process is used as a subheading to identify the process stage. Within each stage description, the description follows the logical work order:

There are three fundamental methods of commercial carpet installation: (1) The tackless strip method of installing carpeting over a separate pad; (2) the glue-down method of installing carpeting either with an attached pad or no pad; and (3) the use of double-sided adhesive tape.

NOT-SO-TACKLESS STRIP METHOD
Actually, the tackless strip method isn't tackless at all since it involves wooden strips filled with long protruding tacks angled to the walls. The strips are secured to the floor by nails or adhesives.

After the strips are fastened according to the

specific instructions in each case (as given by manufacturers), carpet is then stretched over the pad and tucked behind the tacks. Carpet should be stretched uniformly, at least 1% over the length and width of the carpet—about 1½ in. over 12 ft. Lengths exceeding 10 ft. should be power stretched. Knee-knickers and power stretchers are indispensable tools to achieve proper installation by this method in large areas.

GLUE-DOWN METHOD

In this method the carpet is glued directly to the floor, with or without a pad or cushion. All floors should be clean, dry, and reasonably smooth, with all protrusions leveled and sanded down. All cracks more than 1/16th in. wide should be filled with a latex emulsion compatible with the carpet adhesive.

THE USE OF DOUBLE-SIDED ADHESIVE TAPE

This tape is laid down around the margin of the space to be carpeted, removing the covering of the lower side of the tape only as the tape is unrolled.

A double row of the tape should be put down for all seams, so that each edge of the carpet has a full-width tape strip. Strips of tape should be laid at 3-ft. intervals across a room in one direction, and a strip should also be laid across the center of each doorway.

After the carpet has been cut to fit the space, it is laid in place. One edge is rolled back for three or four ft., and the top covering of the tape is removed in the open area. The carpet is then relaid, with pressure being applied to the carpet along all taped areas. The carpet is then rolled to expose the balance of the tape. As the tape covering is stripped off, the carpet is rolled back into place.

A Technical Description

Figs. 8.2a & b illustrate a more complex technical description—of a "Multiple-Tube Fire-Detection System"—in a text accompanied by two schematic diagrams.

Figure 3A shows an experimental aircraft installation consisting of a control unit, a test-alarm unit and 3 parallel detectors. Each detector can monitor a specific volume, causing a circuit alarm when sufficient uv radiation from a fire actuates a uv tube. The detector package includes an incandescent test lamp whose envelope is transparent to uv radiation. Thus, each detector can be individually checked by actuating its test lamp. Intensity of radiation from the test lamp is voltage adjusted to simulate signal levels of fire.

The detectors are connected in parallel by a two-conductor individually shielded cable. Figure 3B shows how to eliminate cable shunt capacitance effects. Any capacitance shunting the tube terminals would decrease the system signal-to-noise ratio. The twin-wire, twin-shield cabling, plus the location of output transformer T_2, eliminates the cable capacitance problem usually associated with remote detectors.

The distributed cable capacitance of cable 1 (represented by C_2) is continually grounded by the cable shield. This capacitance does not shunt the tube and provides no signal power to transformer T_2, Capacitance C_2 does load power-supply transformer T_2 but this load is easily accommodated. The distributed shunt capacitance of return cable 2 (represented by

C_2) provides no shunt path across the tube. Thus C_2 provides no signal power to T_2. When the uv tube conducts due to uv radiation C_2 resonates in series with the leakage inductance of T_2. As long as the time constant introduced by C_2 and the reflected impedance of the integrating network is less than the ½ cycle time of the operating supply frequency, no ill effects result.

For example, using adequate safety factors on a 400-cps system, the cable shunt capacitance should be limited to 5,000 pf for each cable. Commercially available cable has a nominal shunt capacitance of 25 pf per foot. Thus, tube and control box can be at least 200 feet apart. Such systems have been constructed and proved practical.

The system of Fig. 3A will alarm with a delay time of 1 to 2 seconds on a nominal signal of 10 counts a sec. The delay is reduced to 50 milliseconds when the signal level is at saturation (800 counts a sec).

The application of a rapid response system to line-of-sight communications involves consideration of the transmitter radiated power required to saturate the receiver at distance x, atmospheric attenuation and beaming technique. In such a system the uv tube can function as a transmitter as well as a receiver. Other radiation sources with gas filling can also be used.

FIGURE 8.2a Technical description of a multiple-tube fire-detection system. (Reprinted from **Electronics**, May 26, 1961, p. 52. Copyright 1961 by McGraw-Hill.)

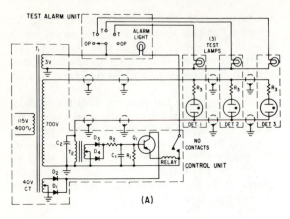

TEST ALARM UNIT

(A)

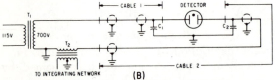

TO INTEGRATING NETWORK   (B)

FIG. 3—Multiple-tube fire-detection system (A) has self-checking feature. Remote tube connection circuit (B) compensates for cable capacitance

FIGURE 8.2b Schematics accompanying the technical description in Fig. 8.2a. (Reprinted from **Electronics,** May 26, 1961, p. 52. Copyright by McGraw-Hill.)

STUDY QUESTIONS FOR FIG. 8.2a&b

1. Why must the prose description be cross-referenced to the illustration, as it is in Fig. 8.2a?

2. What techniques for cross-referencing are used in Fig. 8.2a?

3. In what specific ways in both the text and the schematics is an *overview* or *prediction* given? How does the text follow up on the overview and prediction?

4. What method of organization does the text follow: spatial (the placement of units in the appliance), temporal (according to a sequence of events in time) or functional (according to the functions of units of the appliance)?

5. What references are made to placement of units? To the timing of actions or responses?

6. How is the operation of the circuits related to the purpose of the appliance or to some activity of the operator?

7. What features or advantages are described?

Description of a Manufacturing Process

Fig. 8.3 shows a *flowsheet* for a mill that was designed to separate pure bits of copper from the rock in which it was naturally embedded. The flowsheet shows all of the steps in the process from the time the rock was delivered to the mill until the freed copper was loaded aboard a carrier and the "tailings" (waste rock) were dumped onto a rock heap.

The prose description that accompanied this flowsheet explained in detail the steps in the process, which are labeled on the flowsheet. This description began with an overview that examines the whole mill in brief:

The Ahmeek Mill is located on Torch Lake at the base of a steep hill. The ore comes into the mill on railroad cars, which use a trestle at right angles to the mill and are eighty-four feet above the mill floor. There is a drop of 106 feet from the trestle to the lake level, allowing for a gravity flow of the ore-bearing rock in its various stages as it is processed ("pulp") from the mill bin to stamps, to jigs, to ball mills, and to the concentrating units (concentrates, or "conc.," are the pieces of pure ore ready for smelting). The final tailings must be elevated to a launder (conduit) for movement to the stockpile.[1]

Within the description, stages in the process are identified by topic sentences at the beginning of paragraphs.

Ore is fed into the stamp from the bin by gravity. . . . The stamps are of the Nordberg type. . . . The stamps strike 104 blows per minute . . . From the stamps, the crushed rock passes through mortar grates to tromells. . . . Dorr jig-classifiers separate the pulp into sand and slime. . . . The rake product from the Dorr classifiers is treated on a Woodbury jig. . . . Grinding is done at 75 percent solids.

[1] From C. Harry Benedict, *Lake Superior Milling Practice,* Michigan Technological University, 1955, pp. 123–27.

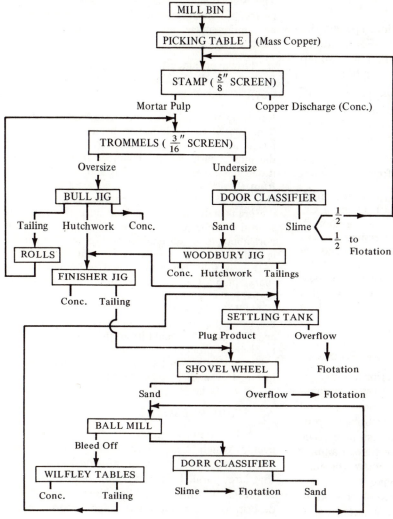

Ahmeek Mill Flowsheet
(Crushing And Gravity Concentration)

FIGURE 8.3 Schematic description of a manufacturing process. (Reprinted from C. Harry Benedict, **Lake Superior Milling Practice,** Michigan Technological University, 1955.)

. . . The entire mill product is treated by flotation. . . . The flotation concentrates are pumped to a drag classifier. . . . The dried product is discharged directly into 50-ton hopper bottom cars . . .[2]

Within this process description, specific description is inserted as necessary. For example, here is the way in which a description of a "stamp shoe" is fitted into the process description:

The stamps are of the Nordberg type. Moving parts, without the stamp shoe, weigh 7000 pounds. When new, the stamp shoe weighs 835 pounds. The shoes are made of chilled cast iron containing 10 percent nihard. . . .[3]

A description of a "mortar die" follows:

. . . The mortar die is circular, 24 inches in diameter, 6 inches high. It is held in place by a circular horizontal ring fitted snugly in the mortar, which is lined with vertical staves resting on this ring. The staves are slightly wedge-shaped, and the king stave is bolted through the mortar casting, holding them all in position. One stave has a cored hole at an angle of 45 degrees. The hole serves as a discharge for any copper nuggets too large to go through the mortar screens.[4]

Description of a Simultaneous Process

The milling of copper ore, described above, is essentially a linear process—one in which stages take place in a direct sequence. However, you will be called on to describe operations or processes in which stages of the process take place in parallel sequences at the same time. Familiar examples of this sort of operation are the telephone call or the automobile engine.

When you write descriptions of this kind, the introduction and overview are important if the reader is to visualize the whole process and relate the several steps to each other.

In the following description, the diagram (Fig. 8.4) serves as the overview. If there had

been no diagram to provide an overview, the description might have begun as follows:

The NSU-Wankel rotary engine goes through five cycles: a fuel injection cycle, a compression cycle, an ignition cycle, an expansion cycle and an exhaust cycle.

However, since the illustration shown in Fig. 8.4 was used, the description proceeded in this way:

Referring to fig. [45A], the cycle starts when the flank of the rotor (indicated by a heavy line [adjacent to the direction arrow]) is just uncovering the intake port, and the chamber formed between it and the curved casing wall is about to be cut off from the exhaust port by the adjacent rotor apex [X]. Fig. 45B shows the rotor turned clockwise 60°, the crankshaft advanced a half turn, the crescent-shaped chamber at maximum value, and the intake port about to be covered by the rotor. The charge is undergoing compression in Fig. 45C, and in Fig. 45D it is fully compressed and is ignited by the spark plug. The expansion or power-producing period is under way in Fig. 45E and is completed in Fig. 45F as the shaft completes its second turn with the exhaust port partially uncovered by the rotor apex [X]. An additional turn of the shaft is necessary to push the products of combustion out through the exhaust port, return the rotor to its initial position in Fig. 45A, and complete the cycle.[5]

STUDY QUESTIONS

1. The description writer often must describe events which take place both simultaneously and in sequence. He must indicate relationships that are parallel in time and sequential relationships in time. How has the writer of this description accomplished this requirement? Underscore all passages in the description that call your attention to simultaneous happenings and circle all passages that describe sequential happenings.

2. This engine operates in complete cycles.

[2] Ibid.
[3] Ibid.
[4] Ibid.

[5] Reprinted by permission from the *Encyclopaedia Britannica,* Vol. 12, p. 392, 1973.

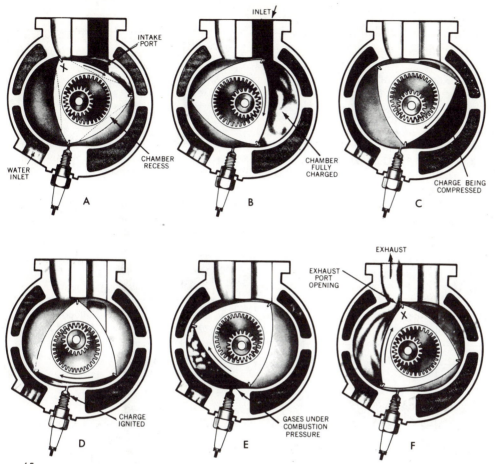

FIG. 45—OPERATING PRINCIPLE OF NSU-WANKEL ROTARY ENGINE ILLUSTRATED BY FOLLOWING ONE SEGMENT OF THREE-SECTOR ROTOR (DESIGNATED BY HEAVY LINE) THROUGH COMPLETE CYCLE

(A) Intake begins (dotted lines indicate chamber recesses in rotor faces); (B) intake ends, chamber at maximum volume; (C) compression begins, chamber volume decreases; (D) chamber at minimum volume, charge fully compressed and ignited; (E) expanding gases produce clockwise thrust on rotor; (F) exhaust begins as rotor uncovers port

FIGURE 8.4 An illustration introducing a description of a simultaneous process. (Reprinted by permission. Copyright © 1973 by the **Encyclopaedia Britannica.**)

Where did the writer begin his description of the complete cycle? Where did he end his description? Why?

Description by Tabulation

In Chapter 6, you saw that specifications and standards could be tabulated. Tabulation can also be used as a kind of description; in this case, the tabulated figures come from the item being described. In tabulated specifications, the specifications come first.

Fig. 8.5 lists tabulated descriptions of standard (full) sizes of Ford automobiles. If you were to write a description of one model (the

								CURB WT. (LBS.)	TRUNK CAP. (CU. FT.)	FUEL CAP. (GALS.)	MODEL NAME	BODY TYPE

Standard (Full) Sizes of Ford Automobiles

MODEL SPECIFICATIONS											MODEL NAME	BODY TYPE
INTERIOR ROOM (INCHES)								CURB WT.	TRUNK CAP. (CU. FT.)	FUEL CAP.		
FRONT				REAR				WT.		CAP.		
HEAD	LEG	SHLDR	HIP	HEAD	LEG	SHLDR	HIP	(LBS.)		(GALS.)		
37.6	41.8	62.0	62.3	36.7	35.7	60.6	61.0	4066	18.2	22.0	Galaxie 500	2-door hardtop, formal roof
37.4	41.7	62.0	62.3	36.5	35.6	60.6	61.0	4133	18.2	22.0	LTD	
37.4	41.7	62.0	62.3	36.5	35.6	60.6	61.0	4159	19.2	22.0	LTD Brougham	
39.1	42.0	62.0	62.3	37.3	38.7	61.8	62.3	3899	18.2	22.0	Ford Custom	4-door sedan
39.1	42.0	62.0	62.3	37.3	38.7	61.8	62.3	3904	18.2	22.0	Custom 500	
38.8	41.8	62.0	62.3	37.4	38.3	61.8	62.3	4066	18.2	22.0	Galaxie 500	
37.9	41.8	62.0	62.3	37.0	38.3	61.8	62.3	4121	18.2	22.0	Galaxie 500	4-door hardtop
37.7	41.7	62.0	62.3	36.8	38.2	61.8	62.3	4184	18.2	22.0	LTD	
37.7	41.7	62.0	62.3	36.8	38.2	61.8	62.3	4214	18.2	22.0	LTD Brougham	
37.7	41.7	62.0	62.3	36.8	38.2	61.8	62.3	4189	18.2	22.0	LTD	4-door pillared hardtop
37.7	41.7	62.0	62.3	36.8	38.2	61.8	62.3	4219	18.2	22.0	LTD Brougham	
39.3	41.7	62.0	62.3	37.0	32.5	60.9	59.4	4261	15.9	22.0	LTD	2-door convertible
									Cargo			
39.3	42.0	62.0	62.3	39.9	37.2	62.0	62.4	4425	96.2	21.0	Ford Custom Ranch Wagon	Station wagon, 4-door
39.3	42.0	62.0	62.3	39.9	37.2	62.0	62.4	4435	96.2	21.0	Custom 500 Ranch Wagon	
39.0	41.8	62.0	62.3	39.5	37.1	62.0	62.4	4450	96.2	21.0	Galaxie 500 Country Sedan	
38.8	41.7	62.0	62.3	39.3	37.1	62.0	62.4	4510	96.2	21.0	LTD Country Squire	
									Cargo			
39.3	42.0	62.0	62.3	39.9	37.21	62.0	62.4	4485	96.2	21.0	Custom 500 Ranch Wagon	Station wagon, 4-door (dual facing rear seats)
39.0	41.8	62.0	62.3	39.5	37.1	62.0	62.4	4500	96.2	21.0	Galaxie 500 Country Sedan	
38.8	41.7	62.0	62.3	39.5	37.1	62.0	62.4	4560	96.2	21.0	LTD Country Squire	

FIGURE 8.5 Description by tabulation.

Galaxie 2-door hardtop) from the tabulated figures, this is what you might write:

The Galaxie 500 2-door hardtop weighs 4066 lb as delivered, has a trunk capacity of 18.2 cu. ft. and a fuel capacity of 22.0 gal. Its front interior dimensions are: 37.6 in. at the head, 62.0 in. at the shoulder, and 41.8 in. at the leg. Its rear interior dimensions are: 36.7 in. at the head, 60.6 in. at the shoulder, and 35.7 in. at the leg. At the hip, the front interior dimension is 62.3 in.; at the hip, the rear interior dimension is 61.0 in.

STUDY QUESTIONS

1. When would you find it more useful to write a description of an object as in the paragraph above? When would you find it more useful to tabulate?

2. Which method of description (tabulation or text) makes comparison easier?

3. Redesign the tabulated description so that the list of model names and body types runs across the top of the table rather than down the column. What kinds of problems do you run into? What does this attempted change tell you about preparing tables?

4. Why are the vertical columns set off by rules, while not all the horizontal columns are?

5. If you were to convert this table to text, would the following be a good predictor sentence?

Model specifications in the standard (full) size Ford automobiles depend on the model and body types.

6. Write a predictor sentence and/or overview sentence on the assumption that you are about to convert this table to text.

Description Primarily by Illustration

In some cases it is possible to rely entirely on illustration for description: a photograph, a blueprint, an electrical schematic. If the illustration gives all the understanding needed, why not let it stand by itself?

It is also possible to rely largely on illustration, with some added explanatory text for description. Look at Fig. 8.6. Could you manufacture this Dutch hutch with no more information than the picture provides? If your answer to the question is no, what additional information would you need?

The Parts List

The parts list is a special kind of description. It exists to help purchasing departments, production supervisors, parts department managers, and customers to order the parts they need.

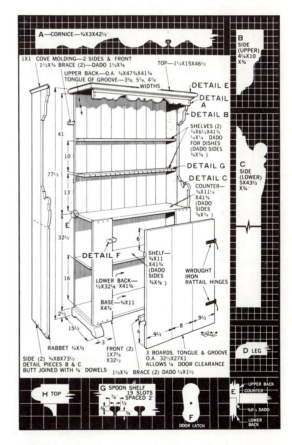

FIGURE 8.6 Description primarily by illustration. (Reprinted from **Mechanix Illustrated.** Copyright © 1971 by Fawcett Publishers, Inc.)

Parts lists should be prepared first for the complete assembly (a model, an automobile, a record player), and then for each subassembly. Fig. 8.7 will show you how to group subassemblies under basic headings. Note that for each assembly there is a title, a part number, a figure number (where an illustration is used), and a page number.

The parts list should have two sections—an exploded drawing (Fig. 8.8) and the actual parts list. In the exploded drawing, each part is shown as it actually appears, and its relationship to all other parts is established. The parts list (Fig. 8.9) is numbered to correspond to the numbers in the exploded drawing.

In the drawing, each part is given a key

Table of Contents

	Description	Assembly	Page
	Power Train Group		
1	LOWER POWER TRAIN ASSEMBLY (Transfer Case to Axle)	AL-P409	7
2	UPPER POWER TRAIN ASSEMBLY (Continental F-163 and Warner Transmission)	BL-P662	8
3	UPPER POWER TRAIN ASSEMBLY (Continental F-163 and Funk Transmission)	BL-P663	9
4	UPPER POWER TRAIN ASSEMBLY (International UB-220 and Warner Transmission)	FL-P172	10
5	UPPER POWER TRAIN ASSEMBLY (International UB-220 With Funk Transmission)	FL-P171	11
6	UPPER POWER TRAIN ASSEMBLY (Wisconsin V465D and Warner Transmission)	BL-P664	12
	Axle Group		
7	WHEEL AND TIRE ASSEMBLY	FL-P230	13
8	FRONT AXLE ASSEMBLY	AL-3315	14
9	REAR AXLE ASSEMBLY	AL-3336	15
10	DIFFERENTIAL AND CARRIER ASSEMBLY (Front and Rear Axle)	AL-P369	16
11	AXLE BRAKE AND DRUM ASSEMBLY (Front and Rear Axle)	BL-P606	18
12	RZEPPA JOINT ASSEMBLY (Front and Rear Axle)	AL-P366	19
13	TRUNNION ASSEMBLY (Front and Rear Axle)	AL-P368	20
14	STEERING CYLINDER ASSEMBLY	BL-P588	22
15	STEERING CYLINDER ASSEMBLY	BL-P665	23
16	PARKING BRAKE ASSEMBLY (Axle Mounted)	BL-4421	24
17	PARKING BRAKE HANDLE ASSEMBLY		25
	Power Train Accessories Group		
18	TRANSFER CASE ASSEMBLY (Model 170)	LL-2663-126	26
19	UNIVERSAL DRIVE SHAFT (Transfer Case to Front Axle)	BL-929-42	28
20	UNIVERSAL DRIVE SHAFT (Transfer Case to Rear Axle)	BL-929-20	29
21	UNIVERSAL DRIVE SHAFT (Transmission to Transfer Case) (Wisconsin V465D Engine) (Continental F-163) (Warner Transmission)	BL-2168-5	30
22	UNIVERSAL DRIVE SHAFT, Transmission to Transfer Case (Continental F-163 and Funk Transmission)	LL-773-175-2	31
23	UNIVERSAL COUPLER, Transmission to Transfer Case (International UB-220 Engine, Warner and Funk Transmission)	LL-773-99	32
24	TRANSMISSION ASSEMBLY, Warner #3 Housing	LL-2389-244	33
	TRANSMISSION ASSEMBLY, Warner #4 Housing	LL-2389-247	33

FIGURE 8.7 Table of contents for a parts list. (Reprinted by permission of Pettibone Michigan Corporation from **Super 4 Cary All Parts Book** (PB-1538), June 1972, p. 4.)

BOTTOM OVEN ASSEMBLY

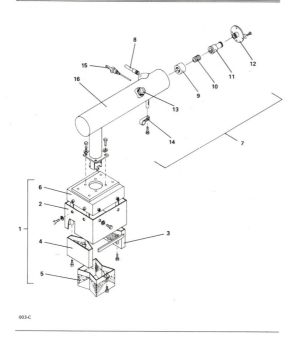

003-C

FIGURE D2

FIGURE 8.8 Exploded drawing accompanying the parts list in Fig. 8.9 (Reproduced with permission of Cherry-Burrell Company, a division of Cherry-Burrell Corporation.)

number. The key number is *not* the parts number. On each exploded drawing, parts are keyed beginning with the number "1" or the letter "A". These key numbers should be listed from left to right, from top to bottom, or in a clockwise or counter-clockwise order (as in Fig. 8.8). Do not list key numbers in a random order; the reader will not be able to find a keyed part if he is working from the parts list to the exploded drawing.

In the parts list, the parts are listed in *numerical* order, according to the key number, or alphabetically, if you are using letters. If you

must have a list of parts numbers in serial order (as for inventory or stocking purposes) make up another list.

Names of parts are listed first by type (screw, shim, nut, cup) and then by function, thus: housing, carrier; shim, medium. The same is true for parts differentiated by size or other quality: lockwasher, $\frac{3}{8}$.

The required quantity is also listed (for the benefit of the purchasing department or a reader who may have mislaid parts during a repair operation).

One part may have several names, according to its use, but no matter what it is called, it always has the same parts number.

Parts numbers may or may not coincide with parts numbers on engineering drawings. But they must coincide with the numbers in the stock room.

STUDY AND WRITING ASSIGNMENTS

1. Write a dictionary definition of a tool or appliance you own and use: a slide rule, a typewriter, a power saw or drill, a sewing machine, a food mixer, or an electric can opener. Restrict your definition to twenty-five words and be sure that your definition will apply to any appliance of the same type.

2. Write a specific description of the same item, giving all the details necessary to identify this item as your own. Begin your description with an overview, or predictor.

3. Write a specific description of a laboratory or shop in which you work or have worked. Be sure to begin with an overview, or predictor.

4. Write a chronological description of the solution of a technological problem on which you have worked: a problem using a transit, an oscilloscope, or whatever. Describe the equipment used and relate the equipment to the solution of the problem.

5. Describe a process or operation in which several events happen simultaneously; printing one typewriter character on paper; stitching cloth

Bottom Oven Assembly

Index	Description	Part No.	Qty X	Qty A	Qty S	Use Code	Attaching Parts Hardware	Qty
1	Oven Housing Assembly	705-8639	2				952-1337	8
2	Shroud, Housing	705-9818		1			952-1001	8
							957-0023	2
3	Oven Element, End	705-8611		1			952-1321	2
4	Oven Element, End	705-8614		1			952-1321	2
5	Oven Element, Center	705-9349		1			952-1001	2
6	Housing	705-8639		1				
7	Burner Assembly, Right			1				
8	Hose Adapter	705-9371		1				
	Burner Subassembly			1			952-1009	4
							957-0023	4
9	Nozzle, Burner	590-1569			1			
10	Nipple, Close Pipe, 1"I.P.S.	555-1403			1			
11	Reducing Tee, Pipe	555-3292			1			
12	Cap, End	705-9887			1			
13	Sightglass	590-1365		1				
14	Clamp, Teflon Cable, 0.25"D	551-1354		1			953-1073	1
15	Electrode, 14mm x 1.25mm S.A.E. thread	551-1273		1				
16	Elbow, Burner	705-9359		1				
	Burner Assembly, Left		1					
	Parts complement same as item 7 with following exception:							
	Elbow, Burner	705-9358		1				

QTY X—QUANTITY PER BOTTOM OVEN ASSEMBLY

QTY A—QUANTITY PER ASSEMBLY

QTY S—QUANTITY PER SUBASSEMBLY

FIGURE 8.9 Parts list accompanying exploded drawing in Fig. 8.8. (Reprinted with permission of Cherry-Burrell Company, a division of Cherry-Burrell Corporation.)

with a sewing machine; throwing a Frisbee; sailing a boat; the functioning of a 2-cylinder motorcycle engine or a 4-cycle automobile engine through one complete cycle.

6. Find a picture of a technical object. Write a description of the object, using the picture as overview, partial explanation, or both.

7. Make a schematic drawing of an electrical appliance, a mechanical device, or a production line that you know about. Write the necessary text to explain it.

8. From sales material given to you by an automobile company, write a description of an automobile. Begin with an overview, or pre-dictor. Make the description completely your own.

9. Prepare a tabulated description of several models of stereo sets, TV sets, bicycles, or motorbikes.

10. Make a detailed drawing of some project you have built—a stereo cabinet, a gun case, a tool chest, a bookcase. Put as much of the description as you can into the drawing. Add whatever text is necessary. Check your work for completeness.

11. Bring to class examples of good and bad descriptions of the types mentioned here or of types you do not find mentioned here.

9 | "How-to-do-it" Information

The United States is the greatest consumer society the world has ever known. But Americans rarely produce the goods they use. It is more likely that we manufacture goods, processes, and systems in one place for use elsewhere. Sometimes the consumption location is halfway around the world from the place of manufacture. In many cases, each part of a machine or system is made in a different place, and the final assembly takes place in still another place. In other cases, unassembled objects (a bicycle, a model airplane kit, an electronics kit, a piece of ordnance) are assembled by the user. In almost every situation, the user must be told how to use the goods or system and how to keep it going.

In any of these instances, therefore, "how-to-do-it" information must accompany the product. The information may be on a label fastened to an object; it may be printed on a plastic or paper envelope containing small parts; it may be printed on a single sheet of paper; or it may be contained in a manual of several thousand pages.

When this information need not necessarily accompany the product, it may be sent in a letter or appear in a magazine such as *Elementary Electronics* or *Popular Mechanics*. It may appear in a book such as *Chilton's Auto Repair Manual*

or be printed on a box or crate. It may be shown on a motion picture screen or on closed-circuit television.

The information may serve one or more of the following purposes:

1. furnish a parts list
2. give instructions for assembly or operation
3. instruct in use or operation
4. instruct in repairs, adjustments, or maintenance
5. teach skills, such as selling, explaining, writing, soldering, painting, wiring
6. instruct in unpacking and shipping
7. give procedures for ordering parts, optional attachments, tools, and so on

What Is "How-to-do-it" Information?

How-to-do-it information (usually called either *directions* or *instructions*) is a special form of the *process paper* discussed in Chapter 8. The written and illustrated material is basically like other descriptive material. Like the process description you saw in Chapter 8, it may contain descriptions within it. Like other process descriptions, it must be adapted to the purposes of the writer and his reader.

When you write how-to-do-it information, you become a teacher. But unlike most teachers, your "students" may be far away—both in place and time. In a classroom, a student may raise his hand and ask the teacher to repeat, to explain, or to illustrate a point. Your student-reader can't do that. Instead, he must write a letter that may waste valuable time, or make an expensive telephone call. If his first inquiry is incomplete, more time and money will be wasted. Or, if he decides to go ahead on his own and try his luck and if his luck is bad on this occasion, disaster may strike.

The Language of How-to-do-it Information

Voice

The language of instructions *may* be like that of other process papers. But when you are telling someone to do something, you do not use the *descriptive voice*:

The reader will do what he is told.

You use the *command voice*:

Do exactly what I tell you.

To illustrate the differences between the descriptive voice and the command voice, here are two paragraphs that contain the same information:

1. The installer must cut a 3″ × 5″ opening in a vertical flat surface of the plenum 3″ above the furnace outlet to permit inspection of the heating element. This heating element must be positioned 1⅜″ from the furnace casing to the center of the element and 1½″ from the top of the heat exchanger to the bottom of the element. After proper inspection through this opening, the opening is covered with the 4″ × 6″ plate and the screws provided. The plate should be screwed tight to eliminate air leaks.

2. Cut a 3″ × 5″ opening in the vertical flat surface of the plenum 3″ above the furnace element to permit inspection of the heating element. Position the heating element 1⅜″ from the furnace casing to the center of the element and 1½″ from the top

of the heat exchanger to the bottom of the element. Cover the opening with the 4″ × 6″ plate and the screws provided. Screw the plate tight to eliminate leaks.

Remove the plate whenever you need to inspect the heating element.

STUDY QUESTIONS

1. Which of the two preceding paragraphs is written in descriptive voice? What evidence do you have?
2. Consider the phrases "should be screwed tight" and "screw the plate tight." Do you find any difference in these phrases other than in the voice?
3. What is the implied relationship between writer and reader in each of the two paragraphs?

Vocabulary

You must write how-to-do-it information for the people who will read it. Therefore, you must use the language of your reader. You must define technical terms or terms that your reader doesn't know, particularly words or terms used in a local or special sense. Use the techniques you learned in Chapter 7.

Because instructions use a great many illustrations, you can often define by "pointing":

. . . to permit inspection of the heating element (1, Figure A) . . .

Be specific about locations of objects or places. When you use the words *top*, *bottom*, *left*, *right*, *below*, *above* and so on, be sure your reader knows your point of view:

As you face the machine, the volume knob is in the upper right-hand corner.

Hold the cylinder in the horizontal position with the door bracket at your left. The air valve screw is at the left end of the cylinder, adjacent to the door bracket.

Use the words *clockwise* and *counter-clockwise* to specify directions of turns. Specify amount of turn in degrees:

Rotate the control valve clockwise 145°. Tighten the valve locking nut by turning it counter-clockwise until it is firmly seated.

Never change the meaning of a word within a given context. Do not use synonyms or more than one name for a technical item because you are concerned that you are repeating yourself. If a name is used in a parts list, use that name in your instructions.

Do not write:

If the unit replaces coal-fired *equipment,* the chimney must be thoroughly cleaned. No other heating *appliances* should be piped into the vent.

Write:

If the unit replaces a coal-fired *appliance,* clean the chimney thoroughly. No other heating *appliance* . . .

Do not use the words *should* or *may.* The intent of these words is to give the reader options. Be specific about whether something is to be done or is not to be done.

Don't write:

The worker should not smoke while he is using the cleaning fluid.

Write:

Do not smoke while you are using the cleaning fluid.

Many small parts have more than one name, according to their function in a specific assembly. Always use the name that pertains to the specific use:

Remove the small *by-pass plug* from the muslin bag that is attached to the burner. Remove the *pipe plug* at the oil return line connection (4, Figure 2) and install the *by-pass plug.* Tighten the *by-pass plug* securely.

Clarity

Remember that everything in your reader's situation is strange to him. He has not had the opportunities you have had to learn about the subject you are explaining. You may think you are making something clear; he may find your instructions confusing.

Here is an example of confusing instructions:

Make a fold along the dotted line of the envelope. Place template against door with folded flap against edge of door.

These instructions raise some questions in a reader's mind:

Are the the envelope and the template the same thing? Is the folded flap half of the envelope I have just folded, or is it the flap of the envelope? Which of the eight edges of the door do these instructions apply to?

DISCUSSION ASSIGNMENT

Bring to class examples of how-to-do-it information that you have found to be incomplete or confusing. Tell briefly what problems you had because of the defective explanation. Then, if you can, show your improved version of the instructions.

Before You Write

Know Your Subject

Before you can begin to write instructions, you must know everything about the subject.

1. Study the pertinent engineering drawings. Read the specifications and the parts list.

2. Examine the subject itself. If there is something that must be assembled, assemble it. If it is already put together, take it apart and put it back together, if possible.

3. Ask the project engineer why the subject came into being, what its purposes are, who will use it, and under what circumstances. Find out which are its good and bad features. Learn which elements are likely to wear out, break, malfunction, or cause problems. Find out how worn or broken parts are replaced.

4. If the sales department is involved, discuss the subject with a member of the department. What uses, advantages, and features will salespeople emphasize?

5. If the subject is to be packed for shipment, discuss packing and unpacking with someone in the shipping department. Be sure you know exactly how the package will look to the reader and what tools will be needed.

6. Find out what warranties and guarantees the subject will have. Get written copies of these.

7. Note: do not trust your memory in this learning process. Take all the notes you can. Get copies of engineering drawings, photographs of the subject, copies of advertising and sales materials, parts lists, specifications, and whatever else may be useful. You can always discard unwanted material. But if you quote anything, keep that material in your file as your authority for what you write.

Gather Materials

As you go along, try to picture what the completed instructions package will look like. If similar instructions have been prepared for other projects, get copies of those and study them. Or, maintain a file of good how-to-do-it materials from various sources.

Decide which photographs and parts drawings you will need. Have the photographs taken by competent photographers. Arrange for cutaway photographs, retouched photographs, inset photographs, "exploded" photographs, and so on (see Chapter 14 for explanations of these terms). Have the parts drawings made in sharp black-on-white by competent artists.

Get copies of standard clauses written for other projects that are usable for yours. Have parts lists typed, following the procedures outlined in Chapter 8.

Analyze Your Subject

Before you begin the final preparation, analyze your subject. Divide the whole into its main parts, keeping in mind the advice from Chapter 8. Do not have more than five main divisions.

Individual stages might be: unpacking, assembly, operation, and maintenance. If you are preparing a manual on repair and maintenance, the divisions might be: day-to-day service—cleaning, oiling, and adjusting; replacement of broken or worn parts; preventive maintenance; factory overhauls. If you are preparing a teaching manual, the divisions might be: theory and principles of operation; application of theory and principles; self-testing. Whatever the case, the analysis will depend on the subject matter, your purpose, and the needs of the reader.

If further division is needed, divide the main stages into main subdivisions, and if the subdivisions are too large, divide these into sub-subdivisions. Within each division or subdivision, set up the individual steps of the operation, decide the order of the steps, and number the steps in order.

Next, make up a list of such items as tools and materials that your reader will need. Be sure this list is placed at the beginning of the instructions. Don't get your reader up a ladder with a piece of material in his hands and then tell him that he will need a hammer and some tenpenny nails.

Then, make up a list of whatever precautions your reader will have to take. Divide these into classes, and label each class clearly and distinctly:

DANGER—This label, boldly printed, will apply to any stages or operations that could lead to loss of life or serious injury if proper care is not taken. If your reader is required to use any flammable or poisonous materials, this signal must be used. If high voltages are involved, this signal must be used.

This label must be applied to the subject itself, to any packages in which the subject is contained, to the first page of the instructions, and within the instructions where appropriate. If you must err in the use of this label, err on the side of plenty. If there is any doubt about this matter, consult a lawyer.

WARNING—This label is used to single out any stages or steps where damage could occur to the object itself if instructions are not followed. Here is a sample warning statement:

WARNING—Rosin-core solder is supplied with your kit. This type of solder *must be used* for all soldering in the kit. The use of other types of solder, such as acid-core solder or paste fluxes, will cause corrosion of parts.

CAUTION—This label will apply to any stages or steps where faulty or minimal results will occur if instructions are not followed:

Caution—Where minimum clearance is desired, two ventilation openings should be provided, six inches from the top and bottom of the front door. Each opening must be one-half of the total area shown in the table below . . .

NOTE—This label will be applied to any stages or operations where you must alert the reader to potential problems:

Note—If it is necessary to remove the crate sides in order to get the unit through any doors, the rest of the crate, particularly the crate base or skid, should not be removed until the unit has been brought to its final location.

ADVICE—This label will be applied to any suggestions you can give to make your reader's work easier:

Advice—Lay out parts so they will be handy when you assemble your kit. Muffin tins and egg cartons are ideal for holding small parts.

Writing and Illustrating Technical Instructions

First Stage: Labeling

1. Be sure that whatever the length or style of your instructions, their purpose is plainly marked:

Kit Builders Guide—steps to easy Heathkit assembly
Installation instructions—Newell no. 005—Al door closer
Installation instructions for predrilled doors
Baseboard heater—installation, operation, and repair parts

2. Instruction sheets, manuals, or labels become "parts" that must be stockpiled and inventoried. Have the parts department assign a part number and print it on the item.

3. Instruction materials often contain proprietary information. In such cases, be sure to copyright the materials.

4. Put the date of publication and the address of the supplier (in case the supplier is not the manufacturer) on the materials. Be sure to include the Zip Code

5. List all models or operations to which the instructions refer and clearly describe the differences among them.

Second Stage: Table of Contents

If the instruction materials run to several pages, include a table of contents. This will be the last item you write, but be sure to include space for it in your layout and title each stage accordingly.

A table of contents need be no more elaborate than this:

• Unpack 1 • Tools 2 • Resistors 3 • Parts 4 • Assembly 5 • Soldering 6 • Integrated Circuits 7 • Service Information 8 •

Or, a table of contents may be as elaborate as the one shown in Fig. 8.7.

Third Stage: Introduction

If the purpose of the appliance is obvious and the instructions are very brief, the title may serve as the entire introduction. But in many cases, an introduction is valuable; it gives your reader an overview of the product, the project he is about to begin, or both. It may reassure him that he has done the right thing in dealing with you. It may motivate him to do a good job of reading and following the instructions.

Here is a sample introduction:

This manual contains instructions on the operation, maintenance, and service for the Prufrock Super 3 Series Fork Lift.

Full benefit of the long life and dependability built into this machine can be realized through proper operation and maintenance. Of equal importance is the use of proper procedures during machine operation.

Personnel responsible for machine operation and maintenance should study the section of the manual pertaining to their particular duties.

Here is an introduction designed to be more persuasive:

The Heathkit Model GD-48 Metal Locator is a reliable instrument for finding buried or hidden metals. A single SENSITIVITY control provides easy operation and enables the operator to pinpoint buried metal objects such as silver, gold, iron, and so on with accuracy. Lightweight enough to be easily handled by youngsters, it can provide many exciting hours of "treasure hunting."

Fourth Stage: Parts List

Where it is appropriate in an instruction manual, a parts list should be provided. Parts lists serve three functions in these manuals:

1. They help the reader locate and identify individual parts.

2. They help him identify and order replacement parts.

3. If, through accident, a part is missing, the reader can see that the part is missing, he can identify it, and he can order a replacement.

Figs. 8.8 and 8.9 illustrate a good parts list and good parts illustration procedures.

Fifth Stage: List of Materials

List the tools and materials your reader will need and put these lists at the beginning of the instructions. Be as helpful as you can. Remind him, for example, that large, infrequently used tools and equipment can be rented. Try to anticipate his problems in locating tools and materials with some helpful advice:

It will be necessary to purchase a 9-volt battery (NEDA #1602 equivalent). A smaller metal-cased battery will not last nearly as long.

Use a high-grade lubricating oil on all moving parts (Standard Oil Finol or equivalent).

You will need about 50 no.6 brads. These can be obtained at a store that sells picture-framing supplies.

Sixth Stage: Aids for Reader

1. Label each major division of the instructions.

2. Number each step in turn.

3. Use illustrations as much as possible and key the illustrations to the text.

4. Place a check bracket opposite the number of each step so that the reader can mark off each step as he completes it.

5. Use exploded drawings or photographs where necessary.

6. Refresh the reader's mind on precautions as necessary.

7. Place all illustrations as close to the text as possible. Label illustrations with the same step numbers as the text.

8. Simplify each step as much as possible. Confine each step to one task.

Figs. 9.1 and 9.2 illustrate superior instruction manual practice.

Seventh Stage: Operating Details

Include necessary operating details after assembly or unpacking instructions. Fig. 9.3 illustrates a page of "Operating Instructions" from a Navy manual.

STUDY QUESTIONS

1. How does the numbering of the steps in the Navy manual differ from the numbering in the Heathkit manual?

2. Why do you think the producers of the Heathkit manual have not numbered steps (notice that "pictorials" are numbered)?

3. How does the Navy system of call-outs (cross-references between text and illustrations) differ from those in the Heathkit manual? Which system do you like better?

4. Which manual makes more effective use of illustrations?

STEP-BY-STEP ASSEMBLY

Before starting to assemble this kit, read the Kit Builders Guide for complete information on wiring, soldering, and step-by-step assembly procedures.

CIRCUIT BOARD ASSEMBLY

Install components on the circuit boards by following the steps on Pictorials 1 through 5.

Assembly of the audio circuit board (#85-307-1) will be followed by the assembly of the search coil circuit board (#85-388-1). The entire circuit board is shown on each Pictorial.

Resistors will be called out by their resistance value (in Ω or kΩ) and color code. Capacitors will be called out by the capacitance value (in pF or μF) and type (disc, mica, Mylar, and electrolytic).

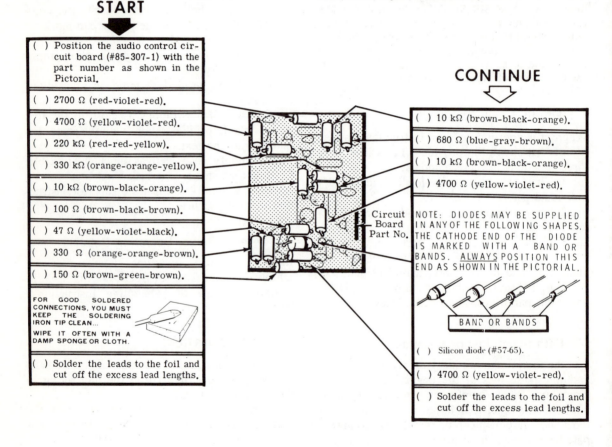

START

( ) Position the audio control circuit board (#85-307-1) with the part number as shown in the Pictorial.

( ) 2700 Ω (red-violet-red).

( ) 4700 Ω (yellow-violet-red).

( ) 220 kΩ (red-red-yellow).

( ) 330 kΩ (orange-orange-yellow).

( ) 10 kΩ (brown-black-orange).

( ) 100 Ω (brown-black-brown).

( ) 47 Ω (yellow-violet-black).

( ) 330 Ω (orange-orange-brown).

( ) 150 Ω (brown-green-brown).

FOR GOOD SOLDERED CONNECTIONS, YOU MUST KEEP THE SOLDERING IRON TIP CLEAN...

WIPE IT OFTEN WITH A DAMP SPONGE OR CLOTH.

( ) Solder the leads to the foil and cut off the excess lead lengths.

Circuit Board Part No.

CONTINUE

( ) 10 kΩ (brown-black-orange).

( ) 680 Ω (blue-gray-brown).

( ) 10 kΩ (brown-black-orange).

( ) 4700 Ω (yellow-violet-red).

NOTE: DIODES MAY BE SUPPLIED IN ANY OF THE FOLLOWING SHAPES. THE CATHODE END OF THE DIODE IS MARKED WITH A BAND OR BANDS. ALWAYS POSITION THIS END AS SHOWN IN THE PICTORIAL.

BAND OR BANDS

( ) Silicon diode (#57-65).

( ) 4700 Ω (yellow-violet-red).

( ) Solder the leads to the foil and cut off the excess lead lengths.

FIGURE 9.1 Good instruction-manual practice. (Reprinted by permission of Heath Company. Copyright © 1969 Heath Company. All rights reserved.)

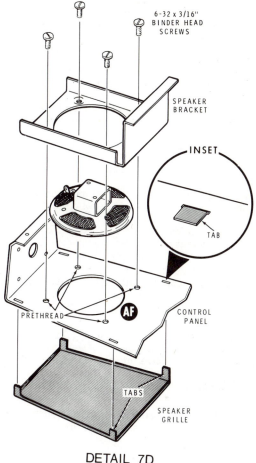

( ) Locate the 6-32 x 1/2" self-tapping screw and thread the four holes around the control panel cutout AF. Then, remove and save the screw. It will be used later.

( ) Insert the speaker grille tabs through the front of the control panel. Then refer to the inset drawing on Detail 7D and bend the tabs over to secure the grille to the panel.

( ) Position the speaker over cutout AF in the control panel with the speaker magnet parallel to the rear apron and with the terminals positioned as shown in Pictorial 7.

( ) Place the speaker bracket over the speaker and secure it to the control panel with four 6-32 x 3/16" binder head screws, as shown in Detail 7D. NOTE: Do not overtighten, or the control panel will bow.

DETAIL 7D

FIGURE 9.2 Good instruction-manual practice. (Reprinted by permission of Heath Company. Copyright © 1969 1969 Heath Company. All rights reserved.)

5. In which specific ways have the two manuals used such cautionary labels as "warning," "caution," and "note"?

6. What is the function of the "operating instructions"?

7. What voice is used in the "operating instructions"? In the Heathkit manual?

Eighth Stage: Possible Difficulties

Where the situation calls for it, include information about the kind of difficulties your reader may experience. Such information is usually listed under three headings:

Difficulty noticed
Possible causes
Possible remedies

Fig. 9.4 shows an example of a troubleshooting chart. The boxed form is a good form to follow. Each item of difficulty is set off with its "possible causes" and "possible remedies" from every other item.

4.0 OPERATING INSTRUCTIONS
4.1 Preparation for Use (See figure 2-1.)
4.2 Perform the following operational checks and adjustments prior to using the breathing apparatus.

  a. Lay the breathing apparatus on a clean work surface.

  b. Remove canister assembly (7) from back plate (18) by removing cylinder spreader bar (24), disconnecting control block to canister hose (15) at air inlet block (16), and unthreading hoses (25 and 26) from breathing bag and vest assembly (17).

  c. Remove regulator assembly (13) and control block assembly (14) from the back plate by disconnecting pull rod (27) and loosening regulator yoke assembly (22).

  d. Recharge cylinders (9) with the proper gas mixture selected for dive as follows (See figure 4-1.):

    (1) Open manifold shut-off valve (1) to bleed off any gas that may remain in cylinders (2).

WARNING

Avoid all contact with oil and grease. Oil coming in contact with high pressure connections may result in an explosion. Mixed gas cylinders should be treated the same as oxygen cylinders, USE NO OIL.

    (2) Connect charging line assembly (3) to manifold valve assembly (4).

    (3) Slowly open valve of high pressure gas source and fill cylinders to desired pressure (3000 psi maximum).

CAUTION

Charge the cylinders at a rate not to exceed 500 psi per minute. Since cylinders will become warm during charging, allow cylinders to cool and complete charging if maximum pressure is desired.

    (4) Close manifold shut-off valve (1) and the high pressure gas source valve. Bleed the charging line assembly at the high pressure source.

    (5) Disconnect charging line assembly (3) from manifold valve assembly (4).

    (6) Check stem gauge (5) for approximate cylinder pressure indication.

    (7) After charging, tag the cylinders to indicate the exact composition of the gas mixture used to fill the cylinders and the pressure to which the cylinders were pressurized.

Note

When changing the gas mixture previously used in the cylinders, empty the cylinders and flush thoroughly with a 100 psi charge of the new gas mixture prior to recharging to desired capacity.

  e. Remove access cap (28, figure 2-1) from control block, install appropriate resistor orifice (8 LPM, 12 LPM, or 21 LPM) with gasket, using allen wrench supplied with service kit (see figure 6-8), and replace the access cap.

FIGURE 9.3 Operating Instructions. (Reprinted by permission from **Service Manual for Mark VI Underwater Breathing Apparatus** (Navships 393-0653), Bureau of Ships. U.S. Department of the Navy, Washington, D.C., 1963, p. 4-1)

Ninth Stage: Warranty Notice

Factory repair service and warranty notices may be called for. A warranty notice may exist in your organization as a standard clause. If one has to be written, it should be written with the advice of lawyers and engineers.

Tenth Stage: Quality Control

No matter how careful or how concerned you may be, errors, omissions, or unclear statements may appear in your instructions. Therefore, you should always have clearly defined procedures for controlling the quality of your instructions. These quality controls should be similar to those on a factory production line.

1. Step-by-step control:
As each step of the instructions is completed, it should be reviewed by someone other than the writer.

2. Over-all control:
When the instructions are completed, they should be reviewed by:

a. The project engineer. Moreover, one of the draftsmen should check all details against engineering drawings and specifications.

Troubleshooting Chart

Difficulty	Possible Cause
No sound in the speaker when the unit is turned on.	1. Battery dead. 2. Phone jack wired incorrectly. 3. Transistors or other components incorrectly installed. 4. Pickup coil leads shorted.
Sound is heard from the speaker, regardless of Sensitivity setting.	1. C3 not adjusted for null. 2. Transistor Q5 defective, or improperly installed. 3. Search coil or pickup coil improperly wired. 4. Capacitor C3 faulty.
Unable to obtain a minimum reading during adjustments.	1. See steps 2 through 4 above. 2. Damaged pickup coil.
Meter does not indicate properly. Audio circuits operate properly.	1. Capacitor C18 faulty or incorrectly installed. 2. Faulty meter.
Meter indicates backward.	1. Meter leads reversed. 2. Improper alignment (refer to Adjustments section).
Poor Sensitivity.	1. Weak battery. 2. Improper alignment (refer to the Adjustments section). 3. Transistors Q4, Q6, Q7, or Q8 faulty or incorrectly installed. 4. Search coil or pickup coil has shorted windings.

FIGURE 9.4 A troubleshooting chart or check list. (Reprinted by permission of Heath Company. Copyright © 1969 Heath Company. All rights reserved.)

b. The sales department, if the instructions accompany something to be sold.

c. A typical user. Have someone who is unfamiliar with the subject of the instructions go through them step-by-step. The writer should be present ready to take notes, but he should remain silent.

d. If the instructions are to accompany something to be unpacked upon delivery, the shipping department should review the instructions for unpacking.

e. In any case, the instructions should be checked carefully against the actual object, process, or system.

f. Provisions should be made for immediate changes in the instructions should any change occur in the subject of the instructions. If changes are made in the instructions, *all* parts of the instructions should again be subjected to quality control.

3. Cross-reference control:

All cross-references in the instructions (such as references to figure and page numbers) should be checked. If later changes are made in the instructions, all cross-references are re-checked.

Example of Good Student-Written Instructions

Appendix 1, page 167, shows a set of well-written instructions for an assembly operation. This set, written by a student at Michigan Technological University when he was a freshman, is modeled after instruction manuals furnished with kits manufactured by the Heathkit Company of Benton Harbor, Michigan.

Operations Check Sheet

Another form of instructions is the *operations check sheet*. It is used to make repeated routine checks or verifications and to insure that every required step or operation has been completed in turn. Such check sheets are used in "preflighting" aerial flights of commercial, military, or private aircraft. They are also used in many other process and equipment operations.

The example shown in Fig. 9.6 is one page of a sheet used during an Apollo space mission.

STUDY QUESTIONS

1. What are the purposes of this activity?
2. What is the "systems configuration"?
3. What change in "voice" takes place in the check sheet? At what point does the change take place?
4. In the section "Egress Preparation," what do the letters "C," "B," and "P" stand for?
5. What characteristic of language do you notice in the "Configure Cockpit" section? What are the reasons for the use of this style?
6. Prepare a glossary of all the terms you

PURPOSE:
1. To evaluate the operation of the extravehicular life support system (ELSS)
2. To evaluate the handheld maneuvering unit (HHMU) for maneuvering in space
3. To perform the S-9 and D-16 experiments
4. To retrieve Apollo sump tank cameras from the adapter section
5. To attach tether between spacecraft and Agena

SYSTEMS CONFIGURATION:
1. S/C-Agena-docked
2. S/C powered up (with exception of computer)

UMBILICAL EVA
EGRESS PREPARATION:
C Verify tape recorder loaded with fresh tape
B Remove life vests
P Unstow ev gear from r/h aft food box
   Remove Hasselblad and hand to cp
   Stow gloves in Hasselblad pouch
   Stow S-11 bracket if req'd
C Velcro Hasselblad to l/h overhead torque box
   Assemble Ev 16mm camera
P Restow Hasselblad pouch, Eva camera pouch & life vests in r/h aft food box and close vent

   Velcro Ev 16mm camera assembly to r/h sidewall below r/h sidewall pouch

CONFIGURE COCKPIT AS FOLLOWS:
P Check o/h & r/h c/b panels
   Elss pwr c/b—open
   Att ind lt c/b—closed
   Acme bias pwr-pri
   Cabin air recirc—up (open)
   Inlet snorkel—up (closed)
   Cabin vent lanyard—in (closed)
   Cabin vent—up (closed)
   Water seal—up (open)
   O_2 high rate recock—up
   Suit fan—No. 1 & 2
   Pri (a) & sec (b) pumps—on
   Clock lt-iris open
   Cryo qty gage-O_2
   O_2 htr-auto
P H_2 htr-auto
   Prop gage-f
   No. 1 & No. 2 audio-uhf
   C-ADPT-CMD
   C-RNTY-CMD
   UHF-No. 1
   HF T/R-off
   T/M-R/T & ACQ
   Keying-cont int/ptt

FIGURE 9.5 Operations check sheet. (From **Final Gemini XI Flight Plan,** prepared by T. A. Guillory, C. L. Stough, and Warren J. North of Missions Operation Branch, Flight Crew Support Division, Manned Spacecraft Center, NASA, 19 August 1966, p. 61. Reprinted through the courtesy of the National Aeronautics and Space Administration, Washington, D.C.)

will use. Be sure that each term has one meaning only and that it accords with standards for naming. List these terms in alphabetical order. For each term, give the necessary explanation or description and the standard abbreviation and style.

7. Although this example does not have a checkoff box before each step, the use of checkoff boxes ought to be considered. They are frequently used in operations check sheets.

8. Notice how indentations are used to set off and identify the second line of an instruction. This practice is the opposite of usual indentation practices. Why?

WRITING ASSIGNMENT

1. You are planning to take a long trip in your automobile. Prepare an operations check sheet that you will use before you start on the trip and at intervals. (Remember the case of the man who drove three hundred miles and then discovered he had left his wife in the motel!)

2. Assume that you are conducting a final examination in a driver's school. Prepare the operations check sheet that will be used in evaluating the student.

Instructions that Are Primarily Illustrations

Usually, good instructions represent a carefully drawn balance between text and illustrations. In some cases, most, if not all, of the instructions can be given through illustrations. In some cases, the instructor relies too much on illustrations.

A Major Distinction Between Instructions and Description

The principal difference between instructions and description is in the style. Description is usually written in paragraph-long segments, while instructions are written in sentences. Instructions use the command voice.

Although you may have to insert paragraphs of description in a set of instructions, you should differentiate clearly between description and instruction.

You should not mix up the narrative style used in description and the command style used in instructions, as was done in this example:

The feet were ripped 1½ in. wide from 2 × 4 stock and then beveled 45° at the front. These, in turn, were glued to the lower feet and the leg setup was then fastened to the cabinet below with flathead screws.

Edge (cove) molding is fastened to the plywood top so that it sits above the plywood the thickness of the tile and mastic. With the molding placed before the tile, the former can then serve as the leveling guide when you lay the tile. Apply the mastic with a notched trowel and then let it set about 15 minutes.

As you position each tile or square, tap it lightly with a hammer and clean wood block to assure a tight bond. Allow this to dry overnight before you apply any grouting.

STUDY QUESTIONS

1. There are two distinct style changes that take place in the above text. What are they and where do they take place?

2. Rewrite the three paragraphs as instructions.

WRITING ASSIGNMENTS

1. Write a set of instructions for dismantling and reassembling your bicycle or motorbike.

2. Write a complete set of rules for conducting team "gut Frisbee" contests, or "hot dog" ski contests. Include rules for the contest area.

3. Prepare an operations sheet covering starting a car, driving the car from a driveway onto a street, proceeding onto a freeway, reversing directions on the freeway, returning to the same driveway, and stopping the car.

4. Prepare a set of instructions for testing the electrical circuits on your television or stereo set.

5. Lay out a course on which a student may practice the use of the transit. Write the directions the student will follow at each point on the

course. Include directions for use of all equipment.

6. In a workmanlike fashion, prepare an illustration or set of illustrations that *shows* all necessary information for: changing an automobile tire or wheel; lacing a pair of shoes or a tennis racket; replacing the ribbon on a typewriter; making a calculation with a slide rule; using a transit or an oscilloscope.

Whichever assignment you choose, follow the directions in this chapter and exercise quality control.

10 | The Routine Technical Report

The technical report is one of the most common examples of technical information. Technical reports are presented orally and in writing every working day, and they are given and written by everyone concerned with technical matters.

You will make technical reports in person, you will write technical reports, and you will read technical reports. It is important that you know about a kind of technical information that you will encounter in your work.

What Are Technical Reports?

Reports are oral or written records of the following kinds:

Situations that need correcting
Problems that exist
Work that is planned, must be done, is being done, or has been done
Tests that have been conducted
Meetings that have taken place
Conversations that have taken place
Decisions and *choices* (judgments, evaluations) that have been made or must be made
Comparisons that have taken place
Drawings, designs, models that have been made
Trips that have been taken

Changes that have been made or must be made
Failures that have taken place; "dead ends" that have been reached
Studies and *investigations*
Research

Reports can take any one of these patterns:
Face-to-face conversations
Telephone calls
Oral presentations to committees or groups
Short or long memoranda
Letters
Printed forms
Reports of telephone calls or visits
Minutes of meetings
Narrative reports for in-house distribution
Narrative reports for distribution outside the place of employment
Reports for publication in journals and magazines

Two Requirements for the Report

When you prepare reports, then, you must remember two basic requirements for the report: the subject matter and the form it must take. Subject matter will vary, of course, although it will usually fall within one of the categories mentioned above. But report forms are often standardized or conventional. You must learn what the standards and conventions are, many of which follow in this chapter and in Chapters 11 and 12.

The Audience for the Report

You must also be concerned about the audience for the report. It may consist of any, many, or all of the following:

Engineers, technologists, and technicians
Salesmen and advertisers
People who work in public relations or who are trying to develop the public "image" of the organization
People concerned about money and costs
People in charge of production
People who buy the materials you need
People who hire workers to help you
People in shipping and receiving departments
Laboratory workers in chemistry and metallurgy
People who work in parts and tool departments
People who type and edit your reports
People with more or less education than you have
Employees of city, county, state, and federal governments
Members of the military establishments

You must be concerned about your audience because:

they know more or less about the subject than you do;
their ideas may differ from yours;
their standards and conventions may not be the same as yours;
they may use a "different" English than you use.

Brevity and Completeness

Your reports must be as brief as possible, yet complete and must contain all the pertinent information that your readers want or need.

Here, for example, are two very famous brief reports:

Veni, vidi, vici (I came, I saw, I conquered)—
Julius Caesar
We have met the enemy and they are ours—
Lord Nelson

Although these reports have been admired as models of brevity, at least some of us have some questions:

What is the date of Caesar's report? To what place did he come? What did he see? Whom did he conquer?

Of Lord Nelson, we ask: When and where did he meet the enemy? Who were the enemy?

In both cases, we have additional questions: How many people and battles were involved? What were the costs in men, money, and materials on both sides? What problems next presented themselves?

Patterns for Reports

Finally, you must organize your materials. In general, there are two patterns of report organization:

1. A pattern that derives from the subject of the report;
2. A conventional or standard pattern into which you must fit the materials of your report.

The first instance is like fluid that is poured out on the ground. It goes its own way, flowing here and there as it will, forming its own pattern. Gravity and obstacles shape its path.

The second instance is like the fluid that you pour into a test tube, a beaker, a can, a bottle, or a jug. The fluid will always conform to the shape of the container.

In some cases, the report will follow the first pattern; in some cases, it will follow the second. *If a standard form is required* by your employer, your reader, or by convention, *you will use the standard form.*

Face-to-Face Reports

Face-to-face reports tend to be like the first type and are informal, for the most part. Nevertheless, when you are reporting face-to-face, you should realize that the person to whom you are reporting is busy, with many subjects on his mind. Your first obligation is to *establish the context* for the report.

Don't report like this:

"Mr. Smith, I got your work done."
    "What work?"
    "The test you asked me to make."
    "What test?"
    "The test on the shell plate."
    "What shell plate? . . ."

Report like this:

"Mr. Smith, we tested the samples from the lot of steel you ordered for the Bayonne Street molasses tank, and they meet all of the specifications—plate thickness, minimum yield strength, design stress, hydrostatic test, and Charpy V notch values for both transverse and longitudinal requirements."
    "Good. What about the Rockwell hardness?"
    "That's not in the specs, Mr. Smith."
    "Oh, sure. Well, thank you. And send your report over to my department, will you?"
    "Right, Mr. Smith."

In person-to-person reports:

1. Establish the context first—what was done, what needs to be done, who did it, or who will do it. Answer the questions who, what, where, when, why, how. Include authorizations for the work and a brief description of results or consequences.

2. Be as brief as possible, but give all necessary information. Try to anticipate your listener's questions.

3. Stick to the point.

4. Follow up with a written report that records what you said in your oral report. In your written report, cross-reference your oral report so the recipient won't think the written report is something new:

This report records oral information given to R. W. Smith, Superintendent of Construction Engineering, on Tuesday morning, November 23, 1974.

WRITING ASSIGNMENT

Prepare and give to your class a three-minute report of work that you have done in a class, in a laboratory, or on the job. Limit your discussion to one task—a test, an inspection, a determination of some fact. Don't tell how you did it unless the task required unusual techniques.

When you have finished, deliver a memorandum report to your instructor (see Chapter 4) that contains the same information. Do not read from this memorandum when you make your oral report. However, you may use notes for technical information.

The Telephone Report

When you make a report over the telephone, remember that some of the advantages of the face-to-face report are lost. Your listener cannot see you or your body gestures. You do not necessarily have his whole attention (his secretary may be at his desk taking dictation or someone else may be in his office). The technology of the telephone may act as a filter or an obstruction. If either of you has a recorder on your telephone, a sense of restraint may be introduced.

First, introduce yourself:

"Mr. Smith, this is Rob Roy of the materials testing lab."

After you have given him time to acknowledge that he knows who you are, state the purpose of your call:

"I'm calling to report the result of sampling the aggregate materials for the Madison Avenue bridge project. You ordered this work done in a memo of the 24th."
    "Right."
    "You asked us to call you when the information was ready. We sampled the aggregate the afternoon of the 24th and the morning and afternoon of the

25th, according to the specs in the contract. All the samples meet the specs."

"Good. Send me a report, will you?"

"Will do, Mr. Smith."

Before you make a telephone report, have all the information you will need at hand. Don't trust your memory for details. Don't put yourself in the position of having to ask your listener to wait while you get information out of the files.

The manner in which you do your work is important; the manner in which you report your work is equally important. Remember that as far as the other party is concerned, the work hasn't been done until he has received the report.

When you write your report, you may have to include more information than you furnished in the call. For example, in the above conversation, the caller reported that the work was done according to the "specs." Mr. Smith indicated by his response that he was familiar with the specifications. But this may have been only a general familiarity. So, in the written report, it would be a good idea to detail the specifications.

The Report of a Telephone Call

Whenever you make a telephone call about your work, write a report of the details you discussed over the telephone. This stipulation applies whether you are supplying information or receiving it. Even though you are not required to send a follow-up written report, write the report and put it in your file. Or, if you are keeping a journal of work done, put the report in the journal. When you write your report, you will, of course, have the information you had at hand when you made the call.

If many details are to be covered, as an aid to your memory you might do one of the following:

1. Ask your secretary to listen in on the call and take notes.

2. With the permission of the other person, attach a recorder to the line.

3. Have a cassette recorder available and transfer information from the caller to the cassette by repeating it. This repetition will also enable your caller to verify your listening accuracy.

Be prepared to take notes on a note pad. If you take notes, repeat the information back to the other person as you write. This will give you time to write the notes and will also give your party an opportunity to verify the information.

Write the report as soon as possible after the call, while you still have total recall. Put this information in your report:

1. Date and time of the call

2. Names, titles, addresses, telephone numbers (including extension numbers and area codes) of both parties to the call

3. Subjects discussed, orders given, and decisions reached. Limit paragraphs in the report to one subject. Number each paragraph and begin the paragraphs with a subject heading, if possible.

4. Arrangements for follow-ups

5. Distribution of call reports by name and address, if pertinent. One copy of the report should be retained by the caller and one copy should be sent to the other party. Distribution of other reports will be according to established procedures within the organizations.

Reports of Meetings

Reports of meetings follow one of these patterns:

1. A semiformal report pattern that summarizes the problems discussed, the decisions made, and the directions chosen;

2. A formal report pattern that details a meeting according to an agenda.

The first pattern is used for reports of committee meetings, small group discussions, project meetings, meetings to discuss possible solutions to problems ("brainstorming" sessions), and so on.

The second pattern is used for formal meetings of departments, organizations, formally organized groups (such as an association of engineers) with charters, and so on.

Reports of Semiformal Meetings

These meetings are usually of an *ad hoc* nature—called as needs arise to discuss one-time activities. These activities may be to discover a fact, to define a problem, or to resolve a problem. The meeting is reported primarily for the record. If more than one meeting is necessary, the reports help to create the continuing historical record that is necessary to insure accuracy and make sure that nothing is overlooked or done twice.

These reports contain the following information:

1. Time and place of meeting and name of authorizer or chairman.

2. Names, titles, and departments of those present.

3. Distribution of report, usually to all those present plus others with a "need to know."

4. Problems and situations discussed, summarized as much as possible. It is not necessary to note everything said or who said what. Usually, such meetings proceed without motions, seconds, amendments, and other formal meeting procedures.

5. Conclusions reached and actions agreed upon. These should be listed in detail. When an obligation is placed on someone to do something, the person should be named and his obligations specified.

Following is an example of a typical semiformal meeting report.

Report of R & D Department meeting, June 3, 1974
Present: H. Irving, W. Lynn, S. Fox, W. Hootnagle (R & D), F. Church, H. Mayne (Cost Accounting), B. Winters (Purchasing), J. Sommers (Plant)

Purpose of meeting: To discuss possible cost-growth in account DOD-622 because of design changes and consequential additional testing of SHE-105mm shell.

1. Irving reported that changes in the design of the basic weapon meant that previous rifling configurations were no longer suitable and that it would be necessary to implement new designs, construct new models, and conduct additional testing at the Rockbound Arsenal.

2. Lynn estimated that three additional months would be required for new designs and for accompanying calculations. Three engineers, six draftsmen, and two technicians would be continued on the project full time during that period.

3. Fox estimated that six days of testing would be required at the Arsenal and that this testing would require the time of two engineers and one technician who would be at the Arsenal during the test period.

4. Hootnagle estimated that three weeks (five working days, three shifts each day) would be necessary to produce test models.

5. Winters stated that because of an earlier duplication in a materials order, adequate supplies of steel and brass were in stock, but transfers in account responsibility would have to be made.

6. Sommers agreed to release machine-shop time in the amount estimated by Hootnagle and agreed to furnish accurate cost estimates by June 4.

7. Church and Mayne will prepare cost estimates by June 15, at which time they will meet with Irving, Linn, and Mr. Etten. Linn will transmit estimates to DOD.

8. Fox will secure time and equipment cost estimates from the Arsenal.

WRITING ASSIGNMENT

1. You will be assigned a class meeting time and write a report of the business conducted during the meeting.

2. Or, if you wish, you may substitute a report of activities in another class, a laboratory, or a meeting of a group to which you belong.

For this assignment, you should concentrate on a meeting in which there is student participation and discussion. Discuss your situation with your teacher before writing the report.

Minutes of a Formal Meeting

Formal meetings are held from time to time, usually on a regular time schedule, and follow a standard agenda, as follows:

1. Call to order by chairman and determination that a quorum is present

2. Reading and approval of minutes of previous meeting (amendments to minutes, if any, are made at this time)

3. Treasurer's report, if one is in order

4. Report of old business carried over from previous meetings

5. Report of new business

6. Committee reports are made for matters other than new or old business

7. Adjournment

Within the old and new business sections, items are taken up one at a time, either according to the whims of the chairman or upon inquiry or motion from the floor.

As a student, you are probably familiar with the formal meeting; you may have seen it in honor societies, clubs, fraternal organizations, and student professional societies. Or perhaps you have been a member of the student council or the student senate.

The minutes of a meeting follow the order of the agenda faithfully. But beyond that, there must be compression. The record of presentations, reports, motions, amendments, debates, and voting of a one-, two-, or three-hour session must be compressed to perhaps 300 to 500 words.

Still, for all the need to compress, sessions of organizations are of a legal nature and the record must report all significant details:

1. Time and place of meeting and name of the chairman are recorded.

2. Roll is called, if specified. The statement that a quorum is present may replace the roll call.

3. Statements are made that minutes of the previous meeting were read and approved. It is customary to make copies of these minutes available to members before a meeting. Some organizations require that the names of the mover and seconder of motions for approval be recorded.

4. Treasurer's report is presented, sometimes in summary in the minutes with a complete report attached for distribution. Membership approval is reported.

5. Items of old business are reported in the order they are taken up. Reference should be made to earlier discussions. It is not necessary to record all the debate on each item, but major directions should be identified. If called for, names of all movers and seconders are given, with their motions. Disposition of each item is reported. If required, individuals are identified according to their votes; otherwise, only results are given: The motion carried, or the motion carried by a vote of 13 to 7.

6. Items of new business are reported in the order taken up.

7. Committee reports are made. These are often summarized in the minutes, with complete committee reports attached to the record. Action taken on committee reports is noted.

8. Motion to adjourn is made.

9. Signature of the reporter is given.

Fig. 10.1 shows minutes of a typical student organization meeting.

WRITING ASSIGNMENT

If you belong to a group that holds regular formal meetings, you should attend a meeting, take notes of activities, and submit a set of minutes to your instructor. If you do not belong to any group, then attend a regular public meeting of a campus organization such as the student governing body. Take notes and submit a set of minutes to your instructor.

Trip Report

Trip reports are another kind of report that technologists write. These reports are very similar to reports of telephone calls, since trips often result in changes in procedures. Sometimes trips are made to test sites, and the trip report becomes a report of the trip and of the testing.

Trip reports include:

1. Name(s) of person(s) making the trip

Student Association Council
Student Union, 4 p.m.
October 3, 19_

Regular Meeting #9
19_ - 19_ Series
Garry Andreen, Presiding

REPRESENTED

Applied Technology
Army ROTC
Civil Engineering
Electrical Encineering
Forestry
Bio. Sciences

Geology and
     Geological Engineering
Mathematics
Social Sciences
Humanities
Physics

The meeting was called to order to 4:09 p.m., First Vice President Andreen having determined that a quorum was present. He replaced President Ed Stinnett, who had been called home on personal matters.

The minutes of the meeting of September 25 were approved in the form distributed to members.

Treasurer Carl Margaret presented a written financial report, which was approved on motion by Lowe and was seconded by Buoy (copy attached).

Annual Christmas Party: Stegler reported that the Council's Annual Christmas Party would be held on December 9 at the Wyoming Club. Council members will be allowed to invite one couple each as guests.

Sno-Ball: Winchester announced plans for the Sno-Ball. It will be held in the Student Union ballroom on December 8 from 9 p.m. to 1 a.m. Music will be provided by the Blackboard Jonglers, and dress will be semi-formal. No sneakers will be allowed, and all men must wear ties.

A debate followed on this last requirement. A motion to uphold the requirement carried by a vote of 7 to 5.

There being no other business, the meeting adjourned at 5:59 p.m.

Respectfully,

Wayne A. Torgerson, Secretary

FIGURE 10.1 Minutes of a student organization meeting.

MTU STUDENTS VISIT CHICAGO FIRM

Houghton--Nine technical writing students in the Department of Humanities at Michigan Technological University toured printing and publishing facilities in the Chicago area last week.

The trip was financed by a special grant from the Reader's Digest Foundation.

On Thursday the group visited the printing and binding facilities of the Hall Printing Co., where they saw some of the eight million copies of the May issue of Playboy being assembled alongside the current Ward sales catalogue. Later the students went to the Chicago Sun-Times for a tour and a special talk by science writer Arthur Snyder.

The second day was spent at Technical Publishing Co. in Barrington, publishers of Plant Engineering, Datamation, Pollution Engineering, Power Engineering and Research/Development. There the students heard the editors stress the need in technical writing for people with engineering backgrounds. The editors expressed a keen interest in the new technical writing program at Michigan Tech that allows students up to 60 hours of engineering courses within the technical writing degree option.

Additional field trips are planned.

Among those making the trip were Charles A. Beck, a sophomore student from Pellston.

FIGURE 10.2 Report of a student trip.

2. Place(s) visited and name(s) of person(s) with whom meetings were held

3. Inclusive dates of trip; time(s) of actual meeting(s)

4. Purpose(s) of trip

5. An event-by-event report of meetings, discussions, tests, work done, decisions and agreements made, changes considered or agreed upon

6. Provisions, if any, for future trips to continue work done on the reported trip

As a student, you will probably not make the same kind of trips that you will make when you work. But it is likely that you will make trips with other students to industries, mines, field sites, meetings of national student groups, and so on. When you make such a trip, it is good practice to keep a diary of all of the events of the trip. Then when you return, you can write a trip report summarizing all you have seen.

Fig. 10.2 shows a student trip report written by one of the students who made the trip. This report was published in a local newspaper as the student wrote it.

STUDY QUESTIONS FOR FIG. 10.2

The account in Fig. 10.2 is a newspaper story, and newspaper stories have special patterns.

1. What is the function of the first paragraph? How is this function related to the patterns discussed in Chapter 8?

2. How many sentences are in each paragraph? How many words in each sentence? What do you conclude?

3. What are the functions of the third and fourth paragraphs?

4. What are the functions of the second and the final paragraphs?

WRITING ASSIGNMENTS

1. Write a report of a student trip you have taken. Use either the newspaper style shown above or follow the formal outline in the "Trip Report" section.

2. Assume that you are on the staff of your college magazine and that you have attended a meeting in New York City of magazine staffs from colleges all over the country. Among the items discussed were:

a. Increases in the annual dues to the national organization by each magazine;

b. Replacement of Professor Robert A. Duff who has served as a full-time professional advisor to the national group for ten years by a student committee elected annually;

c. Termination of the agreement between the national organization and the J. Thomas Frenchie Agency of Columbus, Ohio. The Frenchie Agency handles advertising contracts on a nationwide basis for college magazines and acts as go-between for the magazines and national advertisers such as IBM, GE, GM, 3-M, DuPont, Monsanto, Ford, and Chrysler. If the agreement were terminated, each magazine would solicit its own advertising.

Write a trip report, including the results of the voting in each case. Add whatever else you think would be of interest.

3. The colleges in your state are thinking about an annual intercollegiate Frisbee contest to be held on a different campus each time. You went to a meeting of representatives from the colleges at a town about 100 miles from your campus. The student council paid your expenses and is now asking you to file a trip report. Write it.

The Report to a Group

You will occasionally be called upon to take part in committee meetings and to make reports either to the committee or to members of an *ad hoc* group. Both of these activities involve talking rather than writing.

When you make such informal oral reports, it is not necessary to exercise some of the precautions that a more formal presentation requires. However, anything you do adds or detracts from your presentation and attracts or distracts your listeners.

Try not to fidget. Speak rather slowly and distinctly. Throw your voice to the back of the room. Talk to those in the meetings rather than to yourself. Don't mumble; speak up. Don't read your talk. Outline your points on a notecard and refer to the card to make sure you touch all bases. Repeat or emphasize major points, or summarize them at the beginning and the end. Periodically, ask your audience if it has any questions. Watch for any show of hands. Also watch for signs of restlessness. Don't waste unnecessary time apologizing for anything. Don't tell people you will speak for a couple of minutes if you will need twenty minutes.

Use audiovisual aids as much as possible. Don't attempt to develop long formulas. Rather, duplicate your proofs in advance and hand out copies. Outline your points on a blackboard. Draw sketches or diagrams and project them to make your points clear.

Begin with an overview or introduction. Then present the problem briefly. Give the background. Remember, in an oral situation, the audience can ask you what it doesn't know or what it wants to know.

Limit your report to a brief discussion of the main points. Don't elaborate on equipment or the method unless it was unique. Have duplicated detailed descriptions at hand for those who might want to think about your work.

If you are reporting judgments or decisions, begin with them. Then explain the available choices. Follow that with a brief discussion of the main criteria (specifications, standards) for your choice. Don't go into the minor points of difference or advantage unless you are asked to. Again, if you think that some people in your audience might like a complete discussion, have handouts available.

Always focus on the busiest person in the audience and don't keep him any longer than necessary. Some explanation can be given to other listeners after he leaves.

Above all, try not to bore your audience. Give them the facts they want. All the rest is talk.

The Small Group Meeting

In your work, you are likely to serve in either fact-finding or problem-solving groups, or both. Be sure you know which task is yours.

If you head the group, divide the work among the members as equally and as impartially as you can. However, don't fail to assign work on the basis of individual skills. Be sure to set deadlines for follow-up meetings and maintain them if at all possible. Remember, there will be more work in the future; so whatever your project, hop to it.

Be sure that everyone is heard during a meeting. Don't allow a long-winded, forceful person to dominate the meeting. Make notes of important points raised and make certain these are discussed. Try to develop a summary of what is being said as the meeting progresses. Before you close the meeting, be certain there is a consensus about what has been said and done. Be sure that a meeting reporter has been selected and that he knows his obligation.

Don't allow meetings to break up into smaller, more private discussions. Keep everyone's attention focused on the topic at hand.

Be sure that a meeting report is written and distributed to those attending and to anyone else with a "right to know."

Fact Finding

Before a problem-solving group can function, it needs information. This information may deal with the background of the problem, money, machinery, ordinances, time, and so on. Whatever the case, first be sure you know what is needed.

Then divide the fact-finding work according to skills or on a shared-time basis. Set a follow-up meeting date. In the follow-up meeting, call on each member in turn. A reporter should be ready to take notes. Be sure that every member of the group is aware of what is going on. Ask for a consensus from time to time.

Such meetings are not formal, and there is no need for the machinery of the formal meeting. Each informal meeting usually focuses on one subject. Stick to it. Get it over with. The sooner the work is done, the sooner the group is dissolved and everyone can go back to his regular work. Don't call a meeting unless there is something that needs to be done.

Problem Solving

Problem-solving groups answer these questions:

1. What is the problem? Define it to everyone's satisfaction. Put the definition in writing.

2. When and where did the problem start? What is its history or background? What solutions have been proposed or tried?

3. What information is needed? Can it be obtained by this group, or is a fact-finding group necessary?

4. What are the new proposed solutions? Which of them seem feasible? What advantages and disadvantages does each proposed solution offer?

5. What work will be necessary? Who will do it? Where will it be done and with what equipment, manpower, and money? Who will coordinate or supervise? When must the work be done?

6. When will the next meeting be held? Who will write the meeting reports?

7. What obstacles seem to lie in the way of a problem solution? What can be done about them?

WORK ASSIGNMENT

Give an informal oral report to members of your class on a project you are working on or have worked on. Define the project if you can as one of fact finding or problem solving.

11 | The Informal Technical Report

So far we have been discussing the kind of reporting that is part of the give-and-take of everyday work. This kind of reporting is primarily oral or based on face-to-face contacts. We have also looked at some general statements about reporting.

Now we will consider two kinds of written reports that are not based on face-to-face contacts. The *formal* report is discussed in Chapter 12. In this chapter we will look at the *informal* report, a pattern usually limited to in-house and in-plant reporting. Its *scope* is usually limited to one item or problem or to a narrow part of a large problem. Its *purpose* is usually to inform in-plant and in-house people at lower management levels.

The informal report may inform, request, or recommend action, or furnish preliminary or partial results of work. If the report is about a study or an investigation, the results of the study will be emphasized. If the procedures used were unusual, the informal report will emphasize those.

The informal report is often limited to an audience of a few people—perhaps only one person. These people are usually informed about the subject, so the language can be technical. If, however, the informal report is sent to a nontechnical person, the language of the report must be nontechnical. Although the informal report is primarily intended for distribution within the house or plant, it is sometimes distributed to interested persons outside as well. This is particularly true when one company is acting as a subcontractor for another.

Parts of the Informal Report

Depending upon the complexity of the informal report, it may have the following parts:

I. Introduction

Purpose statement · Problem statement · Scope statement } Sometimes presented in a subject line in a short report

II. Body
Data
Results

III. Conclusions or interpretations, if called for

IV. Recommendations

The introduction to any report tells the reader what he can expect the report to be about. The *purpose statement* tells the reader what the *function* of the report is: to inform, to report, to compare, to evaluate, to recommend, to define, and so on. The *scope statement* tells the reader what the specific *range* or *limits* of the report are: what information is reported, what is compared or evaluated, what is recommended or defined. The *problem statement* identifies the problem and defines it as clearly and as briefly as possible.

You must be sure that the differences among *results*, *conclusions*, and *recommendations* are clear in your mind. A *result* is the end product of a study, test, or work project. It follows from a cause. A *conclusion* is an interpretation of the results. Conclusions come from thinking of the implications in the results. They are the meanings the results show. *Recommendations* are the directions that must be taken next—if a decision is made to accept the recommendations.

The Laboratory Report

The *laboratory report* is a familiar pattern of the informal report. It is used to report tests and experiments that either stand on their own merits or contribute information to a larger study. The laboratory report is also part of the student's learning experience, giving him a chance to summarize something he has learned and giving the instructor a chance to evaluate the student's progress.

The laboratory or "lab" report is often produced on a standardized printed form. These are used for a number of reasons:

1. Forms insure definiteness and completeness. Because the reporter must supply the information required by the form, it is reasonably certain that he will furnish only the information needed.

2. Forms avoid the necessity for tedious rewriting of repeated information (frequent determinations of properties or qualities, for example).

3. Forms imply uniformity. On each report, similar kinds of information are found in the same place. Therefore, readers know exactly where to look for data, and comparison of several reports is easy.

An Example of a Printed Form

Fig. 11.1 shows a form developed from Fig 6.1, the "Specifications for a testing process for wire (NEMA Standards, September, 1973)." If these specifications are not fresh in your mind, turn to them and compare them with the form.

As the first step in producing this form, a list was made of the test specifications:

1. Room temperature
2. Lot number, wire size, shipper, and date received
3. Diameter of the film-coated wire, and the average of the largest and smallest of four readings taken at 45° intervals on the circumference (1.1.1)
4. Diameter of the bare wire taken at the same four points and a parallel average (1.1.1.)
5. Increase in average diameter of the film-coated wire over the bare wire (1.1.1)
6. Adherence (2.1.1)
7. Flexibility (2.1.1)
8. Elongation (3.1.1)

STUDY QUESTIONS FOR FIG. 11.1

1. What other standard information is on the form?
2. Where on the form do you find these items?

WRITING ASSIGNMENT

1. Design a printed form to be used with Fig. 11.1 to report on the testing of film-coated *rectangular* wire. Design the form so that it is easy for a keypunch operator to retrieve the information.

2. Design a form for reporting a laboratory test you have done, such as a test of a circuit, a compression test on concrete cylinders, a test for characteristics or qualities of a compound, or a test of a machine or product.

3. Bring in a printed form used in your area of study. Fill it in with data you have developed on a project.

REPORT OF TESTING OF FILM-COATED MAGNET WIRE (ROUND)			
Lot No.	Wire Size:	Received from:	Date:

1. Number of specimens and length: 2. Ambient temperature:

                                                                            F

3. Diameter of film-coated wire taken at points shown (45° apart):

    a.   b.   c.   d.

    Average of largest and smallest readings   OD

4. Diameter of bare wire taken at same points (45° apart)

    a.   b.   c.   d.

    Average of largest and smallest readings   OD

5. Increase in diameter because of film-coating (subtract 4 from 3):

6. Adherence (sec 2.1)   Satisfactory ☐   Unsatisfactory ☐

7. Flexibility (sec 2.1)   Satisfactory ☐   Unsatisfactory ☐

8. Elongation (sec 3.1.1)

    Travel distance of jaw (average): _____

    Percentage of elongation (average): _____

The wire tested meets NEMA Standard (September 1973) as detailed above: Date of test:

Signed: _____ Inspector

FIGURE 11.1 Form for reporting laboratory tests. This is based on Fig. 6.1.

The Narrative Laboratory Report

When the lab report is of a nonrepetitive nature and a longer report is required because of the complexity of the work, a *narrative laboratory report* is written. A typical pattern of the narrative lab report is as follows:

Introduction
    Purpose, problem, and scope
Apparatus (or equipment)
    This is discussed in detail only if it is un-usual. There is no point in detailing standard laboratory equipment.
Procedures
    If these are standard, they are summarized or named. They are described in detail only if unusual.
Body (discussion)
    Data obtained
    Interpretation of data
Conclusions
Recommendations

```
TO:            Orlando B. Reynolds, Project Engineer          Houghton, MI

FROM:          E.L.Cooley, Metallurgist                   February 13, 19__

PURPOSE:       To furnish results of testing of wire steel for the Hancock Canal Bridge.

PROBLEM:       To determine whether wire steel for the Hancock Canal Bridge meets

               specifications set by the designers.

SCOPE:         Only the properties of the wire steel are considered in this report. Results

               of other tests are furnished elsewhere.

DISCUSSION:    A study has been made of the average chemical properties of the wire steel

               furnished by Hamtramck Steel and Wire Co. for the Hancock Canal Bridge. The

               properties were determined from ladle and check analyses.

               The number of melts for the various wires tested were as follows:

                         Cable wire              735
                         Suspender rope wire      44
                         Hold-down rope wire       4
                         Hand rope wire            3
                         Wrapping wire            11

DATA:          For each of the five types of wires listed above, the amount of each chem-

               ical component was determined.  Chemicals present were carbon (C), mangan-

               ese (Mn), phosphorous (P), sulfur (S), and silicon (Si).  The maximum,

               minimum, and average amounts were determined and were compared to the

               specified amounts.  Table 1 lists these amounts in percentages [see Fig. 6.2]

               In only one case (wrapping wire, check analysis, carbon), did the maximum amount

               of  the chemical component in the wire exceed the specified amount.  In all

               other cases, the amount did not exceed the specifications.

CONCLUSIONS:   With regard to the excess of carbon in the wrapping wire, you have two choices:

               1. You can disregard the discrepancy inasmuch as the maximum carbon content

               is in excess by only .02 of 1 percent.

               2. You could replace the wire containing the excess with wire that would

               have to be ordered from Hamtramck.

RECOMMENDATIONS:
```

FIGURE 11.2 Laboratory report in memorandum form.

STUDY QUESTIONS FOR FIG. 11.2

1. In Fig. 11.2 what is the purpose of the report? What is the scope? What problem led to this report?

2. In what pattern is the data presented?

3. Read the conclusion statement and then decide what recommendation you would make. Write it.

4. What advantages does this form of report have compared to the form in Figure 11.1? What disadvantages?

WRITING ASSIGNMENT

Write a narrative laboratory report of work you have done in a campus laboratory (perhaps as part of a class) or on a summer job.

The Memorandum Report

Memorandum reports are the most common informal report pattern. They are brief, usually concerned with short-range topics, and intended for informal distribution.

Here is a memorandum report written by a student for transmission to his instructor:

MEMORANDUM REPORT

TO: Electronics Department   FROM: E. Friedman
DATE: April 11, 1975
SUBJECT: Results of Experiment #2

Purpose of experiment: To determine the effect of different frequencies on resistors, inductors, and capacitors at a given voltage.

Results:

1. The voltage across a resistor did not change with changes in frequencies.

2. The inductors and capacitors were observed to react inversely with respect to each other. As the voltage frequency was raised, the inductor allowed increased voltages to move across it, while the capacitor allowed lower voltage.

STUDY QUESTIONS

What is the scope of the above report? What is the problem? ·

The Long Memorandum Report

The *long memorandum report* is longer than most because its subject matter is more complex. It also tends to be more formal in order to organize the information clearly. It is designed for in-house or in-plant distribution, although occasionally copies may be distributed externally.

The form of the long memorandum report is similar to the forms of the formal reports you will see in Chapter 12.

STUDY QUESTIONS FOR FIG. 11.3

1. Why is no letterhead used?

2. What distribution was made? Who supervises H. Boyd Phillips and Ira E. Allen directly?

3. How many people worked on the project? Who wrote the report?

4. What are the purpose, scope, and problem?

5. Where are the results and conclusions? The recommendations? Why is this information given before "Basic Data," "Personnel," and "Technical Details"?

6. What differences are there among the results, the conclusions, and the recommendations?

7. What generalization is drawn in this report? What is a generalization?

8. What is the purpose of the "Technical Details" section?

WRITING ASSIGNMENT

The head of your student council has asked you to plan an all-day program of entertainment and contests for a "Skip Day," or a similar all-day holiday from school. Write him a memorandum report of your progress to date. The report should be about 1,000 words long and should follow an appropriate pattern with sections labeled.

Denver, Colorado

August 21, 1975

MEMORANDUM

TO: Robert Sailer

FROM: H. Boyd Phillips and Ira E. Allen

THROUGH: Hedd, Technical Engineering Analysis Section

SUBJECT: [Purpose]   This memorandum reports   stress analysis of pin

plates for the main bearings of the steel arch--Colorado River

Bridge--Glen Canyon Dam--Colorado River Storage Project

Introduction

[Problem]   A study has been made of the stress distribution

in plates used for the bearings of steel arches. Of primary interest

was the change of distribution of stress in the pin plate as its height

was varied. Of secondary interest were the areas of very low stress in

the upper corners of a rectangular pin plate.

[Scope]   The analysis has been made for a rectangular pin

plate seven ft. wide with heights varying from eight ft. to two ft. by

one ft.

Results

Radial and sheer stresses have been determined in

the pin plate, in the vicinity of the pin, or radial lines spaced at

22 1/2° around the pin. Figure 1 gives these stresses. Also indicated

on the same figure are the points along the vertical sides of the pin

plate at which the boundary stress reaches approximately zero. The

radial load distribution around the pin groove is also given.

The stress normal to a line near the base of the pin plate is shown

in Figure 2 for the various heights.

Figure 3 gives the distribution of normal stress on the vertical

center line of the pin plate.

FIGURE 11.3 Long memorandum report pattern. This pattern follows local style requirements. The bracketed words—Purpose, Problem, Scope—were supplied by a later editor and indicate how these parts of the report would be labeled today. (Reprinted by permission of the U.S. Bureau of Reclamation.)

<u>Conclusions</u>

From an inspection of Figures 1, 2, and 3 it can be seen that:

1. The radial stresses in the vicinity of the pin are independent of the height of the pin plate.

2. The stress distribution near the base of the pin plate is almost identical for heights of eight ft. to five ft. Below five ft. the distribution changes rapidly as the height decreases.

3. The distribution of normal stress on the vertical center line is independent of height for pin plates between eight and four ft. high. For heights of three and two ft., the distribution is dependent on the height.

4. For all except the two-ft.-high pin plate, the point of beginning of stress along the vertical sides occurred approximately twenty-two in. down from the top of the pin plate. The distance was fourteen in. for the two-ft. high pin plate.

<u>Recommendations</u>

For the dimensions used in the study, it appears that with a pin plate width of seven ft., the height may be varied between eight and five ft. as desired without appreciable change in the stress condition.

For the sake of appearance or for other reasons, it may be desired to remove the corners at the top of the pin plate. The material so removed should be outside a 45° line intersecting the vertical side twenty-two in. below the top of the pin plate for all except the two-ft.-high one. In this latter case, the point of intersection should be fourteen in. below the top.

The results of this study can be applied to any other size of structure that is geometrically similar to this one.

(Fig. 11.3 continued)

<u>Basic Data</u>

Width of pin plate	7 ft.
Height of pin plate	8 ft. to 2 ft.
Pin diameter	16 in.
Pin groove diameter	16-1/32 in.
Applied load	1 kip per in. thickness

The load was applied to the pin and directed along the center line of the pin plate.

Moduli of elasticity of the pin, pin plate, and foundation were equal.

<u>Technical Details</u>

This study was made photoelastically using the photoelastic polariscope and photoelastic interferometer. The model material was Columbia Resin, CR-39, 3/8-in. nominal thickness. A scale of approximately one to sixteen between model and prototype was used. The pin and the foundation were also made of Columbia Resin, CR-39.

A smooth contact surface between the model and the foundation was achieved by lapping the two pieces together using a very fine grinding compound. . . .

<u>Personnel</u>

This study was made under the general supervision of William T. Moody. John R. Brizzolara, Gerald D. Stone, and H. E. Willmann assisted in taking readings in the photoelastic interferometer. Mr. Willmann also prepared the figures.

[s] H. Boyd Phillips

[s] Ira E. Allen

Copy to: H. C. Olander

Unit Files

(Fig. 11.3 continued)

DETROIT MACHINE DESIGN CO.
Detroit, Michigan
Brooks at Warren
48237

TELEPRINT LETTER

February 20, 1973
Mr. Lea Verne Hansel
Chevrolet Gear & Axle Co.
1840 Holbrook
Detroit, Michigan
48212

                    Ref: Our telcall of February 20, 19_

Dear Mr. Hansel:

    We have determined that the best type of electric machine to be
used in your Waste Disposal Systems is a 100 horsepower, 3 phase,
60 cycle, 575 volts, 900 rpm, Class A spuirrel cage induction motor.

    To date, we have completed the calculations for the prototype
machine and have designed the stator. Work on the design of the rotor
is proceeding.

    Under separate cover we are mailing a progress reprot which details
our assumptions and calculations [see Appendix 3].

    Two design drawings are also included.

    If you approve of our determination, we can proceed with the
manufacture of stators at once. Before we can begin, however, we
need a specific initial quantity order.

    Work on the manufacture of rotors can begin in the next thirty
days. No rotors will be started, however, until you have approved our
rotor design.

    A firm price per machine will be available to you on completion of
the rotor design.

                                        Sincerely,

                                        Terence M. Deford

                                        Terence M. Deford
                                        Project Engineer

FIGURE 11.4   Letter report.

The Letter Report

When a report of one to three pages is sent outside a plant, it goes by letter rather than by memorandum. The motive in writing a letter is usually a concern for the "image" of the organization represented by the letter. A letterhead will be used, and it is likely that the report will be signed by or approved by an executive of the reporting organization.

The *letter report* combines two patterns: (a) one of the semiformal or formal letter patterns presented in Chapter 4, or (b) one of the report patterns described in this chapter. This combination presents no problem since the two patterns complement each other and work well together.

The letter report is likely to be somewhat more complete than the memorandum report. While the memorandum report is usually distributed among the people working on a project or assigned to it as managers, the letter report is sent to the people who commissioned the work. As a result, the memorandum report may imply certain information (for example, the fact that a request has been made for a test). But the letter report will almost always give reasons for each step.

The letter report is a short or condensed form of the long, formal report discussed in Chapter 12. It is used either when there may be a delay in publishing a long report, or when there is not enough information for a long report. It may also be used as an interim report.

STUDY QUESTIONS FOR FIG. 11.4

1. Where are the recommendations in the report in Fig. 11.4? Why are they placed where they are?
2. What work has been done so far?
3. What information is enclosed with the report? Why is this information not included in the letter?
4. What action is requested by the letter writer? At what point in the report does this request come? What does this feature of this letter suggest about the letter report?

WRITING ASSIGNMENT

Assume that you have been awarded a scholarship or given a grant for your expenses by a corporation. Write a formal letter to an officer of the corporation summarizing your progress so far and detailing your plans for the balance of your academic career.

The Comparison Report

From time to time you will be asked to compare objects, materials, or methods and to report your discoveries so that others can make choices. In some cases, you may be given a printed form on which to report. In other cases, you may have to create your own report pattern.

The following information is required in a *comparison report*:

1. Date, place, time of test. If weather conditions, ambient temperatures, or elevations above sea level are important, be sure to record these data.

2. Reason for test and name of person authorizing the test.

3. Descriptions of objects, materials, or methods tested. Be *specific*. Use model numbers, lot numbers, weights, sizes, quantities, horsepower ratings, rpms, formulas, and so.

4. Description of test procedures. If standard test procedures are used, simple naming is enough, or they may be implied as in the phrase, *Rockwell hardness: C65*. If nonstandard procedures are used, describe in detail. (For an example, see NEMA specifications in Fig. 6.1.)

5. Information organized for easy comparison of the results by your reader. There are two basic patterns of comparison. One treats each of the objects or methods tested separately and reports all the results for that unit. The second treats each of the test results in turn and reports them for all the objects. This outline illustrates the difference:

```
Object A              Test result 1
   Test result 1         Object A
   Test result 2         Object B
   Test result 3         Object C
Object B              Test result 2
   Test result 1 . . .   Object A . . .
```

For easier comparison, tabulate data whenever possible.

6. Assurance that critical qualities have been compared. Write your report in terms of those qualities. Omit references to unimportant or irrelevant qualities.

A Sample Comparison Report

Fig. 11.5 illustrates a comparison report written in the pattern of an internal memorandum. If the Conrepco Corporation had been conducting the test for a client or customer, the test results would have been sent in a letter.

STUDY QUESTIONS FOR FIG. 11.5

1. What characteristics of the five drills were examined? Would the report have been improved if these characteristics had been discussed in general in an early paragraph?

2. What information is presented in the first paragraph? Why?

3. What special test provisions were made?

4. Which pattern of comparison was used in this memorandum?

WRITING ASSIGNMENTS

1. Prepare the table described as Figure A in item 4 of Fig. 11.5.

2. Reconstruct and rewrite Fig. 11.5 to focus on qualities rather than on drills. Item 2 will have a new title, Qualities. The first item under 2 will be costs. What order will the other items take? Why?

What changes will you have to make in paragraphs 1, 3, and 4 of the report?

3. After you have completed #2, write a report in which you compare the two memorandum reports—Fig. 11.5 and your reconstructed report. Address this memorandum report to your instructor. Do not make any judgments at this point about the two reports. Simply describe the features of each report.

The Recommendation Report

The comparison report does no more than list comparable qualities. No decisions, judgments, or evaluations are made; these are left to the clients to make on the basis of the information furnished. They will evaluate the information in the context of their needs for it. In many cases, they may not tell you why they need the information.

Occasionally, however, you will be asked to evaluate or interpret the data or to make a choice or decision. This information constitutes the essential feature of the *recommendation report*. It is likely to be written about day-to-day activities and addressed to your immediate supervisor.

You interpret or evaluate data by matching the specifications or criteria to the test or work results. For example, in Table 1, Fig. 11.2, the specifications in column 3 are matched with the test results in columns 4 through 13. You must interpret test results as ably as you can. You will have to bring your best judgments to bear on every case.

You will quickly discover that not all the criteria or test results carry the same weight. For example, go back to Fig. 11.5, the comparison report, and answer these questions:

1. The price range for the five drills is from $24.95 to $39.95. How important is price to you?

2. Only three of the drills have ac-dc capability. How important is that quality? How much more are you willing to pay for it?

3. Two of the drills are of double-insulated construction. Is this feature as important to you as ac-dc capability? How much are you willing to pay for this feature? How much is your life worth?

These are the kinds of questions you must answer when you interpret data.

Conrepco Corp.
Huffton Branch

May 3, 1975
Memorandum
To: Irvine Consumer Products Division
From: I. Levering, Products Testing Laboratory
Subject: Comparison of five single-speed portable electric drills. Your memorandum of April 20, 1975.

I have tested the five drills according to the standards given below. Per your memo, the drills were bought at local retail stores. Results of the test are summarized and then tabulated.

1. All five models have pistol-grip handles, geared-key chucks, and trigger switches with lock. Two are double-insulated as noted. The other three are standard construction with a three-wire cord and grounding plug. The double-insulated drills have two-wire cords and standard plugs. Three of the drills have ac-dc capability as noted. The other two are ac only.

All five drills have a chuck offset of approximately 1 in. The drill lengths shown include handle and open chuck. Weights given do not include cord.

2. DRILLS:

Black River QDP1323 Model Q (Black River Tool Co., Black River, Mich.). $31.50. This drill has ac-dc capability and has double-insulated construction with nonconductive housing. The chuck is insulated from the rest of the drill. It weighs 2¾ lbs, and is 8⅝ in. long. Its full-load and maximum outputs ranged from 125 to 145 watts. Its speed was 1,450 to 1,700 rpm. This drill has sleeve bearings with single-ball thrust bearings.

Chicago A1000 (Chicago Electric Tool Works, Chicago). $39.95. This drill has ac-dc capability. It weighs 3¼ lbs, and is 9⅛ in. long. Its full-load output was 125 to 145 watts. Its maximum output was 180 to 200 watts in short spurts. Its speed was 1,450 to 1,700 rpm. It has ball bearings.

Glencorp 440 Type Y (made by Glensmith Corporation, Brillion, Wisc.). $35. It has double-insulated construction. The chuck is insulated from the rest of the drill. The drill weighs 3½ lbs, and is 8½ in. long. The full-load output ranged from 150 to 175 watts. In short spurts, it ranged from 180 to 200 watts. The speed ranged from 1,450 to 1,700 rpm. It has ball thrust and sleeve bearings.

Slik 220 Type A1 (made by Kenosha Drill Co., Kenosha, Wisc.). $37.95. This drill has ac-dc capability. It weighs 3 lbs, and is 8½ in. long. Its full-load and maximum outputs ranged from 150 to 175 watts. Its speed ranged from 2,000 to 2,300 rpm. It has ball thrust and sleeve bearings.

National Ener-Skill Catalogue number 43105B (National Catalogue Sales, Chicago). $24.95. (In the catalogue this drill is listed at $21.95 plus packing and shipping charges.) It weighs 3¾ lbs and is 8¾ in. long. Its full-load output was 150 to 175 watts. Its maximum output in short spurts was over 200 watts. Its speed was 1,275 to 1,360 rpm. It has sleeve and ball bearings.

3. TESTS:

Watts were measured with a wattmeter at constant voltage. The load applied in each test was similar to loads to be expected in nonindustrial use. A test chart is available showing details of each of the test circumstances and the watts measured. Speeds were measured with a strobe light under the same sets of circumstances.

4. TABULATED RESULTS:

Figure A attached tabulates the results. [Note: see Writing Assignment, p. 128]

FIGURE 11.5 Comparison report, submitted in memorandum form.

The recommendation report will look like the report in Fig. 11.5 or like your reconstructed version made according to Writing Assignment #2. But it will have one important addition. The recommendation report will include paragraphs like the ones below:

I have tested the five drills according to the standards given. In my opinion, the best of the drills is the . . . (At this point, you will write reasons for your choice.)

Per your memo, the drills were bought at local retail and catalogue sales stores, and the prices given are over-the-counter prices.

WRITING ASSIGNMENT

1. To the preceding two paragraphs, p. 129, add your choice of the best of the five drills. Base your choice on your own needs, real or imagined, for a drill.

2. Write your reasons for making the choice.

3. Copy the second paragraph of the two just above. Then place your completed work in Fig. 11.5, so as to convert it into a recommendation report. Be prepared to defend your decision about the location of the two paragraphs in Fig. 11.5.

The Report of Study or Investigation

The *report of study or investigation* deals with research that leads to the discovery of previously unknown information. Such a study may be reported to a fact-finding committee. It may represent a portion of a larger research project. The student most often encounters this type of study in a classroom or laboratory situation.

Following are two investigative reports about the same subject. The first one uses a pattern that grows out of the subject and the investigation (see Chapter 10). The second one uses a formal report pattern (see Chapter 12).

Informal Investigative Report

Armed with the information from lectures and reading, I proceeded to measure my lab partner's blood pressure while he was sitting, standing, and lying down. My first attempts to take his pressures while sitting were disastrous. No heart beat at all could be detected! The subject was quite definitely alive, so the problem had to be with my technique. The subject's arm was fairly heavy, so I suspected the brachial artery was well insulated with fat, and therefore the pulse would be faint. I also took into account the fact that I had never done this procedure before. By the sixth try, I detected the first heart sound around 102 mm Hg. This seemed extremely low, no doubt due to my inexperience at detecting the systolic sound as soon as it became audible. Several readings revealed a consistent 115/80 mm Hg. There was no difference between his sitting and standing pressures. I was slightly surprised that his systolic pressure while lying down was higher than his erect systole instead of lower, but I had probably improved my ability to detect the heart sounds. All three readings fell within a margin of error. The subject's pulse was then counted for 15 sec and multiplied by 4. This gave a reading of 88 beats/min, which was within the normal range.

I listened to the subject's heart with a stethoscope while feeling his pulse at the wrist. Since I was listening from the back, the heart beat was very muffled and was very difficult for my inexperienced ear to detect. The lung sounds (internal noises when the subject breathes) were very loud and tended to mask the heart beat.

I then performed the Harvard Step Test on myself and computed my maximal oxygen uptake at 2.9 liters/min, which is within normal limits.

My lab partner then ran an EKG on me. The heart rate was 120 beats/min, and the blood pressure was 133/85 mm Hg. No abnormalities were apparent although my blood pressure was high (normal 110/80), probably due to my interest in the proceedings.

I participated in the setup and running of an EKG on another student. I also observed a demonstration setup of a rat cardiogram transmitted by radio telemetry and picked up by an FM receiver, which could be heard on a loud speaker.

H. F. Whitten[1]

STUDY QUESTIONS

1. This report uses a pattern "that grows out of the subject and the investigation." What is the pattern of this report? In which order is information presented?

2. How is blood pressure taken? The pulse? How is a stethoscope used? What is the "Harvard Step Test"? How does one run an EKG?

3. For which audience might this report be suitable? Would that audience need more or less information? Which information needs to be added? Which needs to be deleted?

4. What would happen to this report if the last paragraph were deleted? The last two paragraphs?

[1] Courtesy of Hope F. Whitten.

Formal Investigative Report

I. **INTRODUCTION**

This report describes the process by which I learned to use the noninvasive technique for measuring blood pressure. The noninvasive technique is familiar to everyone. It uses the sphygmomanometer, a machine that has three parts: a pressure cuff to be wrapped around a subject's arm, a bulb for pumping air into the cuff, and a device for "bleeding" off the pressure that results from pumping air into the cuff.

Also discussed is the method by which I learned to calculate my maximal oxygen uptake.

A. Purpose

The purpose of this report is to describe a laboratory learning process. This particular process has to do with blood pressure measurement, measurement of oxygen uptake, and production of an electrocardiogram (EKG) for a rat.

B. Problem

The problem was to learn to use the non-invasive technique for measuring blood pressure, to calculate personal maximal oxygen uptake, and to record a rat's EKG.

C. Scope

This report presents only the techniques and results for the first two parts of the problem. The rat's EKG was determined, but is reported separately.

II. **DISCUSSION**

Blood pressure of the subject was measured with a sphygmomanometer while she was standing, sitting, and supine. Using a stethoscope, I listened to the heart while the radial artery was palpitated. The stethoscope was also applied to the back, over the heart.

I performed the modified Harvard Step Test on myself, and used the Åstrand nomograph to estimate my maximum oxygen uptake.

At first, I could detect no heartbeat at all in the subject. I assumed that the subject's brachial artery was well insulated with fat and therefore the pulse felt faint. I also took into account the fact that I had never done this ting a heartbeat.

procedure before. By the sixth try, I was get-

III. **RESULTS**

Blood pressure and pulse of the subject:

Sitting   115/mm Hg.
Standing   115/mm Hg.
Supine   117/75 mm HG
Pulse   88 beats/min
Pulse pressure: 35 mm Hg.

Calculation of maximal oxygen uptake on my-self:

Weight	Pulse	VO_2
62 kg	140 beats/min	2.9 liters/min

IV. **CONCLUSIONS**

I concluded that both the subject and I were in normal physical condition.

STUDY QUESTIONS

1. Could you read this report to an audience? If so, what kind of audience? What problems would you have if you were to read this report to an audience?

2. Is there any place in the report where the organization could be improved? Is the first paragraph of the Introduction necessary?

3. Can you see any reasons for placing the "conclusions" at the beginning of the report?

WRITING ASSIGNMENT

Assume that you have been invited to report an investigation you have made in the laboratory to a high-school class or to a Boy Scout or Girl Scout troop. Write a report of the investigation for presentation to such an audience. Which pattern will you use? Why?

12 | The Formal Report

The formal report is used most often within the company or plant when it is prepared for upper levels of management. It is used outside when the amount of information is three or more pages long and a letter is obviously inadequate.

The format will almost always follow one of the two patterns presented below. It is more likely to deal with major problems, often with policy matters, or with contractual matters. The subject is usually treated in detail since the formal report becomes part of a legal record. Very often the subject of the report is the basis for decision making at management levels.

The formal report is more likely to have a broader readership than the informal report. Although some of its readers may have a technical background, others may not. The feasibility study, for example, may be read by lawyers, accountants, sales personnel, advertising personnel, and others, such as members of city councils, boards of education, and county supervisors.

The emphasis of the formal report is almost always on results and recommendations. If procedures are reported, the purpose is largely to put them on the record. If the procedures are highly technical, they are placed in the appendix and summarized in the body of the report.

The Two Forms of the Formal Report

The formal report may be written in one of two patterns: an older form, which you will encounter in storage centers and which is still used by some reporters, and a newer form.

In both the old and the modern report patterns, the organization should be indicated by certain typographic arrangements—size and style of type used for heading, the use of underscoring, by a numbering system, or both. Each main section should begin at the top of a new page so that a section of the report can be removed or replaced by a revision without disturbing or rewriting other sections.

Main headings should be consistently identified by using parallel typographic styles:

  I. WORK DONE DURING THE PERIOD
 II. WORK PLANNED FOR THE NEXT PERIOD
III. LONG-RANGE PLANS

Similarly, the next level of headings should be treated consistently, with the same type style or number style or both:

A. *Designs*
B. *Models Made*
C. *Tests*

A third level might be:

1. Aberdeen Proving Grounds
2. Picatinny Arsenal
3. Dover Arsenal

The Older Report Form

Listed below are the elements of the traditional report form:

Letter of transmittal
Title page
Table of contents
Table of illustrations and a table of figures
Glossary of terms (some reporters place this at the end)
Body of the report
Results
Conclusions or interpretations
Recommendations

Letter of Transmittal

This is a formal letter that is either attached to the report as a first page or mailed under separate cover, if the report is bulky. Its contents are:

A statement that it accompanies a report or that a report is being mailed

The title of the study, contract number, or both

The serial number of the report (first, second, final, or perhaps the only report)

The period of work or the kind of work covered by the report or both

A paragraph of results or conclusions

A paragraph of recommendations

Title Page

No page number is put on this page, but reserve number *i* for it and number the following pages

```
Report No. _____                        Copy No. _____

                        TITLE IN CAPS

                            Date


                             by


                     Typed Author's Name


                          APPROVED

                     _____
                          Signature
                  Typed Name and position



                      Name of Publisher
                   City, State, Zip code
```

FIGURE 12.1 One pattern of title page for a formal report. The same information may be printed on the cover of the report.

in sequence with lower-case Roman numerals. See Fig. 12.1 for kinds of information on the title page. Notice such items as title, contract number, name of reporter, signature of report authorizer, classification, and so on.

Table of Contents

A table of contents is used if the report is longer than a few pages. It helps the reader find information quickly.

Table of Illustrations and a Table of Figures

The table of contents and other tables are always the last items typed, after all page numbers have been assigned to figures, illustrations, and text. text.

Glossary of Terms and Symbols

See Chapter 6 for an example of a glossary. Be sure to define words that have specific or unique meanings in the report and define symbols used in the report if they are not familiar to the reader.

Body of the Report

These pages should have arabic numbers. The body contains such items as:

Statement of the problem

Context of the problem

History of work or study to date (synopsis, if this is one report in a series)

Discussion of work done, studies made, and so on. Include data and specific interpretations. This part of the report may be organized in one of two ways: chronologically—from beginning to end—or by division of the work into several distinct parts—designs, tests, research. In turn, the distinct parts may be discussed chronologically.

Results, Conclusions, or Recommendations

To include, or be replaced by, plans for future work if the report is one in a series of progress reports.

A Modern Outline for a Report

Many reporters prefer the following report pattern to the older form. This report form is based on a study made in 1962 by Richard W. Dodge.[1]

In this so-called "modern" report form, the letter of transmittal, the title page, the table of contents, the tables of illustrations and figures, and the glossary of terms and symbols are the same as in the report form just discussed. The differences are in the remainder of the report pattern.

Because of the pattern used, this report has come to be known as the "administrative" pattern or the "double-report" pattern. It is called administrative because it is designed for administrators' reading habits (as identified by Dodge); it is called double-report because it reports the same information twice—once in an abridged, or "mini-report," pattern and once in complete detail. The detailed part of the report is written for engineers and technical experts.

The distinctive parts of this pattern are:

Introductory Summary

This abridged, or mini-report, pattern can stand on its own. It summarizes the significant data of the whole study for the benefit of those who have to make decisions. It gives them just the information they need and no more.

The introductory summary is likely to include:

1. A statement of the purpose of the report
2. A statement of the problem that led to the study
3. The data on which the conclusions are based
4. The conclusions themselves
5. The recommendations

[1] Richard W. Dodge, "What to Report," *Westinghouse Engineer,* Vol 22, July–September, 1962.

Three-Part Introduction

1. The *purpose* statement. Such statements usually begin, "The purpose of this report is," and then state the problem as something needing solving, researching, studying, or investigating:

The purpose of this report is to outline progress toward reopening the Copperas Point copper mine at the site of shaft no. 6.

The purpose of this report is to summarize research in improved methods for debarking aspen and maple trees which are to be used for pulpwood.

2. The *problem* statement. The problem must be carefully defined in precise language that allows no misinterpretations. If the problem involves technical matters, the language must be technical.

When you have written your problem statement, try it out on someone else. Ask him to rephrase the problem in his own words. In that way, you will discover whether your statement is as complete and as clear as it must be.

3. The *scope* statement. The scope statement explains the limits of the report, outlines the organization or form the report uses, and emphasizes the items the report features. Be sure to list the items in the scope statement in the order in which they will appear in the report.

Body or Discussion

The organization of this section will depend on the subject matter. It may include such subsections as designs, calculations, models, tests, costs, changes, work done, and so on.

Conclusion

Conclusions represent the most significant inferences that can be drawn from an examination of the data presented in the body or discussion. Conclusions must be so worded that they can be supported in every detail by reference to the data. Everyone connected with the work should agree on the wording of the conclusions.

Present your conclusions in paragraphs, one conclusion to a paragraph. Number the paragraphs in sequence for easy reference.

Recommendations

Recommendations must derive logically from the conclusions and must be supported both by the conclusions and by the body of data in the discussion.

Recommendations must be complete and clearly worded. They must be worded so that either a positive or a negative response is possible. Those who act on them must have no doubts in their minds about what is being recommended.

Bibliography Section

If a bibliography is included in the report, it follows at this point. Complete information about the production and writing of bibliographies is given in Chapter 5.

Examples of bibliographies will be found in the long reports that follow this discussion. Other examples can be found in almost any technical book.

Appendix (Fig. 12.2)

The appendix of any report will contain detailed technical information of the following kinds:

Detailed test reports (summarized in the body)

Drawings, especially detailed drawings. If it is necessary to make a point in the body or discussion, drawings or portions are used there.

Photographs. However, if it is necessary to make a point in the body or discussion, photographs are used there.

Calculations (summarized in the body)

Detailed technical descriptions

Detailed technical reports of work (summarized in the body)

STUDY ASSIGNMENT

Appendix 2, page 177, illustrates a student-written report that follows the modern pattern. Study the report in all its details and be prepared to comment in class on its quality. Be ready to document any praise or negative criticism you offer.

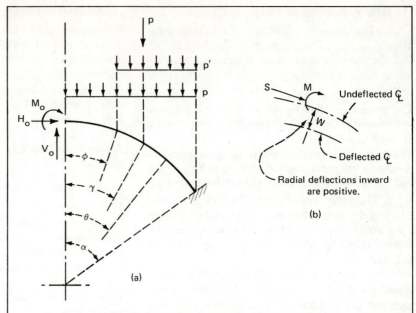

Figure A-1. —Free body diagram of deflected arch.

The differential equation of the arch is:

$$\frac{d^2w}{d\theta^2} + w = \frac{-M'r_o}{EI}$$

Substituting the above value of M′ in this equation and rearranging terms we have:

$$\frac{d^2w}{d\theta^2} = -\left\{1 + \frac{r_o^2}{EI}\left[H_o\cos\theta - V_o\sin\theta + pr_o\sin^2\theta\right.\right.$$

$$\left.\left. + p'r_o\,(\sin\theta - \sin\Phi)\sin\theta + P\sin\theta\right]\right\}w$$

$$- \frac{r_o^2}{EI}\left\{M_o + H_o r_o(1 - \cos\theta) + V_o r_o\sin\theta - \frac{pr_o^2}{2}\sin^2\theta\right.$$

$$\left. - \frac{p'r_o^2}{2}(\sin\theta - \sin\Phi)^2 - Pr_o\,(\sin\theta - \sin\gamma)\right\}$$

Or this may be written

$$\frac{d^2w}{d\theta^2} = -f_1(\theta)w - f_2(\theta) \tag{1}$$

FIGURE 12.2 Material commonly found in report appendixes. This material is highly technical and of interest only to to technical people.

The Periodical or Progress Report

Many firms contract with other firms to do a job that cannot be completed for several months. In such cases, it is customary to furnish periodical reports, usually monthly, about the progress of the work.

Progress reports follow the outlines just presented—either the older pattern or the newer, modern form. Whichever form is chosen initially will be the one used for every reporting period.

Three of the progress reports in any series will have distinctive features.

1. The first report will utilize the body of the report for a detailed statement and definition of the problem and its background. It will outline the work program to be followed and the results that are desired. If a contract forms the basis for the work, details of the contract will be incorporated into the body; a copy of the contract may be placed in the appendix. The report will list proposed expenditures, names of personnel to be assigned, space to be made available, completion dates, and so on.

2. In many cases, the next to the last report becomes a rough draft of a final report. If this is the case, this report will review the work period. The body of the report will list accomplishments, problems that arose, changes that had to be made—a narrative history.

3. When the draft has been corrected, brought up to date, and approved, the revised form will then be written as a final report. This will be the report of record on work; all other copies can then be discarded.

In all other monthly editions of the progress reports, the body will take up the following:

1. A brief statement of the problem, together with such revisions as have been made periodically

2. A brief statement of the general aims of the work and the general directions the work is taking

3. A detailed report of work during the report period

4. A detailed report of complications encountered during the report period, particularly if those complications had not been anticipated

5. A report of any changes made in the original work specifications

6. A statement of work planned for the future. This will be detailed for the immediate future, but summarized for the long-range future.

7. Designs, drawings, photographs, and figures are included at the point in the report where they are referenced if they help the explanation; otherwise, they are placed in the appendix. Reports of trips, meetings, and telephone calls are summarized in the report; if advisable, copies of the complete reports are appended. Reports of tests and discussions of calculations are also summarized in the report; if necessary, the complete reports are appended.

Organization of Historical Materials in a Progress Report

There are two basic ways to report the work history in a progress report. One is a chronological history and essentially reproduces a diarylike account. Work is reported as it took place from day to day during the month, beginning with the first day and ending with the last.

The other method is to subdivide the work into classes and discuss one at a time. For example, categories of work might consist of: planning, designing, drawings, model making, testing, reviewing.

In either case, there should be adequate cross-referencing to tie all the information into a compact package.

Mechanical Treatment of the Progress Report

All aspects of the progress report should be kept uniform from report to report—printing, drawings, photographs, figures, and so on. If the reports are bulky enough to require covers, the covers of all reports should be of uniform weight and color. Covers of reports on other projects should be in a different color for easy identification.

Two letters of transmittal should be prepared for each report. One letter is enclosed with each copy distributed; the other is mailed separately. The enclosed letter is for the benefit of mail clerks, messengers, and so on to insure delivery of the report to its proper reader. The other alerts the reader that the report is on the way.

Finally, because progress reports are often disassembled and sections of the report are handed out to interested persons, each section should stand on its own. There should be no run-over of divisions of the report from one page to another.

A Sample Progress Report

Terence M. Deford's "Report on the Design of a 100 Horse-power Squirrel Cage Induction Motor," Appendix 3, page 199, is an example of a progress report submitted during a short-term project. Because the project was short-term, a more formal pattern was not followed.

The Feasibility Report

The feasibility report is a common type of report. Actually, it is a comparison report of the kind we saw in Chapter 11, but, as generally understood, the feasibility report deals with upper managerial-level decisions involving time, money, suitability, and capability: which of two or more choices will require the least time, entail the least cost, is most suitable? which of two or more choices are we most capable of? And finally, considering all four of these decisions, and the possible variations among them, which of two or more choices is the most feasible?

Example One: Three Highway Routes

Look at the map in Fig. 12.3. It shows a situation that typically leads to a feasibility study and report. On opposite sides of a half-mile-wide navigable stream are the two towns X and Y. X has business district A-A and college C-C. Y has business district B-B. The two towns are connected by drawbridge D. The drawbridge is

necessary because ore boats and oil tankers use the stream as a canal, and a high bridge could not be built at the point where the bridge joins the two towns. Highway 4 comes into X from the east and joins Highway 3 at a junction just west of the business district. Both highways cross the bridge. At the north end, Highway 4 turns left, passes through Y's business district, makes a horseshoe curve, and climbs a steep ridge. At the north end of the bridge, Highway 3 turns east and proceeds along the stream.

X and Y are in the center of a resort area. In the summer, many people come to fish, camp, sail and canoe, and swim. In the fall, there is hunting. In the winter, people come to ski and snowmobile. The merchants of X and Y are happy that Highway 4 passes through the business districts of both towns. They sell a lot of merchandise to tourists.

But a problem has developed. The college is growing in size and has built dormitories on the south side of Highway 4. Students have begun to complain because they have to cross the busy highway to get to classes. At the same time, the amount of traffic on Highway 4 is increasing. The highway commission and college administrators agree that Highway 4 should bypass the college.

Three routes are suggested. Route T could turn off just south of X, cross the stream on a new high bridge, and rejoin the present route north of Y on the ridge. As an alternative, Route S could bypass to the south of the college. As a second alternative, Route R could proceed south of X to a new junction with 3 and then continue north across the drawbridge.

There are problems with all three proposed routes. Bridge O would have to be a high bridge because of the boats and because of the high ridge on the north side of the stream. Moreover, a high bridge would be cheaper to build and maintain than a low bridge. However, if Route T were chosen, an expensive interchange with 3 would have to be built on the slope leading up to the ridge.

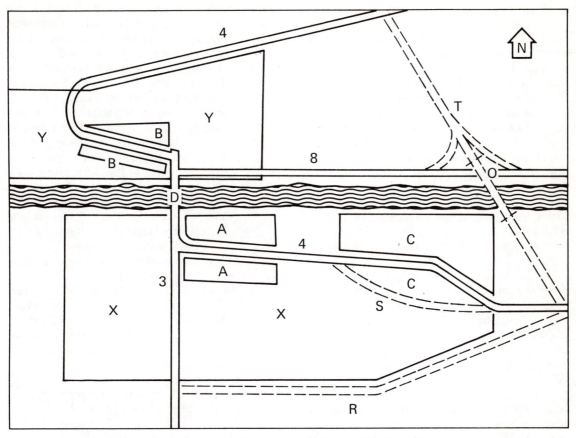

Map showing present and proposed highway routes, business districts, and college campus.

FIGURE 12.3 Map serving as the basis for a feasibility report.

Route S would have to pass through a region of high-priced homes where many prominent citizens live. Route R would be the cheapest and easiest to build, but it is directly in the way of further expansion of X. Moreover, the merchants of X don't want R built, because the traffic would then bypass business district A-A but not B-B. None of the merchants want T built for the same reason—it would bypass both business districts. Meanwhile, the highway commission would like to move all the nonlocal traffic out of the business districts.

A feasibility study is initiated. It prepares cost estimates as follows:

Cost of Route T:
  Purchase of right-of-way
  Building bridge O
  Building interchange with 3 just north of O
  Estimated loss to merchants in A-A and B-B (which would lower tax revenues)
  Cost of grading and paving route T
Cost of Route S:
  Cost of condemning and acquiring prop-

erty, including the possibility of lawsuits and resulting delays

Cost of realigning some city streets in X

Cost of grading and paving Route S

Cost of Route R:

Cost of acquiring route

Cost of grading and paving

Estimated loss to merchants in A-A

Cost of overpass to permit expansion of X

Notice that some items in a feasibility study may be difficult to evaluate. The estimated loss to merchants is one such item; it can be argued that visitors will shop in the towns. The psychological problems of those residents on Route S who are forced to give up their homes and relocate are not easily translated into dollars and cents.

There is also a political factor. How much political clout do the merchants of A-A and B-B have? Interestingly enough, some of those who will support Route S because of their business interests live in houses that would have to be torn down. How will these people vote? In any case, the political factor is not easy to assess in dollars and cents either.

The four choices this particular feasibility study must consider are: leave the highway where it is and put up with the problem of increased traffic in a congested area. Choose either Route R, S, or T as a new route for Highway 4.

Components of the Feasibility Report

When all the facts have been accumulated, a report will be written covering the preceding case. It will be distributed among those who will make the ultimate decision. It will have the following parts:

1. A title page
2. A table of contents
3. A list of illustrations, maps, and so on
4. The introductory summary
   A summary of the problem, the conclusions arrived at, and the recommendations

5. The introduction
   a. The purpose statement: The purpose of the report is to present the reason for the study, the facts in the case, the conclusions, and the recommendations.
   b. The problem statement: A detailed statement of the problem. However, highly detailed, technical descriptions, such as legal descriptions of real estate, will be placed in the Appendix
   c. The scope statement: The scope of this study is limited to this particular stretch of Highway 4 and the four operations described, together with the conclusions and recommendations made on the basis of the evidence
6. Part I: Background information
   A narrative similar to the preceding one, but with complete data
7. Part II: A detailed, four-part description of each alternative. This report covers four alternatives: not changing the present situation, Route R, Route S, and Route T. In each of these parts, the following would be discussed:
   a. Specifications for each proposal
   b. Estimated costs for each proposal
   c. Advantages of each proposal
   d. Disadvantages of each proposal
8. The conclusions
   A detailed set of conclusions based on the evidence presented in the four sections of Part II above
9. The recommendations
   A detailed set of recommendations
10. The appendix
    Highly detailed technical information is presented here. Similar data should be grouped and a table of contents should be used if needed.

Example Two: Recovery of Investment

The previous example looked at a situation where a number of choices were presented. In the course of the feasibility study, each choice was examined in detail, and all the consequences were considered. Ultimately, one of the choices was recommended.

Now, let us consider a feasibility study that might derive from Thomas Zarnke's investigation of Die-Draulics. Let us assume that Mr. Zarnke's report, (Appendix 6, page 225) came into the hands of a manufacturer of power-lawnmower cowlings. The manufacturer would react as follows:

If we were to replace our present horizontal die system with the Die-Draulic system, how much would the changeover cost?

Cost of scrapping present equipment or at least removing it,
Purchase price of Die-Draulic and cost of installation,
Down-time (time when there is no production because equipment is not available).

With the new system, how much would we save per cowling? How much would our production rate increase? Is there a market for this increased production? If not, could we use the new equipment for other work?

At our present production rate, how much would we save per year (savings per cowling times number of cowlings produced per year)?

Considering that the money to be invested in new equipment costs us 8 percent per year, how long will it take us to recover or amortize the costs represented by removing present equipment and replacing it with new equipment?

Should we, on the basis of this study, change to Die-Draulics?

The Recovery of Investment Feasibility Report

The report that would be written after the above study was completed would consider these matters in the body of the discussion:

1. Costs
   a. Cost of scrapping or removing present equipment
   b. Purchase price of Die-Draulic system, F.O.B. plant

c. Down-time
   1. Actual cost
   2. Effect on customer relations. Can conversion be completed during an off season?
2. Savings
   a. Savings on cowlings
      (1) Present cost per cowling
      (2) Estimated cost with new equipment
      (3) Savings per cowling
      (4) Present annual production
      (5) Estimated annual savings (3 $\times$ 4)
   b. Other savings
      (1) Savings on oil drip cap
      (2) Savings in repair, maintenance, less down-time
   c. Total annual savings
3. Estimated time to recover investment: Total annual cost in dollars divided by total annual savings

WRITING ASSIGNMENT

1. Write the feasibility report that would report the study made in the example of the proposed highway relocation. You will find costs for the work in encyclopedias (look up "bridges" or "highways"), handbooks, manuals, or textbooks. Be sure to recommend one of the routes and defend your choice.

2. Write the feasibility report that would be given to the president of the company that manufactures power lawnmowers.

3. Assume that you have been asked to recommend one of two air-conditioning systems (gas or electric) for a two-story, 24' $\times$ 48' house in your area. The machinery will be set outside the house and connected to the present heating system; no new duct work will be necessary.

You can get costs of equipment from a catalogue. You can either estimate costs of installation or ask an equipment salesman what the average installation costs are.

You will have to estimate BTU's to be removed on the basis of the mean summer temperatures (you can find these in an encyclopedia). A catalogue may help you here.

Your feasibility study will also have to take into account:

Initial investment in equipment

Local energy rates

Cost per BTU removed by gas equipment

Cost per BTU removed by electric equipment

Number of BTU's to be removed in average season

This question: over a five- or ten-year expected lifetime which is the lowest-cost system?

Write the feasibility report complete with recommendations.

If you wish, you may substitute a study for heating the same house: coal versus oil versus gas versus electricity.

4. The local Milligan Water Softener Supply Co. has reached the point where its present delivery and installation crew and its present number of trucks is just able to handle the company's business in a 40-hour week. It is faced with two choices—ask the present crew to work Saturdays at time-and-a-half rates (two men per Saturday) or to purchase a new truck and hire two new men. At present there is not enough business to keep additional men and a new truck busy all the time, although some maintenance work could be done. If two new men were employed, the available work would be distributed evenly among all men and trucks.

The men are paid $5 an hour. A new truck costs $10,000. One truck usually covers 100 miles per day at 10 cents a mile for gasoline and maintenance, but not depreciation. The lifetime of a truck is estimated at 5 years. The estimated growth of population in the area served is 10 percent per year. Milligan can expect a proportionate increase in its business each year.

Your feasibility study should consider two matters: Is it feasible at present to hire two men

and purchase a new truck? If not, at what point in time will the additions be feasible?

Whichever study you report, follow this form:

Introductory Summary

1. Introduction
   a. Purpose
   b. Problem
   c. Scope
2. Background Information
3. Cost
   a. Present cost, or cost of one system or object
   b. Proposed cost, or cost of second system or object
   c. Cost of third system or object, if applicable
4. Capability
   a. Present
   b. Proposed
5. Suitability
   a. To writer's organization
   b. To client's organization, if applicable
   c. To the state of the art (see index)
6. Detailed Conclusions (feasibility statement)
7. Detailed Recommendations
8. Appendix
   a. Designs, illustrations, photographs, drawings
   b. Cost calculations
   c. Other technical information

Example Three: Student-Written Feasibility Report

Appendix 4, page 207, is a student-written feasibility report. Study the report and answer these questions:

1. What is the scope of the report?
2. How is description used in the report?
3. Are the "conclusions," conclusions or something else?
4. If you think they are something else, write

your own set of conclusions and bring them to class for discussion.

5. Does the report make good use of the illustration, the table, and the appendix?

6. Do you agree with the recommendations of the report?

The Proposal Report

On many occasions on your job you will be asked to investigate a problem and work out a proposed solution for it. Your proposed solution will be turned over to someone else for a decision about its feasibility. Or, you may see the problem on your own (as T. M. Deford did; his report is in Appendix 5, page 215) and investigate on your own. Many organizations maintain employee suggestion programs and encourage employees to propose new ideas or better ways of doing things. When your proposed solution is presented formally, it is called a *proposal report*.

The informal employee suggestion may be as simple as a short memorandum suggesting that the shop be swept out twice a day to promote comfort, safety, and efficiency. The formal report may range from a one-page memorandum to a book-length report that puts forth a plan for a sewer system, a high-rise building, a supersonic airplane, a power plant, or a computer installation. Whatever the project, proposals are basically the same. For one thing, they will usually be optimistic about what they propose.

Proposals usually focus on three main areas:

1. What is the nature of the work being proposed?
   Implied in this question is the existence of some problem the proposer intends to solve.
2. Who will do the work?
   Implied in this question are such questions as these:
   a. Who will manage the work?
   b. What professional people will be employed?
   c. What other people will be employed?

3. How much will it cost and who will pay? Costs include:
   a. Costs for materials
   b. Costs for the use of equipment and space
   c. Costs for salaries and wages
   d. Costs for overhead and burden
   e. Costs for expense

The Problem

The problem to be solved may be one that has been identified by the party to whom the proposal is made (a city council's decision to build a new sewage system) or one that is being identified by the proposer (someone trying to sell new plant machinery, for example).

Consideration of the problem and the proposed solution will result in discussion of any one or more of these:

1. Materials and supplies
2. Machines and equipment, buildings and space
3. Processes and methods
4. Energy sources
5. Human resources
6. Time needed for the proposed solution (included will be a list of priorities)
7. History or background of the problem
8. Costs, estimated or actual

The proposed solution will essentially be a plan of action to be followed.

Format for the Report

The proposal report will follow the same order as a formal report:

1. Title page
   Not used in a simple proposal, or perhaps not used in an internal proposal
2. Table of contents (for long proposals)
3. List of illustrations
4. List of tables and figures
5. Introductory summary
6. Introduction
   a. Purpose

b. Definition of the problem
Including background and context if applicable
c. Scope of the proposal
7. Body or discussion sections
  a. The work
    (1) History or background
    (2) Materials, methods, equipment, time, other resources (human resources in general)
  b. Who will do the work
    (1) Specifically named human resources
      (a) Managerial
      (b) Professional
    (2) Generally named human resources
      (a) Supporting personnel—guards, caretakers, machine operators, draftsmen, computer operators, and so on
  c. Costs
    (1) Categories of costs—materials, facilities, equipment, salaries, wages, expense, overhead, burden.
    (2) If appropriate, division of the costs. How much will be borne by the proposer, how much by other agencies.
  d. Detailed schedule of work
8. Conclusions
9. Appendix

DISCUSSION ASSIGNMENT

Find as many of the elements of the proposal report as you can in T. M. Deford's proposal report in Appendix 5, page 215.

The Report of Literature Search

In Chapter 5 you learned about searching for information in libraries and learning materials centers. On the job, you will use these skills in two kinds of investigations. The first kind is simply to learn what the state of the art is (see page 42). There is no point in conducting research into a problem if the problem has already been solved. There is no point in beginning research if the state of the art has not yet arrived close to the proposed problem.

The Annotated Bibliography

To learn what the state of the art is, the literature in the subject area is investigated, using the techniques outlined in Chapter 5. Then one of two types of reports is written: the annotated bibliography or the literature review. The *annotated bibliography* is a list of books, articles, and other materials that report knowledge or research in the subject area being investigated. The list consists of bibliographical information about each item followed by an abstract, review, or critique of the work:

Brady, George Stuart. *Materials Handbook*. 9th ed. New York: McGraw-Hill, 1963. 968 pp.

Brief descriptions of raw and fabricated materials used in various industries are given in alphabetical order. Hence, this book, in spite of its title, differs from the typical scientific handbooks and resembles a small encyclopedia. Although intended for engineers, purchasing agents, and executives, it is equally useful for students and others who want concise information on products included—for example, abrasives, cellophane rosin, starch, water glass.

Hopkins, Albert A. *The Standard American Encyclopedia of Formulas*. New York: Grosset, 1953. 1077 pp.

Formulas for the home, factory, workshop. If you want to polish brass, remove ink stains, launder dacron, or a thousand other things, a book of formulas will supply the answer. This one . . . includes over 15,000 formulas . . . (*Reference Books: a brief guide*, compiled by Mary N. Barton and Marion V. Bell, 7th ed., 1970, Enoch Pratt Free Library, Baltimore).

WRITING ASSIGNMENT

In the *Engineering Index* (or a similar index in another subject area, see Chapter 5) locate three articles on a topic that interests you. Look up the articles, read them, and write an annotated bibliography on them.

The Literature Review

The *literature review* is an extension of the annotated bibliography. Because the annotated bibliography usually indexes articles and books alphabetically according to authors' last names, the reader is put to some work to get it all together. The literature review saves the reader that trouble. Here is a typical review:

In the past twenty years there has been considerable work dealing with grass leaf anatomy as related to systematics (Brown, 1958; Tateoka, 1957; Lommasson, 1961; Stebbins and Crampton, 1961; Decker, 1964; Reeder, 1961; Metcalfe, 1960).* The concentrated effort of these workers has resulted in a realignment of the traditional subfamilies Festucoideae and Panicoideae. A major factor in the "new taxonomic system" has been the presentation of new anatomical information, which shows that the two traditional subfamilies were made up of genera that often had very little or no phylogenetic relationship. During the past few decades, most workers (Avdulov, 1931; Prat, 1936; Brown, 1958; Tateoka, 1957; Reeder, 1957) have settled on a taxonomic system that includes six main subfamilies of grasses . . .

No review of literature pertinent to grass anatomy would be complete without mention of *Anatomy of the Monocotyledons* (Metcalfe, 1960). Metcalfe (1960, 1961) studied and described the anatomy of many grasses but also pointed out the need for additional study. . . .

WRITING ASSIGNMENT

Refer to the three articles in your annotated bibliography from the preceding writing assignment. Write a literature review that brings these three articles together as in the above example.

The Report Based on Literature Research

A standard assignment in technical schools is the report based on literature research. There is a good reason for the assignment; industrial and business leaders say over and over again that they want the people they hire to have training in the skills involved in producing this type of report.

Thomas Zarnke's "Progress of the Progressive Die" (Appendix 6, page 225) is an example of the report based on literature research. It is a good report, particularly because Mr. Zarnke was interested in his topic. As a result, he did a good job of researching, organizing, writing, and illustrating his paper.

STUDY QUESTIONS FOR APPENDIX 6

1. What does Zarnke's first paragraph do?
2. What form of definition does Zarnke use in his second paragraph? What form of definition does his report represent?
3. What do the next two paragraphs of his report do? Are these two paragraphs presented in any logical order?
4. What do the next three paragraphs do? What logical process is Zarnke using here? Is Zarnke merely informative here, or is he trying to do more than inform? If he is doing the latter, what techniques is he using?
5. How, where, and when does Zarnke use an example?
6. How does he end his report?
7. Does Zarnke make effective use of illustrations?
8. What were Zarnke's sources of information?

---

* The names and years refer to articles that would be found in the bibliography accompanying this review. Thus, "Brown, 1958," refers to this item:
   Brown, W. V. 1958. Leaf anatomy in grass systematics. *Bot. Gaz.* 119:170-178.
The following bibliographical note is an example of a bibliographical item which is *not* annotated: Sutton, Dale D. Leaf anatomy in the subfamily *Eragrostoideae. Mich. Acad.,* Winter 1973, pp. 373–374.

WRITING ASSIGNMENT

Pick a machine or device that interests you and that represents some advance in the state of the art. Write to the manufacturer for brochures about the item. Perhaps you can find information about it in magazine advertisements or in *Sweet's Files*. Or, you may find information in a catalogue or at a local dealer's office.

Write a report on the item, following either the outline used by Thomas Zarnke or an outline of your own invention. Do not use the formal report outlines discussed earlier in this chapter. They are inappropriate for this kind of report.

13 | Writing for Magazines

On many college campuses, there is either an engineering magazine, written by and for engineering and technology students, or a general magazine, either of which is always looking for publishable reports. A good magazine-type report, written by someone like you and published in one of these magazines, helps build the status and prestige of technology on your campus.

Once you are working, you will discover that "publish or perish" is a theme that is not limited to college teachers alone. Engineering and industrial firms want their engineering employees to publish in magazines or journals specializing in the areas in which they work.

Lynn V. Jeske's article on p. 148, "The ME 262," is an example of the magazine report. Jeske was a freshman at a technological university when he wrote this report. He had built a flying model of the ME 262 several years earlier and was impressed by the flight characteristics of the aircraft. So he decided to do a magazine report on the subject.

Jeske began by reading the materials listed in the bibliography. Then, he decided to use a pattern that developed out of his subject—the same kind of pattern used by H. F. Whitten in the first of her two investigative reports in Chapter 11 and by Thomas Zarnke in his report on the progressive die in Appendix 6.

STUDY QUESTIONS

1. How does Jeske begin the report? What is his purpose in placing the incident at this point in his report?

2. How does Jeske build suspense and anxiety into the report? Why?

3. What is the chronological order of events in Jeske's report? Can you see an advantage in deviating from the order of events as they happened?

4. How might some of the problems he reported first be of interest to engineers and engineering students?

5. How does Jeske use some of the history of World War II?

6. What do you learn about the top policy management in that war?

7. Where are Jeske's sympathies—with the Germans or the allies? How can you tell? How does this use of "voice" compare with Whitten's in her two reports or with Zarnke's in his report?

8. How does Jeske end his report? Do you find his ending effective?

WRITING ASSIGNMENT

Pick a topic in engineering history that interests you. Such a topic might deal with the Sterling engine, the Wankel engine, the steam turbine, the diesel engine, or even the internal-combustion gasoline engine. It might be about the building of a bridge, such as the Verrazano Narrows Bridge or the "Big Mac." Or, it might be about the development of the laser, the transistor, or radar.

Limit your coverage of the topic to aspects that will produce a report about as long as Jeske's. If you plan to write for a college magazine, ask how long the report should be. Don't try to write about the history of suspension bridges, engines, or electronics. Narrow your topic to subjects such as cable spinning, a particular plane or engine, or one electronic item. Readers want specific information; they do not want to read broad generalizations.

Locate your source materials and take notes, following the procedures in Chapter 5. When you have gathered your material, think about it for a while. Think about the "voice" of your report. What point of view will you adopt? How will you sustain it? It is a good idea to make an outline before you begin to write to insure that the report follows a clear and logical development. Then, where is the best place to begin? Is there a pertinent incident or anecdote in your material that will catch and hold your reader's attention? Can you devise good "funnel" paragraphs for the introduction and for the ending? How will the report end? (Some writers say they always plan the ending of a report first and then go to the beginning.)

<hr>

The ME 262
by
Lynn V. Jeske

Shortly before 08:00 on July 18, 1942, an aircraft waited at the extreme end of the runway of Leipheim Airfield, near Gunzburg on the Danube. The runway was only 1,200 yards long, and every yard was needed.

Fritz Wendel, flight captain and chief test pilot with Messerschmitt, acknowledged the farewell wishes of the men on the ground with a nod of his head and closed the roof of the cockpit. The sound of the engines rose to an ear-splitting scream.

On this machine, the traditional feature of every other aircraft to date was missing: the propeller. Nor were the engines themselves of the conventional type. Instead, beneath the wings were two thickly-cowled jet turbines. From their circular rear openings thundered fiery blasts that sprayed the tail unit with sand and stones.

Slowly and cautiously Wendel pushed forward the power lever. With both feet on the brakes, he held the plane for thirty to forty seconds, until the revolution counter read 7,500. Eighty-five hundred represented full power, and he could hold it no longer. He released the brakes, and the ME 262 shot forward.

With its sharp nose pointing into the air, the machine resembled a projectile. This position had the effect of blocking the pilot's forward vision. He could only keep aligned with the runway by glancing to the side. On the initial takeoff of a revolutionary prototype this was a disadvantage indeed. If only, thought Wen-

del, it had a tricycle-undercarriage. Its undercarriage was, in fact, the only conventional thing about the plane. It accounted for the awkward stance, as a result of which the blast of the engines hit the ground and the pilot could not see. Worse still, the tail unit in this position was aerodynamically "blind": it received no airstream. There was no response from the elevator, and for all its high ground-speed the machine refused to become airborne.

The spectators held their breath. Deafened by its piercing whistle, they watched as it hurtled like a racing car to the end of the runway. Surely it must have attained 110 m.p.h. long since.

That was the speed at which, so it had been calculated, the ME 262 with its five-ton all-up weight must leave the ground. During ground tests early in the morning Wendel had reached it in just over 800 yards, without, however, getting the tail unit off the ground. And the remainder of the distance was only just long enough to stop in. Each time, he had come to a halt close beside the boundary fence. "No plane can fly without a propeller," the doubting Thomases had said. It looked as though they might be proved right.[3]

This time, Wendel put fortune to the test. He had been advised as to how, in such a situation, he could still get the stubborn tail into the air. It was a most irregular and dangerous procedure, but he had to risk it. At 110 m.p.h. and full power he suddenly trod briefly but sharply on the brakes. It worked. The plane tipped on its axis, and the tail came clear of the ground. Horizontal motion at once produced an air-stream, and at last pressure could be felt from the elevator. Wendel reacted swiftly. Very gently, almost automatically, he lifted the aircraft off the ground. The first ME 262 was airborne—and how it flew! The chief test pilot, who had nursed it from the beginning, was at last rewarded for all his trouble. He pushed the stick a bit forward to gain more pace and felt himself pressed backwards into his seat. The Messerschmitt shot like an arrow up into the sky. What was more, the higher it climbed, the faster it flew. The astounded Wendel stared at the instruments. Since he had himself raised the absolute world speed record on April 26, 1939, to 469.22 m.p.h. with the ME 209, it had only been exceeded by his colleague, Heini Dittmar, in the rocket-propelled ME 163. And the veil of secrecy in which wartime rocket development was shrouded, the new record had never been claimed.

Now the third prototype of the ME 262, with its JUMO 004 jets, was soaring above the world-record mark on its very first flight. Five hundred m.p.h. on the clock, without a murmur! Suddenly Wendel felt really happy in this sensational aircraft. He throttled back, then reaccelerated: The engines responded splendidly. Then, in a wide circuit, he swept in toward land, put down smoothly, and rolled to a stop. The first flight of the ME 262 V-3—the world's first jet aircraft ever to reach the stage of series production—had lasted just twelve minutes.[3]

"She's wonderful!" beamed Wendel, as Professor Messerschmitt came up to meet him. "I've never enjoyed a flight more." In the afternoon he flew the machine again. If time was to be made up, the real tests must begin at once. Messerschmitt had waited a long time for the engines. The air-frame had been flown by Wendel as long ago as April, 1941—powered by an old piston engine that was quite inappropriate to the new streamlined frame. But it was at least a start, and it enabled some of the flying characteristics to be gauged. Six months later, the first turbojets arrived from B.M.W. in Berlin. They ran satisfactorily on the bench, and on March 25, 1942, were submitted to their first flying test. For this occasion, the ME 262 V-1 presented a curious spectacle. Besides the turbines under the wings, the old piston engine was still in the middle. For Wendel this was just as well, for he hardly reached 150 feet before both the former cut out one after the other, and he got down again only by using the conventional engines full power. The turbines had not withstood the strain: In both cases, the compressor blades were broken. Such "teething" troubles were to be expected, but it was a long wait before fresh engines became available, and meanwhile the V-1 prototype stood like an orphan in a hangar.

Finally the JUMO 004s arrived, and, as we have seen, were successful. On its first jet-powered flight the ME 262 revealed a performance that its creators had hardly dared hope for. Now Wendel tested its every feature, had small modifications made, and flew again. After the tenth flight, during which the plane reached well over 500 m.p.h., he advised the factory management to get ready for series production. Such a decision could not, of course, be taken by Messerschmitt alone. Until now, the contract had been only for three prototypes, nothing more. So the supply chief in Berlin, Milch, was put in the picture, and he, in turn, set the wheels turning at the official Rechlin test center.

On August 17th, just one month since the ME 262's initial flight, an experienced test pilot, Staff Engineer Beauvais, arrived from Rechlin to submit the new plane to exhaustive trials. As he wedged himself into the narrow cockpit, Wendel reminded him once more of the trick with the brakes to elevate the tail. He, [Wendel] would take up station at the 800-yard mark to indicate when Beauvais should execute this maneuver. Then he watched as the machine approached. But its speed was too low—nothing like 110 m.p.h. Nonetheless, as he came abreast, the pilot braked. The tail wheel came up, but then fell impotently down again. Beauvais tried it a second time, then again just before the airfield perimeter. Somehow the machine became airborne and whizzed over the ground at perhaps three feet, but much too slowly ever to gain height. Seconds later a wingtip touched a refuse heap, and with a loud report the Messerschmitt crashed on top of it in a cloud of dust. Miraculously the pilot climbed out of the wreckage almost unscathed.

This accident put back the ME 262's final development by months. Though a replacement air-frame was rapidly constructed and even new engines were available, the Reich Air Ministry in Berlin had no confidence. The whole project, it was argued, was still too much in its infancy. There could be no question of sanctioning any series production. And no one pressed for this as an urgent matter. Milch merely urged intensified production of those aircraft types that had already proved their worth in the past. New projects stood in the way of such an aim being realized: they simply funnelled off productive capacity.[3]

By the summer of 1942, the Americans had been in the war for nine months, and their first four-engine bombers were appearing over the continent. In 1943, they would number hundreds; in the following year, thousands. At this vital moment, a German fighter had been created that was 125 m.p.h. faster than any other fighter in the world, enough to alarm all Germany's enemies. It could have been operational within a year to cope with the Allies when they opened up their main offensive over Germany. Thus, it could be supposed that, given top priority, Germany would have ultimately won the air war. Yet no one in the Luftwaffe took upon himself the responsibility of saying as much or even seemed to be aware of the unique opportunity.

It wasn't until December, 1942, that a production program was forwarded, and then only for 1944 at a planned output of twenty planes per month. The fastest fighter in the world was set aside. It seemed that the Luftwaffe had no interest in it.

With the last ditch reached, an attempt was finally made to defend the Reich with the "world's fastest fighter," despite Hitler's hatred to speak of it as a "fighter." An experimental unit was formed and was headed by an ace, Major (Professor) Walter Nowotny, who scored 258 kills and was a holder of one of Germany's highest honors, the Oak Leaves with Swords and Diamonds.

At the beginning of October, 1944, Nowotny and his unit, now a gruppe, were making daily sorties against the enemy formations and their mammoth fighter armadas in numbers of three or four. Yet, in a month, these few jet aircraft knocked out twenty-two aircraft. But by the end of a month, they themselves had been reduced from thirty to three serviceable planes, very few as a result of enemy action. On November 8, 1944, five Messerschmitt 262s of Nowotny's unit took off from their bases near Osnabruck to give battle to American bombers. Day after day their airfields had been subjected to attack by United States fighter-bombers, so much so that they had only been able to take off and land under the protection of a whole gruppe of FW 190s and concentrated flak.

On this day, Major Nowotny had been forbidden to take off, but when the returning bombers were reported, he ignored the order and led the last of his serviceable ME 262s into action. A few minutes later he reported a victory—his 258th of the war. But his next report on the radio boded ill: "One engine has failed. Will try landing." The men at operations H.Q., among them Adolf Galland, Fighter General, rushed out into the open. The whine of Nowotny's jet was heard approaching. Then he appeared low over the airfield, but with a whole flock of Mustang fighters on his tail. They were hunting the crippled ME 262 like a pack of crows after a wounded eagle. For Nowotny to attempt to land would be suicide. Instead, with one engine only, he decided to fight it out.

Climbing steeply up, he turned and came down after them just above the ground. But suddenly, there was a piercing flash and an explosion. No one knew whether he had been hit or whether the wild chase had brought him into contact with the earth. In any case, Walter Nowotny was dead at the age of twenty-three. Exit gallant ace.[3]

Yet in the final weeks of the war, one other ME 262 unit was formed. This was called the so-called Jagdverband (JV) 44. Though its strength in machines was no greater than a single squadron, it was led in person by the fighter general, Adolf Galland, a holder (like Nowotny) of the Oak Leaves with Swords and Diamonds, with 103 victories. From February, 1945 on, the records of a few known battles are as follows:

In the last week of February, JG 7, equipped with R4m 5 cm. rockets, alone destroyed forty-five four-engine bombers and fifteen long-range fighters, with minimum loss to themselves. Attack by jets had for a long time been anticipated by the American command, in mid-March, 1945, and at this time its full impact was ecountered. On the 18th, 1,250 bombers set course for Berlin to deliver the heaviest attack of the war. Despite difficult weather, German fighter control was successful in bringing thirty-seven ME 262s of JG 7 against the enemy. Though the bombers were escorted by no less than fourteen fighter groups of the recently superior P-51 Mustang, the jets pierced their defensive screen without trouble. Outclassed by the easy, elegant flight of the ME 262s, the Mustangs had suddenly become ponderous and outmoded airplanes. The jets claimed nineteen certain victories plus two probables, at the loss of two of their own aircraft. The actual American figures were twenty-four bombers and five fighters.[3] On April 4, forty-nine ME 262s of JG 7 attacked a formation of 150 bombers over Nordhausen, claiming ten certainly, and probably fifteen, though on this day the Eighth A.A.F.'s attack was in the Hamburg region. The next day, Galland's JV 44, taking off with only five ME 262s, accounted without a loss for two bombers out of a large, heavily escorted force. The terrific advantage enjoyed by jets against piston-engined fighters was probably given its best demonstrations on April 7. That day, the Luftwaffe, under code-name "Wehrwolf," directed its attack, not against the bombers as usual, but against their fighter escort. Without mentionable loss to itself, JG 7 alone claimed as many as twenty-eight fighters. Only three days later, however, the German jets paid the penalty. Formations totaling 1,200 bombers entered the Berlin area and devastated their airfields and bases by carpet-bombing. Though the jets knocked down ten of them, they were obliged with their airfields gone, to withdraw to others as far distant as Prague.

The bomber streams now over Germany often numbered over 2,000 aircraft at a time. The rate of success of some forty jet fighters was but a pin-prick. Of a total of 1,294 ME 262's built, perhaps only a quarter ever became engaged with the enemy. Many failed to survive their numerous test commandos, but most never got off the ground—even though fuel for its jets was one item Germany was never short of. No longer were a few stout-hearted German pilots, however superior in their planes, in a position to challenge the Allied sovereignty of the air.

Developed already before the war, for years neglected and even banned by Germany's supreme military director, and then thrown into the struggle at the eleventh hour, Germany's jet fighter remains a tribute to German inventiveness at a time of true crisis.

Bibliography

1. Hirsch, R. S., and Uwe Feist. **ME 262**. Fallbrook, Cal.: Aero Publishers.
2. Brian, J. Ford. **German Secret Weapons**. New York: Ballantine Books.
3. Bekker, Caius. **Luftwaffe War Diaries**. Garden City, N. Y.: Doubleday & Company.
4. Shirer, William L. **The Rise and Fall of the Third Reich**. New York: Simon & Schuster.
5. Speer, Albert. **Inside the Third Reich**. New York: Macmillan.
6. Galland, Adolf. **Luftwaffe**. New York: Ballantine Books.

14 | Technical Explanation with Illustrations

Individuals who are uncertain about their writing abilities, who dislike work, or who place too much confidence in technology often try to rely on substitutes for words by assuming that "A picture can save a thousand words." There is no doubt that a picture often replaces words or that a well-made drawing can save unnecessary verbal explanations. But it is just as often the case that an illustration raises a lot of questions: *Playboy* magazine center spreads seem to reveal a lot, but the questions they raise usually require several pages. When comprehension is necessary, words must supplement illustrations. In spite of these realistic cautions, illustrative aids should not be overlooked, and they should be used as often as indicated.

Types of Illustrations

Ordinarily, you will have access to the following types of illustrations. Some of these are readily available, others are expensive or take time to produce, and still others present some reproduction problems.

Charts, Graphs, Tables

These are useful for presenting comparisons, for summarizing data, or for illustrating abstract facts. Tables can be prepared by a typist; graphs

will need the services of a draftsman; charts may require someone with some artistic ability. The following types are among those possible:

1. Line graphs—for representing continuous processes. Be sure that every potential point on a line graph is an actual point (Figs. 14.1, 14.2 and 14.3).

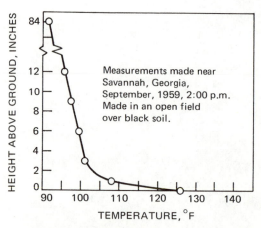

Fig. 3. Experimental temperature distribution in a warm air layer near the ground.

FIGURE 14.1 A conventional line graph. Note the caption. (Reprinted by permission from Clarence D. Cone, Jr.'s, "Thermal Soaring of Birds," **American Scientist**, 50:1, 1962.)

2. Bar graphs—for representing absolutes. Two or three absolute quantities may be compared on each bar of the graph (Fig. 14.4).

3. Pie graphs—for showing percentages (Fig. 14.5).

4. Cartoons—for dramatizing or illustrating comparisons or abstract concepts.

5. Map graphs—for making geographical comparisons (Fig. 14.6).

6. Flow charts—for illustrating, in an abstract way, the steps in a process (Fig. 14.7).

7. Schematics—serving the same function as flow charts, but usually illustrating even more abstract concepts, such as the flow of electrical current (Figs. 14.8 and 14.9).

8. Scatter graphs—for showing the location of every coordinate in a test pattern. They are used in place of a line that might show an average or in addition to a line that shows an average, a mean, or a median. They are useful when the number of test results or samples is small (Fig. 14.10).

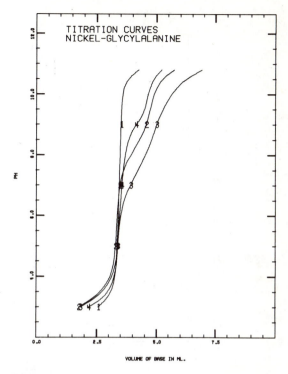

FIGURE 14.3 Line graph drawn by a computer. (Reprinted by courtesy of Michigan Technological University.)

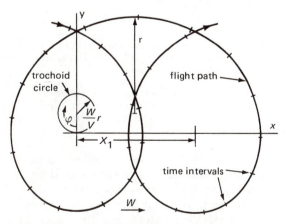

Fig. 5. The trochoidal flight path of a circling Cheel.

FIGURE 14.2 An unconventional line graph. Note the caption.

Photographs

Although they have their limitations, these are useful for illustrating actual objects. They cannot always illustrate inner recesses or fast-moving objects. Nor can they illustrate objects that have ceased to exist or do not yet exist.

Photographs are good for showing unique objects—people, machines, and so on. They also are effective in presenting the *overview* discussed in Chapter 8.

To be of value, photographs must focus on the subject so that it is emphasized. Distracting elements must be eliminated; an industrial photographer should always carry a broom and some gray sheets with him. The pictures must be clear;

153

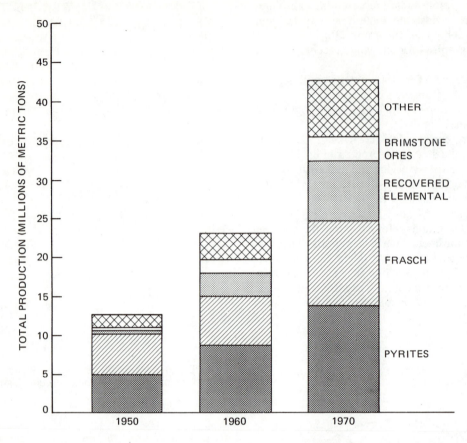

Production of Sulfur has nearly tripled since 1950 and the proportion of the various sources has altered. Pyrites are minerals containing iron and sulfur in combination. Much of the increase in the category labeled "Other" is attributable to the recovery of sulfur from sour natural gas, which in turn reflects the increasing demand for sweetened gas.

FIGURE 14.4 Bar graph used for a dual purpose—to illustrate absolute quantities and to compare percentages of production. In bar graphs, the usual practice is to set fixed or control points (in this case, points in time) on the **x**-axis and the variables (in this case, the absolute quantities from year to year) on the **y**-axis (Reprinted by permission from "Sulphur," **Scientific American,** 222: May 5, 1970.)

they must have sufficient contrast so that the desired details stand out. Irrelevant details can be cropped out when the prints are made.

Photographs can be made up in pairs—an overall view of the subject with an arrow pointing to a desired detail and an accompanying closeup showing an enlarged view of that detail (Fig. 14.11).

Photographs can be retouched by a specialist, who can emphasize desired details or delete or deemphasize irrelevant or secondary details. Retouching provides greater contrasts than in the original photograph, and they reproduce very well. Since retouching is expensive and takes time, it must be done by a qualified person with the appropriate equipment (Fig. 14.12).

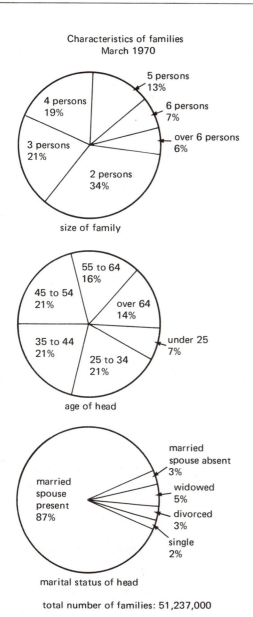

Characteristics of families
March 1970

size of family

age of head

marital status of head

total number of families: 51,237,000

FIGURE 14.5 Pie graphs are used to show percentages when the combination of the percentages equals 100%. A pie graph helps to demonstrate relationships among percentages. (From the U.S. Department of Commerce, Bureau of the Census. **Current Population Reports.)**

Overlays using arrows, letters, and numerals can be prepared and placed on the photograph before reproduction. There are several kinds of transfer type and symbols available. Some care must be exercised in applying them. Key letters can be placed in the margin, with an arrow pointing to the desired detail. If the detail area is dark, the superimposed symbol must be white to stand out (Fig. 14.14).

If you are publishing your own material, photos can be pasted on the page with rubber cement, if they are the 4″ × 5″ conventional size. In that case, save a place on the duplicated page for them. If the 4″ × 5″ size is not large enough, have a photographer make 8½″ × 11″ prints (rather than the 8″ × 10″ he will suggest). This larger size is the same as a standard-sheet size, and the photographs can be bound in with the printed pages.

Be sure that your photographs are good and that they serve a purpose. Not long ago, the editor of a trade publication lost his job because he kept taking pictures of company engineers shaking hands with other people. The trouble was that the most visible element was someone's broad back. A few years ago, an engineering college magazine ran an article on expressways. The only illustration was a full-page photograph of a cement mixer! It would have been far better to have illustrated the article with drawings or photographs of diamond-shaped and clover-shaped interchanges—the kind of information people did not know about then.

It is a good idea to show the scale of some objects in photographs or drawings. Use a familiar object, such as a hat or a hand, or use an actual scale, such as a ruler in a photograph.

Engineering Drawings

These are good for supplying precise technical details. The problem is that these drawings tend to be large. Reductions of them fit into reports, but small details are lost in the process. If the drawings are folded to bind into a report, the result is a bulky package. One solution is to put the

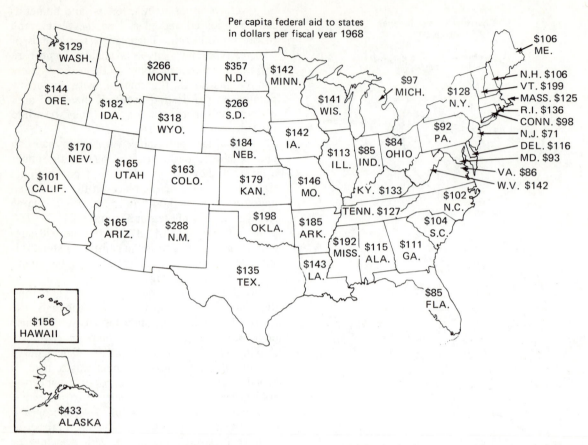

Per capita federal aid to states
in dollars per fiscal year 1968

$129 WASH.
$106 ME.
$144 ORE.
$266 MONT.
$357 N.D.
$142 MINN.
$97 MICH.
N.H. $106
VT. $199
MASS. $125
R.I. $136
CONN. $98
$182 IDA.
$266 S.D.
$141 WIS.
$128 N.Y.
N.J. $71
$318 WYO.
$184 NEB.
$142 IA.
$92 PA.
DEL. $116
MD. $93
$170 NEV.
$113 ILL.
$85 IND.
$84 OHIO
VA. $86
W.V. $142
$101 CALIF.
$165 UTAH
$163 COLO.
$179 KAN.
$146 MO.
KY. $133
$102 N.C.
$165 ARIZ.
$288 N.M.
$198 OKLA.
$185 ARK.
TENN. $127
$104 S.C.
$192 MISS.
$115 ALA.
$111 GA.
$135 TEX.
$143 LA.
$85 FLA.
$156 HAWAII
$433 ALASKA

FIGURE 14.6 Map graph. (Reprinted by permission from the Congressional Quarterly Inc., **Note to Editors**, Copyright 1969. All rights reserved.)

reduced drawing at the appropriate place in the report and put the folded drawing into a pocket in the report cover (Fig. 1.2).

If you are going to reproduce drawings, alert your draftsmen to the need for lines and symbols that will be sharp enough to reproduce in the reproduction process.

Drawings by Artists

These must be secured whenever photographs or engineering drawings will not serve your pur-

pose. They are generally expensive and take time to prepare. Schedule your work and your budgets accordingly. It is not good economy to try to save money by hiring amateurs. Moreover, some artists do well at one kind of illustrations and others do better with another kind. Discuss your problem with someone who knows what he is doing (Figs. 14.14, 14.15). Remember that poor illustrations not only waste money, but they may detract from your report instead of enhancing it.

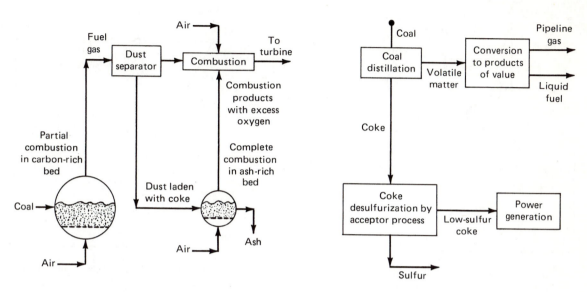

Fig. 4 (left). Scheme to supply CO for combustion ahead of a gas turgine.

Fig. 5 (right). A "Coalplex."

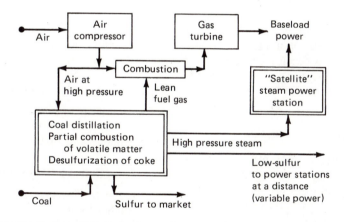

Fig. 6. A pioneering Coalplex (25) directed toward recovery of sulfur and generation of clean power.

FIGURE 14.7 Three flow charts: Figure 4 might also be called a "schematic" (see Figure 14.8). Figures 5 and 6 are both flow charts for different versions of a "coalplex" and show how flow charts may be used to compare elaborate abstractions. (From A. M. Squires, "Clean Power from Coal," **Science**, 169, August 28, 1970. Reprinted by permission.)

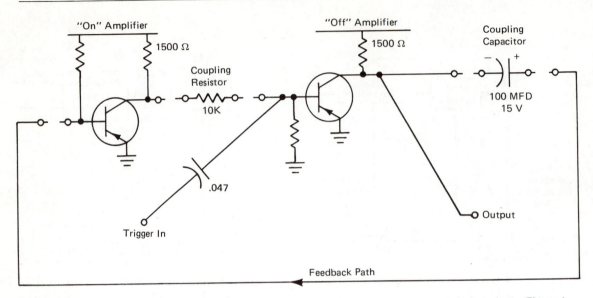

FIGURE 14.8 A schematic illustrating electrical power flows. (Reprinted by permission from **Elementary Electronics**, September-October, 1971.)

Exploded Drawings

These are drawings in which an object is presented as if it had literally been exploded in space (Fig. 14.16). The purpose of such a drawing is to show parts in relation to each other and, at the same time, to show each part in sufficient detail so that it can be identified. Exploded drawings are useful in directions, in explanations, and in parts books.

Cutaway Drawings

They demonstrate the internal mechanisms or operations, while leaving the individual parts in place. Cutaway drawings are useful for explaining operation of a semi-complex object (Fig. 14.17).

Stage Drawings

These drawings show several stages of an operation in sequence. They are especially useful in cases such as in Fig. 14.18, where the stages occupy different areas in space.

Combinations

Almost all of these illustrations can be used in combination. Several kinds of graphs can be combined in one (see Chapter 3 for an example) and photographs can be combined with drawings or graphs.

Oscilloscope Tracings

These show a technician what to expect under certain test circumstances and are useful in maintenance and operations manuals.

Functions of Illustrations

1. Illustrations are aids to the text, not replacements for it.

2. In articles intended for the noncaptive audience, the illustrations may serve as bait. Illustrations break up the monotony of solid text on succeeding pages. They also help persuade.

3. Illustrations provide a general pattern for overview, emphasis, or summary; they also clarify the subject.

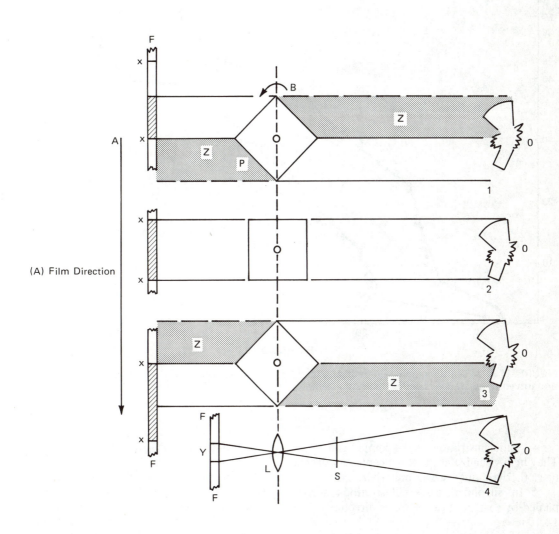

FIGURE 14.9 A schematic illustrating the workings of a high-speed motion picture camera.

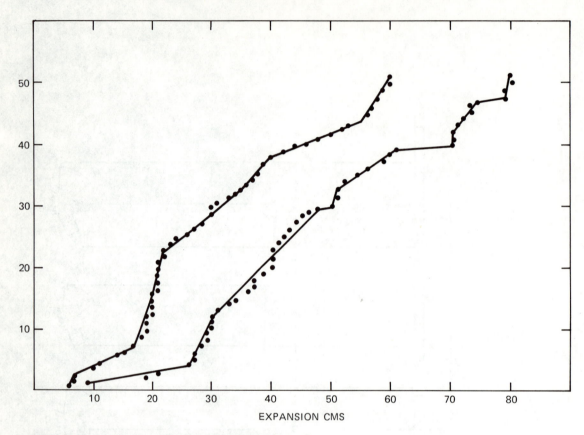

FIGURE 14.10 A scatter graph—all data obtained are shown as points on the **x**- and **y**-axes. The solid lines are arrived at by statistics rather than by algebraic formula.

4. Some illustrations make comparison easier. They help visualize abstract concepts and dramatize otherwise undramatic materials.

5. In simplified cases, illustrations accompanied by some text can serve as directions (Fig. 14.19).

6. They help make the unfamiliar familiar.

7. In the case of x-rays, schlieren photographs, microphotographs, infrared photographs, and similar types of pictures, they show details that are not otherwise visible.

8. They attract attention.

Placing the Illustration

The illustration should always be placed as close to the text as possible, except in those cases where it is used as bait. In a printed book, this is not difficult to do. In internally reproduced publications—publications printed by mimeograph, offset, ditto, Xerox—the task is somewhat more difficult.

If the illustration cannot be placed on the same page with its text, it might be placed on the facing page or on the following page. If neces-

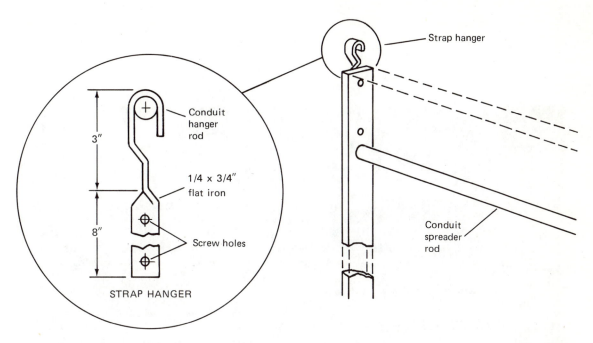

FIGURE 14.11 A closeup, illustrating a small detail of a drawing. (Reprinted by permission from **Popular Mechanics,** copyright © April 1971, The Hearst Corporation.)

sary, several pages of illustrations can be placed in sequence following the pertinent text.

In general, however, you should avoid interpolating pages of tables, charts, photographs, or drawings between pages of narrative. You should consider placing such sequences in the appendix, with a summary in the text.

DISCUSSION ASSIGNMENT

Bring to class samples of illustrative materials, together with the captions and supporting text. Discuss the ways in which text, caption, and illustration support, complement, and explain each other. Of the several functions of illustration enumerated here—summary, substitute, emphasis, clarification—which do you find exemplified?

You are preparing an article for publication. It is about an item that is unfamiliar to the reader. Which of these three illustrations should you use? Why?

A photograph of a pretty girl in a bikini holding the item

A photograph of the item

A photograph of the item in use

WRITING ASSIGNMENT

1. Investigate a duplicating or printing process (mimeograph, ditto, offset, letterpress) or a process for preparing illustrations. Write a report of your investigation, focusing on the liabilities and assets of the process in terms of supplying illustrations for technical papers.

2. Take photographs of a part of your car engine, such as the carburetor or the spark plugs, or of a simple process involving your car, such as changing a tire or shifting the stick on a "four-on-the-floor" model. Bring your pictures to class for examination. Write a critique of your pictures or of those taken by another member of the class.

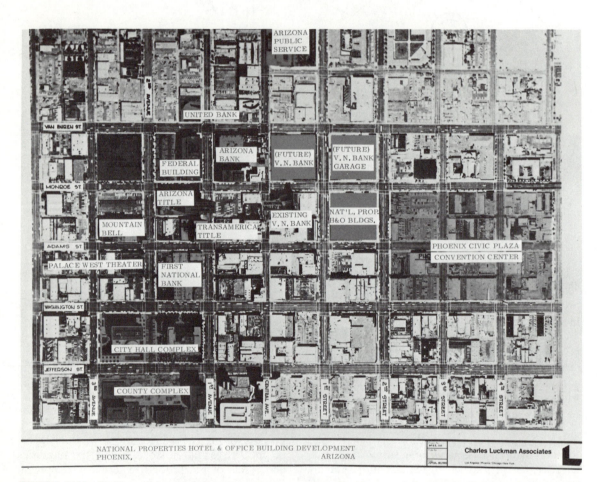

FIGURE 14.12 Photograph to which overlays have been added. To single out important features of the photograph, typewritten labels were pasted to a glossy 8″ × 10″ aerial view. Overlays were also used in Figure 14.13.

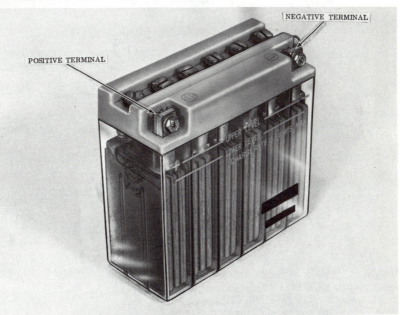

FIGURE 14.13 "Before" and "after" pictures of a product. The top photograph shows the object as the camera saw it. In the bottom picture, irrelevant details have been airbrushed out. Highlights have been added for emphasis, and details have been sharpened and accented. (Reproduced by permission of Ken Cook Transnational.)

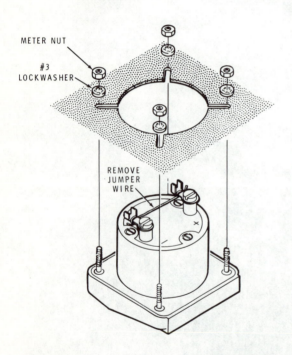

METER NUT

#3
LOCKWASHER

REMOVE
JUMPER
WIRE

FIGURES 14.14 and 14.15 These illustrations are good artwork by skilled artists. Drawings used for external reports should be of this quality, to provide good communications and impart a sense of integrity. (Fig. 14.14 rendering property of Haverhill's. May not be reproduced without written permission. Fig. 14.15 reprinted by permission of Heath Company. Copyright © 1969 Heath Company. All rights reserved.)

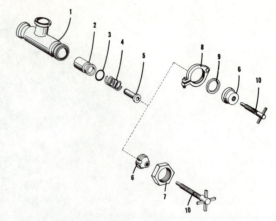

FIGURE 14.16 Exploded drawing. (Reproduced by permission of Cherry-Burrell Company, a division of Cherry-Burrell Corporation.)

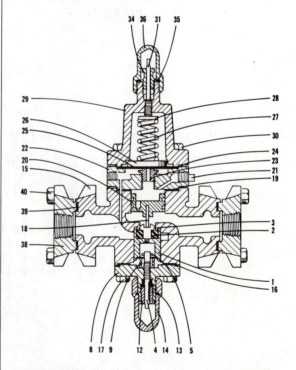

FIGURE 14.17 Cutaway, or cross-sectional, illustration. (Reproduced by permission of Cherry-Burrell Company, a division of Cherry-Burrell Corporation.)

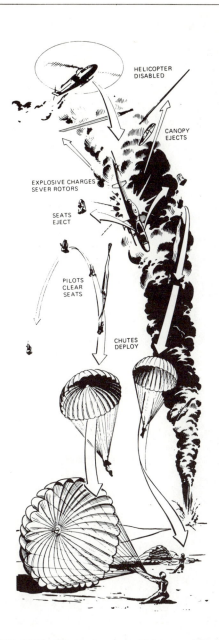

FIGURE 14.18 Stage drawing. This one illustrates a proposed method of rescuing crews from disabled helicopters. (Reprinted by permission from **Popular Mechanics,** copyright © September 1971, The Hearst Corporation.)

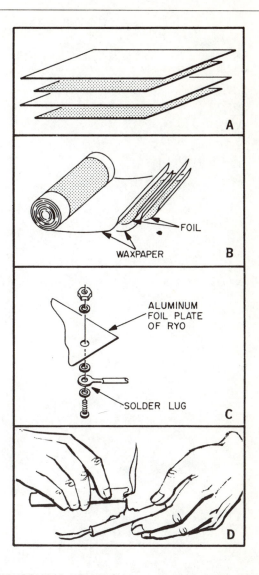

FIGURE 14.19 Illustrations accompanying directions for making capacitors. (Reprinted by permission from **Elementary Electronics,** September-October, 1971.)

Good
Student-written
Instructions

```
                    ASSEMBLY INSTRUCTIONS

                          for the

                    Tool-Lite Kit TLK-1


                            by

                      Stephen Clark
```

Appendix 1: Reprinted by permission of Stephen J. Clark.

ASSEMBLY INSTRUCTIONS FOR THE TOOL-LITE KIT TLK-1

Introduction

The TLK-1 Lamp is made up of high quality parts and, when assembled, will provide the user with an adaptable light source for use with machine tools and work tables.

PARTS LIST

PART NUMBER	PARTS PER KIT	DESCRIPTION
INS-11	1	Instruction Manual (TLK-1)
BAS-22	1	Clamp-on base
SOK-33	1	Lamp socket and switch
SHA-44	1	Shade
ARM-55	1	Flexible arm
COR-66	1	8-ft cord with plug
CON-77	2	Flexible arm connector
NUT-88	3	Nut, 3/8 in.
LOK-99	3	Lockwasher, 3/8 in.

PARTS PICTORIAL

TOOLS NEEDED FOR ASSEMBLY

1. Screwdriver, 3/16-in. blade

2. Wrench, 3/8 in.

3. Knife, pocket

4. Ruler, standard

page 1

ASSEMBLY INSTRUCTIONS

Note: Read each step all the way through. When the step is
          completed, check the space provided ( ).

Note: All figures referred to in the instructions are in
          Figure B.

( ) Fasten Clamp-on Base (BAS-22) in a convenient place.
     Attach base to work table or to machine tool (Figure 1).

( ) Fasten Connectors (CON-77) to Flexible Arm (ARM-55).
     Remove the setscrew from the connector. Place the end of
     the flexible arm into the end of the connector until it
     stops. Hold the flexible arm in this position and insert
     the setscrew. Tighten setscrew securely. Repeat this
     procedure again for the other end of the arm (Figure 2).

( ) Fasten Arm and Connector Assembly (ARM-55, CON-77) to Base
     (BAS-22).
     Place the threaded end of the connector into the hole in the
     base. Place a lockwasher (LOK-99) on the threads. Start a
     nut (NUT-88) on the threads and tighten securely with a
     wrench (Figure 3).

( ) Fasten Arm and Connector Assembly to Shade (SHA-44).
     Place the threaded end of the connector in the hole in the
     shade. Place a lockwasher (LOK-99) on the threads. Start
     a nut (NUT-88) on the threads and tighten securely with a
     wrench (Figure 4).

page 2

( ) Thread Cord (COR-66) through the Assembly.

With the base firmly mounted, straighten the flexible arm so
that it is perpendicular to the base. Thread the end of the
cord without the plug on it through the flexible arm. Start
at the hole in the base and push straight up until the end
of the cord appears in the shade. Leave approximately 1 ft
of cord hanging out of the shade to facilitate connection of
the socket (Figure 5).

( ) Wire Lamp Assembly (SOK-33).

Remove the brass shell from the lamp socket. Push the free
end of the cord through the small hole in the brass shell.
With a pocket knife, remove approximately 3/4 in. of
insulation from each conductor of the cord. Back off the
screws on the socket and loop the bare ends of the cord
around these screws. Tighten screws securely and place socket
back inside brass shell (Figure 6).

( ) Assemble Socket into Shade.

Place the threaded part of the socket through the large hole
in the top of the shade. Place a lockwasher (LOK-99) over the
threads. Start a nut (NUT-88) on the threads and tighten
securely with a wrench (Figure 7).

( ) Place Lamp into Socket.

Lamp can be no larger than 75 watts.

( ) Plug in Cord.

Lamp is now ready for operation. Turn the switch on top of
the shade in a clockwise direction.

page 3

IN CASE OF DIFFICULTY

If the lamp fails to light after the switch has been turned, check the following:

1. Is the bulb good? (Try the bulb in another fixture.)

2. Is the lamp plugged in?

3. Is the outlet working?

4. Is the line cord securely fastened around the screws of the socket?

page 4

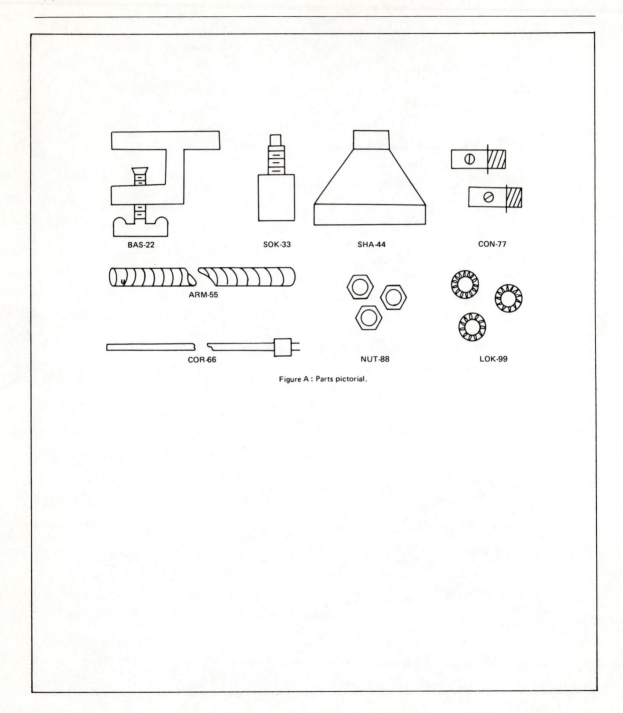

Figure A : Parts pictorial.

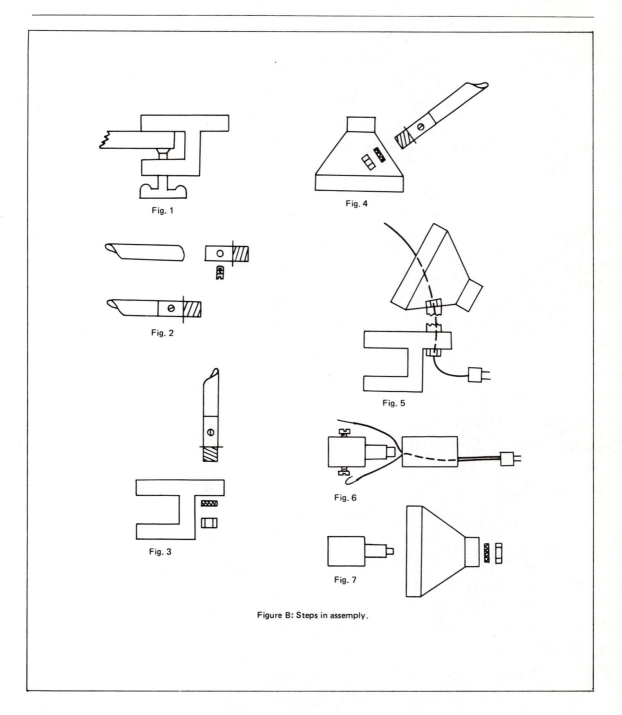

Fig. 1

Fig. 4

Fig. 2

Fig. 5

Fig. 3

Fig. 6

Fig. 7

Figure B: Steps in assemply.

The Formal Report

Pilot Plant for a Partial Water Reclamation Process

by

Gordon Pekkuri

Appendix 2: Reprinted by permission of Gordy Pekkuri.

[THE MEMORANDUM OF TRANSMITTAL]

MEMORANDUM

To: Professor Anson Langenberger   Date: March 23, 19--

FROM: Gordy Pekkuri

SUBJECT: SECOND REPORT OF METHODS FOR DEALING WITH DOMESTIC SEWAGE

    1.   The attached report, entitled "Treatment Methods for Domestic Sewage" is submitted in accordance with your request of March 1, 19--. The first report dealt with the composition and quantities of the contaminants involved.

    2.   This report includes descriptions of treatment methods and a description of a feasible water reclamation system. Data for comparative studies are included.

    3.   We are now working on the third stage, a plan for a closed water-waste treatment system. Our third report will discuss the results of our work.

    4.   We do not claim that the pilot plant described in this report will totally reclaim water. It is possible that our third report will be able to discuss a system for total reclamation.

                        Gordon Pekkuri
                        Gordon Pekkuri

[THE TITLE PAGE]

TREATMENT METHODS FOR DOMESTIC SEWAGE

Prepared for

Professor Anson Langenberger

Department of Applied Technology

Houghton Technological Institute

Houghton, Michigan

By

Gordon Pekkuri

March 23, 19--

[No page number]

TABLE OF CONTENTS

ii

LIST OF TABLES AND FIGURES   Table 1   4

Table 2   5

Table 3   7

Table 4   8

Figure 1   14

[Note: Some editors list the titles of the tables or figures in

this listing.]

iii

GLOSSARY

Ion exchange: method of separation of particles by
                  reversible interchange between ions of
                  like charge

Jar test: laboratory conditions

Stoichiometry: branch of science that deals with laws of
                  proportion and conservation of matter and
                  energy to chemical activity

iv

INTRODUCTORY SUMMARY

Widespread local interest in maintaining the purity of the water in Portage Lake and Lake Superior has led to local interest in domestic sewage treatment. Many of my friends and I think that the Houghton-Hancock sewage treatment plants could be improved to reduce the flow of contaminants into these bodies of water.

In this report, five treatment methods are explored. Included are coagulation-clarification, aeration, reverse osmosis, chemical oxidation, and adsorption on activated charcoal. In each case, I have listed only the basic advantages and disadvantages of each method. In a report to follow, more details about each method will be given.

A pilot plant is proposed. It would utilize these five treatment methods. The plant will not totally reclaim the water, but it is an improvement over present systems. And it can be developed into a total water reclamation system at a later date, using the method to be discussed in the third report.

v

1. INTRODUCTION

    A. Purpose

        The purpose of this report is to present the second of a
series of studies dealing with treatment methods for domestic sewage
in the Houghton-Hancock area. The first study (reported earlier) dealt
with the composition and quantities of the contaminants involved. The
third report (to follow) will discuss a closed waterwaste treatment.

    B. Problem

        Of the five Great Lakes, Lake Superior is now the only one
which is relatively uncontaminated. Some waste is being introduced on
the northern shore (in Canada) and some industrial waste is being
introduced on the southern shore.

        Portage Lake is an arm that cuts across the Keweenaw
Peninsula, an arm of land thrust out into Lake Superior. Midway on
this arm are the twin towns of Hancock and Houghton. One sewage
treatment plant, on the Hancock side of the lake, serves both towns.
It is antiquated, small, and far from efficient. The effluent from it
into Portage Lake is contaminated, even though it has had some treatment.
The imminent growth of both towns will add to the contamination.

    C. Scope

        This report includes descriptions of treatment methods and
a feasible recommendation for a partial water-reclamation system.
Tables for comparative information are included as well as a schematic
for a pilot plant. This information is the basis for any choice of a
unit operation system for waste treatment.

page 1

II.   UNIT OPERATIONS TESTS

   A. Coagulation--Clarification

        Non-settleable and colloidal matter in waste water hinders
effects of all treatment steps. So; it has been proposed to remove this
matter. By using doses of lime, alum, ferric chloride, or other
coagulants, unsettled and colloidal matter can be reduced significantly
Because of organic carbon's high proportion in colloidal matter, it too
is reduced in this step.

        For example, a concurrent effect of lime and alum coagulation
is the removal of phosphates down to about 2-3 parts per million.

        Several ionic, nonionic and cationic organic polyelectrolytes
were tested in doses from 1-5 parts per million, but were found ineffective
as primary coagulants. As coagulant aids used with lime or alum, some
polyelectrolytes made longer floe particles which settled faster than
those without coagulant aids. Thus, it was determined that polyelectrolytes
didn't effectively enhance coagulation.

        Table 1 shows typical data on coagulation and clarification
(purification) of settled domestic sewage with lime. The coagulant dose
can be figured out from stoichiometry and complete knowledge of the waste
water characteristics. But when calculating values based on alkalinity,
phosphate, ammonia, magnesium and pit change, the values are always less
than values found with jar tests.

page 2

Table 1

COAGULATION--CLARIFICATION OF SETTLED DOMESTIC SEWAGE

Contaminants	ORF		Albertson	
	Before Treatment	After Treatment	Before Treatment	After Treatment
Total solids mg/l	650	790	657	772
Conductivity mhos	780	930	1,380	1,560
Ammónia (as N)				
mg/l	35	34	54.4	49.6
Chloride mg/l	84	83	84.0	82.0
Soluble phosphate				
mg/l	48.8	1.0	10.08	0.19
Sulphate mg/l	48.8	57.0	69.0	69.0
Total hardness				
mg/l	153.0	182.0	306.0	392.0
Calcium mg/l	50.0	69.0	60.0	80.0
pH	7.8	11.2	7.4	11.7
TOC mg/l	115	69	186	107
SOC mg/l	75	69	---	---

Buzzel and Sawyer (1) have found an empirical relationship between lime dose and alkalinity of waste. According to their data for alkalinity of waste water, about 100 parts per million ($CaCO_3$) to reach pH 11.0 150-200 parts per million of lime is needed. In a closed system, alkalinity of water is always below 100 parts per million, and the lime requirements thus will be about 200 parts per million.

page 3

B. Aeration

Simple aeration to air is the cheaptest way to eliminate low-molecular hydrocarbons such as acetone and methyl-ethylketone, as well as volatile gases like hydrogen sulphide, methane, carbon dioxide, chlorine,and ammonia. Each substance's volatility will determine how quickly each will be stripped.

While the water is being drowned in oxygen, some organics are oxidized, odors removed, and the taste of water improved. The oxygen present oxidizes and creates hydroxides and oxides of iron and manganese that can also be removed.

Above pH levels of 11.0, the ammoniacal nitrogen is present as dissolved gaseous NH_3 and can be removed by aeration without extra chemical costs. At a cost of 20 cents per 1000 gallons, free and saline ammonia can be reduced by 90 percent. When ammonia is oxidized through breakpoint chlorination, the cost goes up to 7 cents per 1000 gallons for every one part in a million removed.

In addition, by virtue of carbon dioxide present in air, the excess hydroxide alkalinity is reduced, thus reducing the total dissolved solids in treated water.

Table 2 indicates the effectiveness of aeration. It is clear that ammonia, odors, toxal solids, hardness,and organic carbon material are reduced.

page 4

Table 2

AERATION OF CHEMICALLY TREATED AND CLARIFIED DOMESTIC SEWAGE

Contaminants	ORF		Albertson	
	Before Treatment	After Treatment	Before Treatment	After Treatment
Total solids mg/l	790	585	772	570
Conductivity mhos	930	520	1560	945
Ammonia (as N) mg/l	34	9.7	49.6	14
Chloride mg/l	83	84	82.0	85
Soluble phosphate mg/l	1.0	1.0	0.19	0.31
Sulphate mg/l	57	54	69	65
Total hardness mg/l	182	95	392	193
Calcium mg/l	69	43	80	50
Total organic carbon (TOC)	69	66	107	84
Soluble organic carbon (SOC)	69	66	--	--
pH	11.2	9.5	11.7	--

C. Reverse Osmosis

Using cellulose acetate membranes, a reverse osmosis (RO)
process is obtained. In this method, large organic molecules and
polyvalent ions are almost all removed. Divalent ions are removed with

page 5

90-98 percent efficiency, and nonvalent ions such as sodium, potassium, chloride, nitrates, and other low-molecular molecules.

For this reason, RO is described as an advanced treatment process. It is used substantially where water must meet high effluent standards.

Used with electrodialysis and ion exchange, RO can be used to remove inorganic salts from the water solution. Work has been done where RO has been used to get high quality water from pretreated brackish water, from secondary biologically treated and filtered sewage flow, starch wash waters, and chemically treated domestic sewage.

Because RO can be used for demineralization as well as separation of soluble organic carbon material, it is more valuable and useful in a closed water-reclamation system than electrodialysis or ion exchange. Once put into use as a demineralization process, its effectiveness is only a little affected by the presence of soluble carbon matter which usually occurs in lower concentrations than organic salts.

In Table 3, typical product properties and separation efficiencies obtained at Ontario Research Foundation on a commercial RO system are shown, using high-density cellulose acetate membranes.

After 50 tests at Ontario, it was found that the removal efficiency of organic carbon material measured as soluble organic carbon (SOC) at recoveries from 80-95 percent is within 80-90 percent. The higher separation efficiency obtained by Albertson can only be explained by the use of different sewage in these tests.

The tests show that RO alone cannot lower the organic carbon level to drinking level. Further treatment is necessary.

page 6

Table 3

REVERSE OSMOSIS TREATMENT OF CHEMICALLY CLARIFIED

AND AERATED DOMESTIC SEWAGE

	ORF Recovery=95%			Albertson Recovery=80%		
Contaminants	Before	After	Removal Efficiency %	Before	After	Removal Efficiency %
Total solids						
mg/1	585	24	96	570	63	89
Conductivity						
mhos	720	29	96	945	144	90
Ammonia (as N)						
mg/1	9.7	1.3	86	14	2	86
Chloride mg/1	84	8.0	90	85	16	81
Soluble phosphate						
mg/1	1	0.1	90	0.31	0.04	87
Total hardness						
mg/1	95	3.8	96	193	11.0	95
Sulphate mg/1	54	1.1	98	65	2.1	97
Calcium mg/1	73	0.8	98	50	1*	98
Total organic						
carbon	66	11.9	82	84	1.6	98
Soluble organic						
carbon	66	11.9	82	--	--	--
pH	6.0	6.1	--	6.6	7.5	--

* Less than 1, actually

page 7

D. Chemical Oxidation

Chlorine, ozone, potassium permanganate, and other chemicals for years have been used to improve color, taste, and odor qualities, and as disinfectants. They act as oxidants by destroying or altering the structure of noxious organic chemicals. Ideally, the organic molecules would reduce to carbon dioxide, water, oxides of nitrogen or oxides of other elements. Ozone was used in our tests because of the advantages it offers.

Some advantages are:

Almost instantaneous reactions with oxidizable substances

Short contact period to remove odor, color, taste

Ability to remove toxic contaminants (phenol, cyanide)

More efficient in oxidation than chlorine, chlorine dioxide, iodine, potassium permanganate, hydrogen peroxide

Disinfectant

Suitable for precipitation of iron and manganese, and oxidation of hydrophilic colloids

Oxidation of organic colloidal matter

Table 4 shows typical data on ozonation of chemically clarified and aerated domestic sewage.

page 8

Table 4

OZONATION OF CHEMICALLY TREATED, CLARIFIED, AND

AERATED DOMESTIC SEWAGE

Composition	Settled Raw Sewage	After Chemical Treatment	After Aeration	After Ozonation	% Reduction by Ozonation
TOC mg/l	106	64	62	53	14.5
SOC mg/l	66	62	62	52	16.5
Con. mhos	740	910	590	590	---
pH	8.7	11.2	10.6	7.8	---

E. Adsorption on Activated Charcoal

Over a wide range of impurity concentration conditions, activated carbon can remove a high percentage of unwanted contaminants. Expressed as adsorption isotherm, the maximum adsorption capacity of the activated carbon for each contaminant is a function of chemical-physical properties of the organic contaminant and its concentration in a solution.

The composition of the organic carbon matter in sewage changes with each treatment step. Thus, the adsorption isotherm will change with each different sewage process. For example, the adsorption isotherm will vary greatly from raw sewage to RO effluent.

However, test results show that activated carbon is not capable of adsorbing certain organic compounds (concentration in domestic sewage in the range of 5-20 parts per million). But it is

page 9

highly effective in the removal of detergents, insecticides, and odor. Therefore, it is an inevitable operation in drinking water treatment.

After use, activated carbon can be reactivated by high temperature oxidation of adsorbed organics or by desorption with solvents or steam. The selection of the reactivation method depends largely on the characteristics of the absorbed substances.

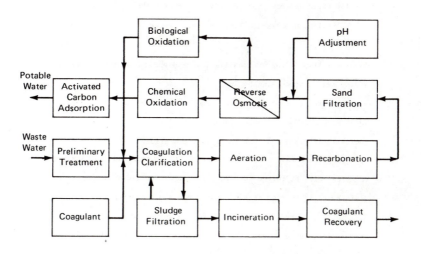

page 10

1. Raw domestic sewage is reduced to small particles, chemically treated, coagulated, and clarified in a clarifier, which will also be used as a storage reservoir for the raw water.

2. The clarified effluent with Ph 11-11.5 is aerated in an aeration column to remove the ammoniacal nitrogen, volatile gases, solvents, and low-molecular-weight hydrocarbons. Precipitated substances are separated and recovered.

3. The effluent from the aeration column is stabilized in a recarbonation unit, excess lime precipitated, and pH reduced to 8.5-9.5 level.

4. After step 3, the effluent is filtered through a sand filter and stored before processing by RO.

5. The water is then processed by RO with product water recoveries 90-95 percent. The concentrated waste, 5-10 percent, will be biologically oxidized and recycled into the clarifier.

6. The product water from RO, to remove toxic compounds and noxious organics, will be further treated by chemical oxidation and disinfected in an oxidation column by ozone or chlorine.

7. Finally, to reduce the organic carbon matter to below .2 parts per million, the effluent from the oxidation column will be polished by activated carbon in adsorption column.

8. Solid wastes can be used for landfill purposes.

page 11

III.   CONCLUSIONS

   This report has answered questions dealing with the effectiveness
of sewage treatments proposed for the Houghton-Hancock plant. As the
tests and studies show, a closed water system is not practical now.
But, using the processes discussed above, a partial water system is.

   The steps to be followed in a pilot plant process, together with
a simplified flowsheet, are presented in Figure 1, above.

IV.   RECOMMENDATIONS

   It is recommended that a pilot plant be constructed to use the
processes described above. This pilot plant should simulate a
closed-system plant as much as possible.

   Furthermore, it is recommended that the present study, leading
to a closed-system plant, be continued.

V.   BIBLIOGRAPHY

page 12

The Progress Report

Report on the Design of a
100 Horsepower Squirrel Cage Induction Motor

Submitted to
Mr. Lea Verne Hansel
Chevrolet Detroit Gear & Axle
1840 Holbrook
Detroit, Michigan 48211
by
Terence M. Deford

Introduction

On February 12, 1973, Detroit Machine Design received a request from the Chevrolet Gear & Axle Company of Detroit for an unspecified quantity of electric motors that would provide the power for hydraulic pumps to be used in waste disposal systems manufactured by Chevrolet Gear & Axle. A major specification was that the motors generate 100 horsepower.

Detroit Machine Design has determined that the best type of electric machine is a 100 horsepower, 3 phase, 60 cycle, 575 volts, 90C rpm squirrel cage induction motor. Chevrolet Gear & Axle was notified of this determination on February 20, in a telephone call from Terence M. Deford, Project Engineer to Mr. Lea Verne Ansel. Mr. Ansel concurred, but asked to see the calculations on which this determination was made. The calculations are furnished below.

At the time of this report, the stator has been fully designed.

Discussion of Work

ASSUMPTIONS

The starting point of any electric machine is with the basic voltage equation:

$$E = \frac{2 [pi] f N \phi k_w \times 10^{-8}}{2}$$

where ϕ is the flux per pole measured in lines. This equation can be expanded, by using ϕ to indicate the total hypothetical flux in the machine, to

Reprinted by permission of Terence M. Deford.

$$E = \frac{2 [pi] n N \phi_t f_d k_w \times 10^{-8}}{60 \times 2}$$

This equation comes about from realizing that ϕ_t is equal to the flux per pole ϕ times the number of poles in the machine divided by the flux distribution factor f_d. The flux distribution factor is an assumption based on the number of laminations of the stator. Furthermore,

$$HP = \frac{Iqp.f. \text{ efficiency}}{746}$$

and,

$$\phi = BD1$$

where B is the peak flux density in the air gap, D is the inner diameter of the stator of the machine and 1 is the length of the stator. Also, N is equal to the total number of conductors divided by twice the number of phases. By substituting into the horsepower equation, we get

$$HP = \frac{[pi]^2 n Z B D 1 f_c k_w Ip.f. \text{ efficiency} \times 10^{-8}}{120 (\text{sq. root of } 2) \times 746}$$

At this point we introduce Q (ampere conductors per square inch of circumference) which is equal to the total number of conductors times the current divided by pi times the diameter of the stator. Typically, Q has been determined by experimental means and by previous experience to follow the curve shown in

201

fig. 1, page 205. This Q can now be incorporated into the horsepower equation:

$$HP = \frac{[pi]^3 \, D^2 \, B \, 1 \, n \, Q \text{ efficiency p.f. } f_d K_w \times 10^{-8}}{120 \, (\text{sq. root of } 2) \times 746}$$

It is now time to remove a few of the constants and to replace certain items with basic assumptions as in the case of f_d and k_w. From previous experiences it was found that $f_d = 0.637$ and k_w (winding factor) = 0.95. At this point we also assume that the p.f. and the efficiency equal 0.90.

Later we will return to determine these actual values. By substituting the known values and the assumed values into the equations above, the following equation is the result:

$$B \, D^2 \, 1 \, Q = 9.2539 \times 10^{10}$$

This will give us a quick and easy reference for the size of the diameter, length of the stator, and the peak flux density as compared to each other.

RULES TO FOLLOW

Before we can start to solve for the diameter and length of our stator, we must realize that we have rules to adhere to. These rules are very liberal, but when followed will provide a good design and a high running efficiency. Since we have a maximum allowable flux in the stator of 100,000 lines per square inch, the flux in the air gap must be smaller. The permeability of air as compared to that of iron is about 40 percent, therefore we must keep the flux density in the air gap above 25,000 lines per square inch. It is best to keep the flux density near 40,000 lines per square inch.

Because the rotor is a mechanical device and has some finite breaking point, we must keep our peripheral speed below 12,000 feet per minute. The equation is as follows:

$$v = \frac{[pi] \, D \times n}{12}$$

This is related to our stator design by the diameter of the stator as equal to the diameter of the rotor plus a sizable air gap to facilitate ease in rotation.

Pole pitch must also be considered, for it is used to determine the ratio of length of pole pitch, which must be kept between 0.6 and 2.0. Pole pitch (T) is found by dividing the circumference by the number of poles. This ratio of length to pole pitch keeps the machine in the relationship commonly used in machines, that is to say the machine will have a diameter of the same order of magnitude as our length and will not be overly blessed in either length or diameter.

The last of the considerations really comes into play at the end of the calculations. It has to do with the allowable flux density in the tooth of the stator and the stator yoke. These flux densities are 130,000 lines per square inch and 80,000 to 95,000 lines per square inch respectively. These are determined from the magnetic properties of the materials used to make the stator and are an important factor in the overall efficiency. Thus if the design of the stator is for maximum flux density our efficiency will be much higher.

CALCULATIONS

The most logical starting point is the determination of the number of ampere conductors possible in this machine. Since there must be two slots per pole per phase and the number of conductors divided by two has to be a whole number (because the windings are distributed so that each slot contains two taped groups of conductors), the number of poles is 8, the number of phases is 3, therefore the number of conductors must be a multiple of 96. A Q of 685 (fig. 1, p. 205) can be substituted into the equation $B \, D^2 n1 \, Q = 9.2539 \times 10^{10}$. This gives us this equation:

$$B \, D^2 \, 1 = 1.3514 \times 10^8$$

Next we assume that B is equal to 39,000 lines per square inch. This produces the following equation:

$$D^2 \, 1 = 3.465 \times 10^3 \text{ cubic inches}$$

By arrangement of some of the previous equations, it can be seen that:

$$B \, D \, L = \frac{E \, 2 \times 60 \times 2 \times q \times 10^8}{[pi]^2 \, n \, Z \, f_c \, k_w} = \frac{3.1438 \times 10^9}{Z}$$

By combining the two previous equations and substituting multiples of 96 for Z, the possible combinations for the diameter and length of the stator of the machine were determined (Table 1, page 203). The flux density shown in Table 1 is the actual flux density determined when using the truncated values of diameter and length. It should be noted at this time that a Z of 384 conductors was determined to be the best possible value for this machine because of the length to pole pitch ratio.

Once the flux density, diameter and length of the stator were known, the total hypothetical flux was determined using this equation:

$$\phi = B \, [pi] \, D \, 1$$

which gave the value 3.429×10^7 lines (providing the proper values are substituted in the equation). This value is used in this equation:

TABLE 1
Possible Combinations for the Diameter and Length of the Stator of the Motor

DIAMETER	LENGTH	B (FLUX DENSITY)	Z
4.21	203.48	39,126.20	96
8.25	50.91	39,000.00	192
12.38	22.60	39,015.00	288
16.50	12.72	39,023.00	384
20.63	8.14	39,900.62	480

$$B_{tooth} = \frac{\phi}{(D - S w_s) (1 \, n_d \, w_d) (0.92)}$$

where w_s is the width of the square stator slot, n_d is the number of 0.25 inch air ducts in the stator that are placed every four inches, and w_d is the width of the air ducts.

The factor of 0.92 is the stacking factor for the lamination of the stator. It is needed because of the lessening of the flux paths because of the lamination. Since the maximum allowable flux density for a tooth in the stator is 130,000 lines per square inch, this is the figure that is used for B_{tooth}. When this figure is used, it will give us the maximum allowable slot width, 0.7173 inches.

From Table 430–150, page 70–260 of the 1971 **National Electric Code,** it is found that the current in the machine is 99 amperes. Since the maximum allowable current density in the windings is 2500 amperes per square inch, the cross-sectional area of a single conductor is limited to at least 0.0396 inches. A square wire was chosen from Table 2 with a cross-sectional area (including the insulation) of 0.0408 inches; its dimensions are 0.165 × 0.307 inches. Using this wire, we have a current density of 2426.47 amperes per square inch. This is well within the allowable limit.

Each slot must be insulated with 0.025 inches of mica to keep the magnetic flux concentrated within the slot. Each slot has two groups of four conductors, and each group is wrapped with tape and insulated from the others (figs. 2 and 3, page 205). With this configuration, a slot of 0.664 inches wide and 0.685 inches deep is needed. This gives us a B_{tooth} of 113,338.31 lines per square inch.

The outside of the stator is determined by the following equation:
where D_o is the outside diameter of the stator, d_{ss} is

$$B_{ys} = \frac{\phi}{(D_o - D_s - 2d_{ss}) (1 - n_d \, w_d) (0.92)}$$

the depth of the stator slot and D_s is the inside diameter of the stator. This equation says that the B_{ys} (flux density in the stator yoke) is equal to the flux per pole divided by the volume of the metal in the stator. Assuming that the maximum and minimum B_{ys} is in the range from 95,000 to 80,000 lines per square inch, it is found that the limit on the outside diameter of the stator is 20.195 to 19.828 inches. The outside diameter of the stator is then taken to be 20.0 inches. This yields a flux density in the stator yoke of 87,344.938 lines per square inch which is within the limits of the machine.

All that remains is to solve for the efficiency of the machine, using the calculated values. It is found that the efficiency of the machine is 0.86 (86%). A complete listing of all machine parameters is in Table 2, page 204.

CONCLUSION

The design of this machine is Class A, normal starting torque, low starting current and low slip. This design has a big disadvantage of having a starting current of 500 to 800 percent of the running currents. Therefore a starting compensator must be used to reduce the starting voltage. Since the starting voltage is directly related to the starting torque, the starting torque of the machine is greatly reduced. However, if the class B, C, or D operation were to be used, the starting current of the machine would be reduced but at the expense of the efficiency of the machine. Since the work of this machine will for the most part be continuous, it is more economical to use the class A operation. Moreover, the class A operation has the advantage that its full load torque occurs a less than 20 percent slip, and it has a maximum torque that is well over 200 percent rated torque. This is also desirable for continuous operation.

This design conforms to all existing NEMA standards for rotating machines.

TABLE 2
Machine Parameters

PARAMETER	VALUE
horsepower	100
voltage	575 line to line
frequency	60 hertz
phases	3
type of connection	wye
amperes	99
poles	8
Z (conductors)	384
ϕ	257.306×10^5 lines
ϕ per pole	2048.799×10^3 lines
S (Slots)	48
B_{tooth}	1.963
length to pole pitch ratio	113, 338.31 lines per sq. in.
v (peripheral speed)	3887.73 fps.
power factor	0.9
efficiency	86%
Q	685
C_w	0.672
f_d	0.637
k_w	0.95
rpm	900
diameter of stator	16.50 inches
length of stator	12.72 inches
B	39,023 lines per square inch
n_d	3
w_d	0.25 inches
w_s	0.664 inches
d_{ss}	0.685 inches
wire	0.165×0.307 in.
	= 0.0408 si
J (current density)	2426.47 amps per square inch
D_o	20.0
B_{ys}	87,344.939 lines per square inch

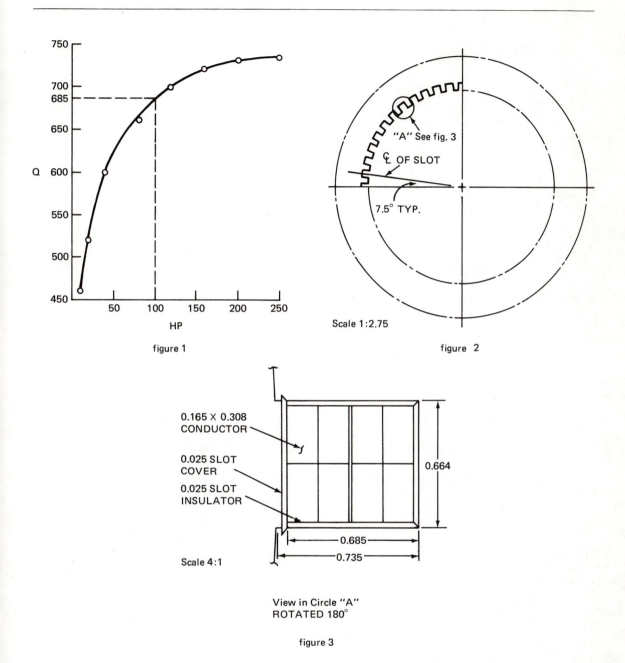

Q

750
700
685
650

600

550

500

450

50   100   150   200   250

HP

figure 1

"A" See fig. 3

℄ OF SLOT

7.5° TYP.

Scale 1:2.75

figure 2

0.165 X 0.308
CONDUCTOR

0.025 SLOT
COVER

0.025 SLOT
INSULATOR

0.664

0.685

0.735

Scale 4:1

View in Circle "A"
ROTATED 180°

figure 3

A Student Feasibility Report

INTRODUCTORY SUMMARY

It is recommended that the electrical contractor continue to purchase and use the 4-terminal side-wired receptacles.

The pigtail receptacle has an excellent installation time, but the added cost does not justify a change.

I.   INTRODUCTION

A. The purpose of this report is to determine whether an electrical contracting firm should continue to purchase and use 4-terminal side-wired receptacles or begin purchasing factory-wired pigtail receptacles.

B. The problem is to determine whether it would be more profitable for an electrical contracting firm to purchase and install factory-wired pigtail receptacles or 4-terminal side-wired receptacles.

C. This report compares a factory-wired pigtail receptacle with a 4-terminal side-wired receptacle. The following characteristics were noted: the dealer cost, the installation cost, the installation time, and the advantages and disadvantages of each type.

II. BACKGROUND INFORMATION

Presently, there are two ways a receptacle is connected to the wires in a junction box. The first method is to use the screw terminals on the sides of the receptacle. The second method, which is relatively new, consists of connecting pigtails (short lengths of wire that are permanently connected inside the receptacle) to the wires in the junction box.

page 1

When installing a screw-terminal receptacle, three operations are performed. First, the ends of the wires in the junction box must have about 1/2 inch of insulation removed. Next, these ends are looped and placed under the screws. Finally, these screws are tightened to secure the wires.

When installing a pigtail receptacle, only two operations are performed. The first consists of removing the insulation from the ends of the wire in the junction box. The free ends of the pigtails have been stripped of their insulation at the factory. The second operation consists of joining the pigtails and the junction box wires with a solderless connector.

III. COSTS

Following is a cost comparison chart of the two receptacles:

	Factory-wired pigtail	4-terminal receptacle
Dealer cost	$1.00	$0.80
Average installation time	2 1/2 min.	4 1/2 min.
Installation cost	$0.38	$0.68
Cost of wire nuts	$0.15	None
Total	$1.53	$1.48

IV. CAPABILITY

The only problem that the contractor would face in switching from his present receptacle to the pigtail type would in replacing his present inventory as it was used. No new tools would be necessary.

page 2

V.   SUITABILITY

    The factory-wired receptacle is of the same quality and rating as the 4-terminal side-wired receptacles.

VI. CONCLUSIONS

    It is recommended that the contractor continue to purchase the 4-terminal side-wired receptacles.

VII. DETAILED RECOMMENDATIONS

    The factory-wired pigtail receptacle is easier and quicker to install, but the savings in labor are offset by the higher cost of the receptacle.

VIII. APPENDIX A

	Factory-wired pigtail	4-terminal sidewired
Model number	1494	382
Manufacturer	Sierra Electric	Bryant Electric
Dealer cost	$1.00	$0.80
Average installation time	2 1/2 minutes	4 1/2 minutes
Installation cost at 0.15 per minute	$0.38	$0.68
Advantages	1. Quicker to install	1. Cheaper
	2. Easier to install	2. A more positive connection with screw terminal
	3. Pre-stripped and tinned pigtail leads	
	4. No screw terminals to short out against metallic junction box	
Disadvantages	1. Cost more to buy	1. Require a longer installation time

page 4

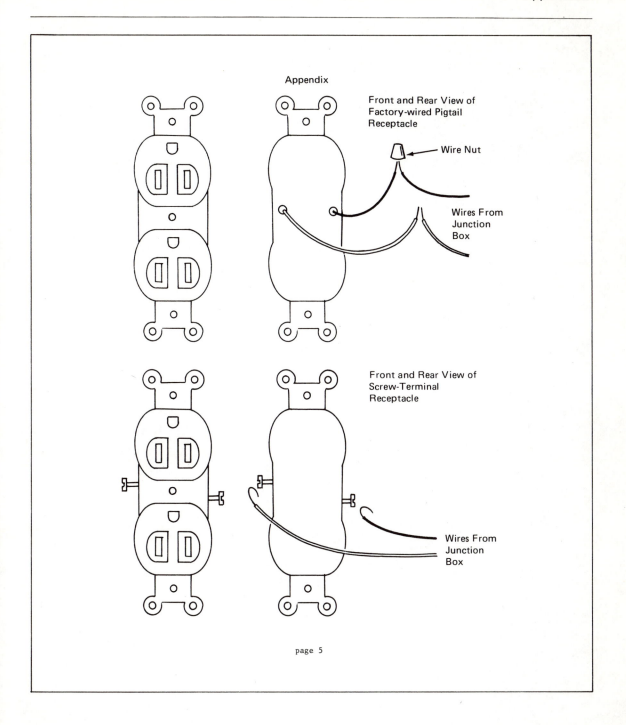

Appendix

Front and Rear View of
Factory-wired Pigtail
Receptacle

— Wire Nut

Wires From
Junction
Box

Front and Rear View of
Screw-Terminal
Receptacle

Wires From
Junction
Box

page 5

The
Proposal
Report

PROPOSAL ON THE DESIGN OF A

LIGHTED COMMUNICATION SYSTEM FOR THE LIBRARY BAR

Submitted to

Jon Davis, Owner

The Library Bar

Houghton, Michigan

January 13, 19--

by

Terence M. Deford

Appendix 5: Reprinted by permission of Terence M. Deford.

434 Wadsworth Hall

Michigan Technological Univ.

Houghton, Michigan 49931

13 March, 19--

Mr. Jon Davis

62 North Isle Royal Street

Houghton, Michigan 49931

Dear Jon:

During the six months that I have been employed by you in the capacity
of assistant manager/bartender, it has come to my attention that a
better method of communication between the kitchen and the saloon is
needed. With the present system, there is a good chance that the food
on the dumb-waiter will become cold before it is taken off. This is
caused by the fact that the bartenders are not always able to hear the
intercom at the end of the bar telling them that there is a food order
on the dumb-waiter. The times of most difficulty are during the busy
evenings when there is a full house and the juke box is at full
volume. A possible solution to this difficulty is a light system
that can be monitored by both the kitchen and the saloon. When an
order is sent up, the kitchen would turn on the light telling the
bartender that there is an order on the dumb-waiter. When the order
is removed from the dumb-waiter, the bartender would then turn off the
light, and the system would be reset.

With the light in a convenient place, the bartender would more readily
see the light than he would hear "order up." This would make for
warmer food, which in turn makes for happier customers and, in the
long run, more customers.

Sincerely,

Terence M. Deford

Terence M. Deford

Assistant Manager - Saloon

CIRCUIT

Installation of the circuit to be used is easy and the design is simple. The circuit discussed below is a single circuit for one bar; two separate circuits would be needed for both floors of the bar. Each circuit is nothing more than the circuit used for controlling the lights of a single room from two separate locations. It consists of two three-way switches (single pole--double throw), shown in Figure 1 and marked S_3, two lamps (120 volt--7.5 watt) marked L, and a three-wire cable which runs between the two floors.

OPERATION

To explain the operation, it must be realized that a closed-circuit or continuous connection is needed for the lamp to be energized. With switch S_3-A in position 1 and switch S_3-B in position 2, both lamps will be deenergized because there is no continuous connection. If either of the two switches S_3-A or S_3-B were to be moved to the alternate position, a continuous connection would be made, resulting in the energization of the lamps.

Therefore with the lamps deenergized, the kitchen could move switch S_3-A to position 2, turning on the lights in both the saloon and the kitchen. When the bartender removes the food from the dumb-waiter, he would then move switch S_3-B to position 1, deenergizing both lights, and the system would be reset.

page 1

The system described is a 120-volt system for economy's sake. If the system were some other value of voltage, a transformer would be needed, but this would cost more than the savings that would be realized from the reduction in wire size and lamp capacity.

INSTALLATION

The installation of the proposed system would be done by me, and I would therefore receive my usual hourly rate for the time spent on the installation of the system. Although I am not a licensed electrician, all work would conform to the standards set by the current National Electrical Code.

BUDGET FOR THE PROPOSED SYSTEM

		Each	Amount	Total
A.	Wages per hour	2.00	2.5	5.00
B.	Equipment (permanent)			
	Switches (120 v--2.5 amp)	1.25	4	5.00
	Lamp sockets (120 v--2.5 amp)	.89	4	3.56
	3 cable--plastic sheathed 300 v	.09 ft	60 ft	5.40
	2 cable--lamp cord 300 v	.03 ft	20 ft	.60
	Male plugs	.19	2	.38
C.	Equipment (expendable)			
	Lamps (120 v--7.5 watts)	.29	4	1.16
	Paint (flat black)	.69	1	.69
	Total project costs			21.79

page 2

The budget shown is for both systems added together. This was
done because the operation of the bar is a total entity and not three
separate systems.

LOCATIONS

It should be noted that the circuit diagram is not to scale.
The location of S_3-A and Lamp A is to be in the kitchen on the side
of the slide for the dumb-waiter that goes to the saloon, while the
S_3-B and Lamp B are to be located in the saloon on the side of the
dumb-waiter shaft in full view of the bar. Therefore, the distance
from the switches to the lamps is relatively short as compared to that
of the distances from switch to switch.

Since there is a dumb-waiter for each floor and each acts
independently of the other, it would be necessary to have two systems
to facilitate the ease of operation. However, in both cases, all
distances are taken into account in the budget, even though the
distance from the kitchen to the saloon is much shorter than the
distance from the kitchen to the Homonyn.

page 3

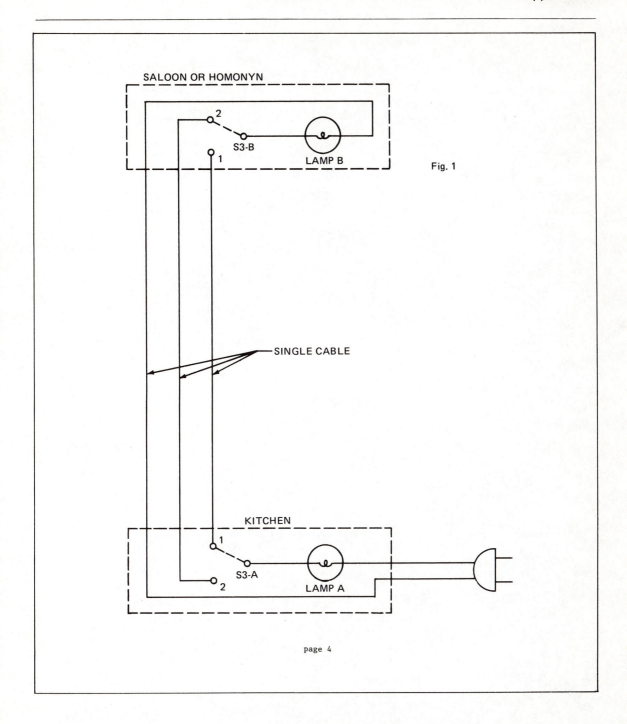

SALOON OR HOMONYN

2

S3-B

1

LAMP B

Fig. 1

SINGLE CABLE

KITCHEN

1

S3-A

2

LAMP A

page 4

The Report Based on Literature Research

Progress of the Progressive Die

Thomas Zarnke

Pressworking with dies has been a major part of industry for many years. Mass production and the assembly line required fast duplication of parts. Die-stamping, with both the one-step and the progressive dies, provided the vast number of small parts needed each day. Today, with accelerated production rates, the use of these dies becomes a hindrance to improving means of production. A man named Barret worked to find newer methods of efficient die-stamping and he succeeded. He became the founder of Die-Draulic, Inc., which in its few years of existence has greatly improved industrial production through its equipment.

What is Die-Draulic? It is a modern method of applying pressure by the use of hydraulics.[1] Another feature of Die-Draulic is its use of vertical progression rather than horizontal progression when working with progressive dies. These are the two main points of Die-Draulic to be discussed here.

Figure 1, page 229, shows the two main parts of a regular die which uses horizontal progression. As the press is lowered, the cam on the left moves toward the right, punching the metal plate lying at an angle. At the same time, the punch on the right moves down to punch the metal piece on the right. As the punch moves upward, the metal plate on the left is removed, and the metal plate on the right slides into the position just vacated by the plate on the left. While the punching process on the right is taking place, the spring or air pad holds the die pad in place. After the press opens, the spring or air pad ejects the punched-out plate, and returns the die pad to its normal position.

Figure 2, page 229, shows the vertical punch method of Die-Draulic. In this system, a piston, controlled by hydraulic oil flow, replaces the spring or aid pad. Air line pressure forces oil in the reservoir (right) through the hose (C) to the area (A) beneath the piston (P). The oil pressure forces the piston and die pad upward to the position shown. When the press closes, it moves the punch holder (B), the punch (E), the stock metal to be punched (S), the die pad (D), and the piston downward. The force of the press then causes the oil to flow back to the oil reservoir through hose (C), and then through a special channel which has a pressure and volume-sensitive valve (V). This valve controls the rate of flow. The valve is set for the pressure required to punch out the metal. This will regulate the flow of oil and keep it constant, thus providing constant pressure for the die pad. Die-Draulic's method, therefore, provides varied pressures to fit the job: full pressure from the start and constant pressure throughout the operation. This control of pressure eliminates parts otherwise rejected because of wrinkles, crimping, or other distortions deriving from unequal pressures found in normal methods.[2]

The usual method of varied punching and piercing by the use of cams (Figure 1, left, page 229) is dangerous for the operator and produces losses of machine parts because it is more subject to failure and breakage. More die repairs and parts replacements are necessary. There is also loss of time and money. Because cams can function in certain positions only, and because they take up a lot of space, their use and the types of work they can perform are limited.

Die-Draulic, on the other hand, has its own piercing unit to replace the cam (Figure 3, page 230). Die-Draulic's piercing units are comparatively small and can be placed anywhere at any angle in the die. The piercing units are independent of the press. They operate off the basic unit and the oil reservoir the same as the pistons under the die pads do. Because these piercing units are completely versatile, they can do an increased amount of varied work. And be-

[1] Die-Draulic, Inc., "Die-Draulic Is the Answer to Your 'Pressing' Problems," Grand Rapids, Michigan, 1965.

Reprinted by permission of Thomas J. Zarnke.

[2] Die-Draulic, Inc., Die-Draulic, Manufacturers of Hydraulic Controls for Stamping Dies, Catalogue 108, Grand Rapids, Michigan, 1969, pp. 2–3.

cause they are operated by the same hydraulic means, their power output and pressure can be varied to meet any requirements.

Die-Draulic, with its method of operation parts design, is preferable to normal dies. There are no parts to wear out since all of the moving parts that are under pressure are in an oil bath. The possibility of die breakage is minimal. If there happened to be interference or a malfunction in the operation, Die-Draulic's air and hydraulic safety releases would prevent pressure from building up and causing breakage. All these features reduce repairs and lost production time, and thus save a great deal of money.

Because Die-Draulic was designed for precise, high-production operations, it is the best solution where progressive steps are needed to produce a part. Normal dies, such as the one in Figure 4, page 230, function with a step-by-step progression of a piece of work through the machine. Each number across the center of the figure represents a step in the production of a metal stamping. Figure 5, page 231, shows a typical piece of metal after it has passed through each die. The numbers under each piece correspond to the numbers in Figure 4. In the process pictured, ten steps are necessary to complete one part, a time-consuming process.

Die-Draulic would combine all of these ten steps into one in its "vertical progression" die. It thus saves time and money and improves the quality of the part as well.

To compare the horizontal method with the vertical Die-Draulic method, we can use the production of a cowling for a lawnmower engine as an example. With horizontal progression, three to four steps may be needed. First, the die would shape the metal. Second, the center hole would be punched out and discarded. The third and fourth steps would pierce mounting holes around the cowl, finish the cowl and eject it. Assuming that the press closes once every ten seconds, it would take about 40 seconds to produce one cowl and the center disc scrap.

Using Die-Draulic, all the above steps would be combined in one. The first part of the stroke could bend and shape the cowl. The next part of the stroke would hit a die pad and the center would be punched out. At any part of the stroke, the piercing units would punch the mounting holes. This is possible, because, as we have seen, piercing units are versatile. The units are timed and operate at a higher velocity than cams,[3] and so they can be used anywhere within the die at any time during the operation.

With the Die-Draulic method, the cowl would be produced in ten seconds. Not only that—the center disc which was punched out could be shaped and formed into another part such as an oil filter cap in the same operation. A double savings of time and money.

In summary, then, Die-Draulic is a superior method of die-stamping over that of conventional methods. Die-Draulic saves time by combining operations and saves money by producing parts out of scrap during the regular production process. The process also saves time and money by the use of superior dies which seldom break down and stop production and require costly repairs. And most important, because of Die-Draulic's design, not only is there higher production, but the quality of parts produced is far superior to that of normal operations.

Bibliography

Die-Draulic, Inc. "Die-Draulic, Amplified Control Hydraulic Die Pad Pressure," Form E-67, Die-Draulic, Inc., Grand Rapids, Michigan.

Die-Draulic, Inc., "Die-Draulic Is the Answer to Your 'Pressing' Problems," Form ANS-65, Die-Draulic, Inc., Grand Rapids, Michigan.

Die-Draulic, Inc., "Die-Draulic, Manufacturers of Hydraulic Controls for Stamping Dies," Catalogue No. 108, Die-Draulic, Inc., Grand Rapids, Michigan, 1969.

Eary, Donald F. **Techniques of Pressworking Sheet Metal** (New York: Prentice-Hall, Inc., 1958).

Hinman, C. W. **Pressworking of Sheet Metals**, 2d ed. (New York: McGraw-Hill, 1950).

Schubert, Paul B. **Die Methods** (New York: Industrial Press, Inc., 1966).

[3] Die-Draulic, Inc., Ibid.

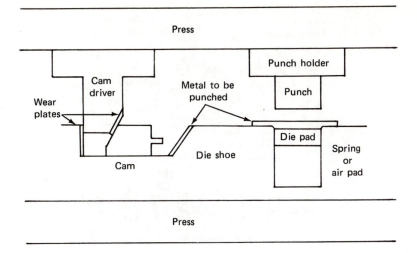

Figure 1 Die using horizontal progression.

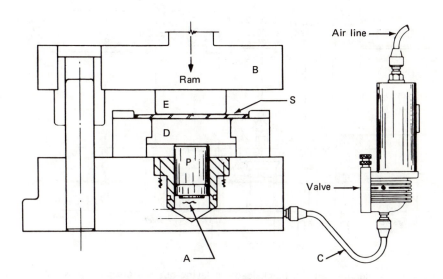

Figure 2 The vertical punch method of Die-Draulic. (Taken from **Die-Draulic, Manufacturers of Hydraulic Controls for Stamping Dies,** Catalogue No. 108, p. 4.)

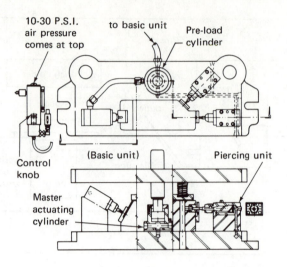

Figure 3 Die-Draulic's piercing unit. (Taken from **Die-Draulic, Amplified Controlled Hydraulic Die Pad Pressure**, p. 3.)

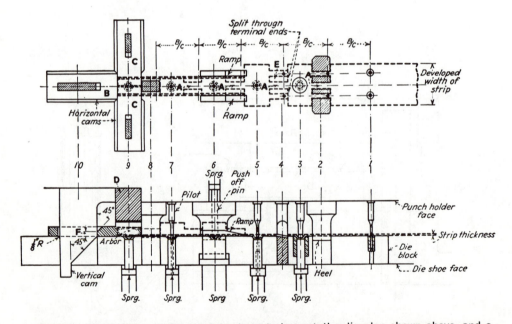

Figure 4 Development of the blank leads to laying out the die plan shown above, and a preliminary front view of the progressive operations shown below. (Taken from **Pressworking of Metals** by C. W. Hinman. Copyright 1941, 1950 by McGraw-Hill Book Company. Used with permission of McGraw-Hill Book Company.)

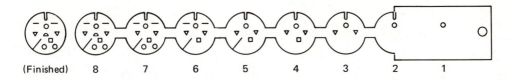

(Finished)   8   7   6   5   4   3   2   1

Figure 5   The progress of a typical piece of metal as it passes through each die.

Index